Materials
and Structure of Music

VOLUME TWO

Materials

William Christ

Richard DeLone

Vernon Kliewer

Indiana University

Lewis Rowell

William Thomson

University of Southern California

and Structure
of Music

THIRD EDITION

Prentice-Hall, Inc. Englewood Cliffs, New Jersey 07632

Library of Congress Cataloging in Publication Data (Revised)
Main entry under title:

Materials and structure of music.

Includes indexes.
1. Music—Theory. I. Christ, William.
MT6.M347 1980   781   79-10594
ISBN 0-13-560417-6 (v. 1)   AACR1

Materials and Structure of Music, Vol. II, 3/E
Christ/DeLone/Kliewer/Rowell/Thomson

© 1981, 1973, 1967 by Prentice-Hall, Inc., Englewood Cliffs, N.J. 07632

Printed in the United States of America

10 9 8 7 6 5 4 3 2 1

Editorial/production supervision by Penny Linskey
Interior design by Mark A. Binn
Cover design by Mark A. Binn
Manufacturing buyer: Harry P. Baisley

PRENTICE-HALL INTERNATIONAL, INC., *London*
PRENTICE-HALL OF AUSTRALIA PTY. LIMITED, *Sydney*
PRENTICE-HALL OF CANADA, LTD., *Toronto*
PRENTICE-HALL OF INDIA PRIVATE LIMITED, *New Delhi*
PRENTICE-HALL OF JAPAN, INC., *Tokyo*
PRENTICE-HALL OF SOUTHEAST ASIA PTE. LTD., *Singapore*
WHITEHALL BOOKS LIMITED, *Wellington, New Zealand*

Contents

Preface

Materials and Structure of Music has been revised for the second time with two paramount goals in mind: 1) to retain basic ingredients—content, procedure, and format—that have made the two volumes useful, and yet 2) to perform major renovations on their presentation, which in earlier editions was at times diffuse and labored. We have added as well as subtracted content. Most notable perhaps is the infusion of musical examples from non-western repertories, consistent with our goal to reveal principles of musical structure, illustrating their most evident manifestations from the broadest sampling of music available to us.

The wisdom and experience of many others have played a significant role in the reorganization of this new edition, and from our teaching colleagues and critics we have gained insights that motivated our re-arrangements, our reductions, and our additions. To all of these we extend our sincerest thanks for their thoughtfulness and concern.

Chapter One

Tonal Structure
and Form

Our discussions of modulation and tonal shift in *Materials and Structure of Music 1* concentrated on the way one tonic replaces another. Now we consider the relationships formed between different keys within a work and how these help to delineate form.

In this sense we can speak of *tonal form*, referring to divisions effected within a composition by the tonality scheme.[1] Tonality changes

---

[1] All musical dimensions are form-creating, and each may be examined as relationships that delineate form.

fulfill a need for variety. In short works, changes often punctuate small form units; in extended movements they delineate large sections as well as small.

In this chapter we shall examine the tonal form of four different movements, our main concern being the sectionalization that results from contrasts of different tonalities. We shall discuss other form-producing elements only as they relate to the tonal form.

Tonal Form of a Baroque Prelude

By tradition, *prelude* refers to many types of compositions that are either independent or introductory to other movements. The prelude that we will discuss is the opening movement of a *suite*. It is a multi-section movement containing many returns of an initial musical idea. As a whole, the prelude consists of continuous rhythmic motion, as you can see in Ex. 1–1.

Ex. 1–1. Bach; English Suite in *F*, Prelude.

Rhythmic invariance[2] tends to make us ignore phrases and restatements of the principal melodic material. Consequently, changes of key are introduced to highlight restatements, as can be heard at measures 5–6 and 10–11.

Considering only the section in Ex. 1–1, the main tonal center is *F*, but other tonal emphases do appear. For example, the dominant, *C*, is a tonal goal in measure 6. In retrospect, the tonal play beginning in measure 3, with its *B*-naturals, changes from *F* to *C*. Measures 12–15 are tonally unstable because three potential tonics (*C*, *F*, *B*♭) appear in a short time span. *F* is reasserted in measure 16, and dominates through measure 20. The tonal structure shapes this section, first by an immediate motion to the dominant tonal region, and second by the rapid succession of secondary dominants.

The next section of this movement introduces new melodic material in association with a rearticulated pedal, as well as chord outlining. Contrary to our expectations, the section (Ex. 1–2a) begins in *F* rather than in a new key, but there is a subsequent modulation to *C* (shown in Ex. 1–2b).

---

[2] Also referred to as *Fortspinnung*. Rhythmic invariance designates continuous rhythmic activity.

Ex. 1–2. Ibid.

Section 3 of this movement, beginning in the second half of m. 27, is a modified restatement of the beginning, but in the dominant key. Like the first section, it opens and closes in the same key.

Ex. 1–3. Ibid.

The fourth section brings back material that was heard in the second section. As before, this section begins in the key of the preceding section (C), but subsequently changes to *d* minor. Furthermore, still another tonal region (*g* minor) connects C to *d*. Thus the tonal design of this section is

Ex. 1–4. Ibid.

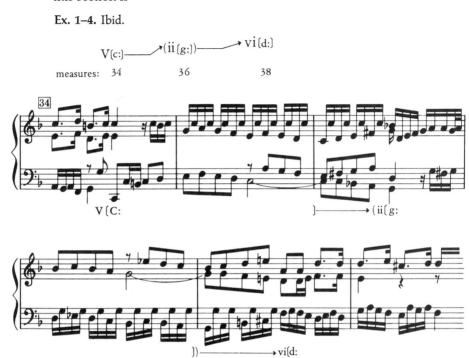

Since we have heard the contrasting material of Ex. 1–4 earlier in a particular formal role, we expect it to precede a restatement of the opening material at a different tonal level. It does, and in this case it is *d* (Ex. 1–5).

Ex. 1–5. Ibid.

Subsequent sections of this prelude contain similar procedures. In short, the formal design unfolds through alternate statements of the initial musical idea and a contrasting idea. In addition, the initial statement usually begins and ends in the same key, while the contrasting idea always begins in the preceding key and then establishes a new key for the next statement. Although space does not permit a quotation of the entire work, listen to the movement to observe the role of tonality in establishing its sectional form.

The tonal form and the consequent key relationships for the entire movement are shown below. Reduced to principal key centers, the tonality scheme is F C d a F. The tonal form, then, consists entirely of near-related keys.

Thus, even though the movement is characterized by rhythmic continuity, tonality changes shape its form. Of particular significance in this composition is the ordering of stable sections and modulatory sections. The latter provide contrast and connect those that are stable.

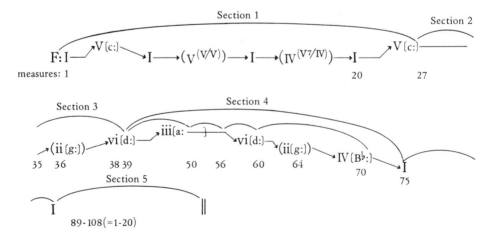

**Key
Relationships
in a Recitative**

By nature, a *recitative* is through-composed. A significant vocal form in opera, it is set to a text that narrates the action of the plot. Since the narration often contains abrupt idea changes, the music also changes character frequently. For example, to give emphasis to a special line of text, a more strictly measured accompanimental pattern might be used.

The tonal form of most traditional recitatives is characterized by constantly changing tonics. At times there is only the suggestion of a tonic, or if a tonic is established, the suggestion of a change soon follows. The general effect is that of successive tonal regions, thereby heightening the arrival of the key of the aria or chorus that follows.

The recitative by Mozart, which we will discuss next, begins and ends in *g* minor (which is reaffirmed in several interior sections). Ex. 1–6 shows the opening eleven measures. As you can see, *g* begins to give way to the subdominant region, *c* minor, in measure 4.

Ex. 1–6. Mozart: *Idomeneo*, Act 1, Scene 1, *"Quando avran fine . . ."*

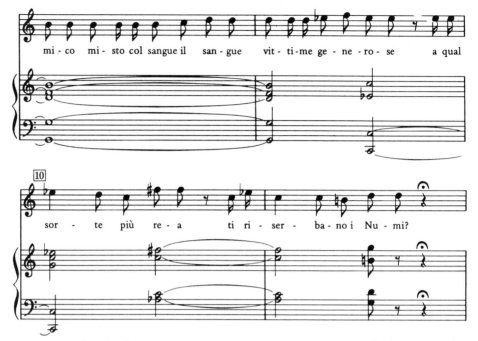

In the first section, *c* minor is an important goal; however, the clear *E*-flat in measure 12 (shown in Ex. 1–7) displaces it. The accompanimental motif of this second section is sequentially restated four measures later. Since it is an exact sequence a major second above, *F* is heard as a new tonic. The return of the chordal accompaniment in measure 21 continues to confirm *F*.

Ex. 1–7. Ibid.

A new accompanimental pattern appears when *g* minor returns in measure 27. Once again, a new reference point (*B-flat* major) appears quickly (Ex. 1–8).

Ex. 1–8. Ibid.

Four suggested keys crowd the space of only five measures in the next section of the recitative. The principal key seems to be *E-flat*, as is confirmed by the last measure of Ex. 1–9.

Ex. 1–9. Ibid.

Changes occur even more rapidly in the next section. Here a sequence in the first three measures of Ex. 1–10 exposes a succession of secondary dominants, each of which implies a tonal region that is not confirmed.

Ex. 1–10. Ibid.

The appearance in measure 51 (Ex. 1–11) of *G* major reemphasizes the principal tonic. The function of the implied *b* minor in Ex. 1–10 now becomes clear; it connects the constant references to *G*. As in the first section, there is a decisive motion in measures 63–65 to the subdominant region, *c* minor. Consequently, the tonal design of the beginning and ending sections is similar, except that the opening consists of *g* minor moving to *c* minor, whereas here it is *G* major moving to the subdominant. The movement closes in *G* minor, which is the key of the aria that follows.

Ex. 1–11. Ibid.

By comparison with our earlier Bach example, the Mozart recitative is quite unstable. The frequent changes of tonic create a tension that is not resolved until the following aria, although *G* acts as an outlining tonic. The following diagram illustrates the tonal form created by the succession of different keys and the relationships of subsidiary tonal centers to *G*. As you can see, the key scheme of the recitative is dominated by tonics related to the principal key by a major third below, a minor third above, and a perfect fifth below.

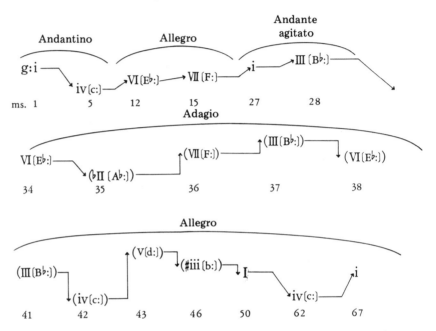

The tonal forms of the two preceding works consist primarily of near-related keys. A design may contain distant key relations as well. The resultant contrasts will usually be more vivid than those with near-related keys.

Both near- and distant-related keys occur in the Schumann movement discussed next. The principal tonic is *D-flat*, and *A-flat* occupies a subsidiary position. By measure 10, a partial restatement of the opening themes is set in the dominant region, clearly dividing this brief section. Thus a simple opposition is brought into play; the melodic material unifies the movement by appearing in four restatements, while the change of key provides variety.

Ex. 1–12. Schumann: *Trio,* Op. 80, II.

Tonal Structure
and Form

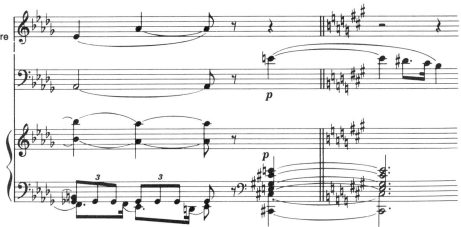

The movement's second section, beginning with m. 17, introduces the distant relation of *A* major (enharmonically *B-double flat*). This establishes strong tonal contrast because it is a departure from the near-related keys that occur in the opening section. Note that the *A* tonic is a semitone above *A*♭, the dominant (enharmonic ♭VI).

Ex. 1–13. Ibid.

Shortly following the *A* in this section, closely related tonal regions occur: *c-sharp* minor, *b* minor, and *f-sharp* major/minor. It is interesting that two of these tonics, *c*♯ and *f*♯, are close enharmonic relatives of *D*♭ (*C*♯).

Ex. 1–14. Ibid.

**Tonal Structure
and Form**

The return to *A-flat* in the movement's third section (measure 33) coincides with restatements of themes of the opening. Reflecting the relationships of the first section, a change to its dominant key, *E-flat*, takes place. The restatement is just an abbreviated version of the original.

Ex. 1–15. Ibid.

**Tonal Structure
and Form**

With the return, in measure 73, to *D-flat* major, the movement's tonal cycle is closed. This reappearance coincides with a restatement of the opening section (with a different accompaniment), including a restatement of the original change to *A-flat*. As could be expected, this key functions as the dominant for the final return to *D-flat* major, which occurs in measure 74.

Ex. 1–16. Ibid.

Tonal Structure
and Form

This movement contains elements of tonal form that are not present in the Bach or Mozart examples. Distant-related keys outline the large formal divisions of the movement, while near-related keys create variety within these divisions. The following diagram may help you to get an overall image of the movement's tonal form.

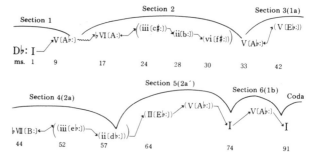

Each of these participating keys is symbolized in relation to *D-flat* major. Considered in this manner, the contrast created by Sections 2 and 4 is readily apparent. This is because they are in keys far afield from *D-flat*. In addition, these two sections contribute extra tonal variety since they also contain passages in minor keys. The gross key scheme, however, is represented by major keys that are framed by *D-flat*.

Each of the three compositions discussed in this chapter reveals various formal roles performed by tonality. Each contains a basic reference point to which all other tonalities and tonal regions can be related. Some of these relationships are *near*, others *distant*. Ultimately, the kinds of tonality relationships that separate formal sections involve factors that distinguish one musical style from another. In general, near-related keys provide greater stability than distant-related keys. Rapid tonality changes are often associated with transitional passages, as are passages that contain fragmented statements of earlier themes. Many forms of music to be studied in subsequent chapters contain the kinds of tonality schemes discussed in this chapter.

Exercises

For more detailed assignments see *Materials and Structure of Music II, Workbook*, Chapter 1.

1. Describe how changes of tonality are produced in the Bach *Prelude* discussed at the beginning of this chapter.
2. Make a tonal form analysis of works such as the following:
   a. Beethoven, *Sonata*, Op. 2, No. 3
   b. Brahms, *Intermezzo*, Op. 116, No. 2
   c. Hindemith, *Mathis der Mahler*, 1
   d. Recitatives from operas by Mozart and Rossini, and from Bach's *St. Matthew Passion*
   e. Copland, *Symphony No. 3*
   f. Bartók, *Second String Quartet*
   g. Barber, *Piano Sonata*
   h. Carter, *Woodwind Quintet*
   i. Berg, *Seven Early Songs*
   j. Stravinsky, *Mass*
3. Write a recitative on a preexisting text or one of your own. Use the Mozart recitative discussed in this chapter as your model.
4. Sketch the basic framework of a composition comparable in length to the last movement of Beethoven's *Fourth Symphony*. Indicate the key relationships in your sketch, and show how the key changes could be brought about.
5. Analyze Ex. 1–12, Ex. 1–13, Ex. 1–14, and Ex. 1–15 to show basic harmony. Then, select at least one of these reductions as the harmonic model for a short piano and flute composition.

Chapter Two

Rondo

Forms in music result from the presentation of musical patterns in schemes of reiteration, variation, and contrast. Every aspect of music (melody, harmony, tonality, pitch register, timbre, loudness, meter, rhythm, texture, tempo, etc.) contributes to the shaping of a musical form. When listeners recognize patterns of like and unlike elements and discern their order of arrangement, they are conscious of the organizational scheme—the *form*.

The rondo is one of the "return" forms we mentioned in Chapter 18 of Volume I. In general, the term *rondo* applies to any return form in which multiple returns occur, such as *ABABA*, *ABACA*, etc. Therefore, it is merely one manifestation of the return principle.

Rondo Principle in Early Music

An extension of the basic idea of statement, contrast, restatement is seen in the medieval *rondeau* of Ex. 2–1. Form is achieved in this piece through two contrasting themes presented in a pattern of repetition and alternation accompanying lines of the text. The form can be represented as A B a A a b A B, the capital letters indicating the music attending the refrain—the repeated text (underlined). Unity is achieved here by repetition of both text and themes.

Ex. 2–1. Trouveres: *En ma dame* (Rondeau).

The main organizational feature of the old *rondeau* was the recurrence of a refrain, a recurring phrase or section of identical text and music. During the seventeenth century an instrumental *rondeau* was developed that was similar to the earlier vocal form. The newer version consisted of a theme whose many restatements alternated with numerous digressions, which usually incorporated a degree of tonal variety.

The seventeenth-century *rondeau* was a direct ancestor of the modern rondo, which adheres to the principle of recurrence but usually differs from its forerunner by having fewer but longer sections.

In the composition that follows (Ex. 2–2), you can find a representative example of the seventeenth-century *rondeau*. Although this piece was not called *rondeau* by its composer, it is clearly organized through the alternating statements of a principal opening passage (the *rondeau theme*), measures 1–12, separated by five digressions, or couplets. The result is a simple reiterative form consisting of the following:

Rondeau theme—couplet 1—*rondeau* theme—couplet 2—
rondeau theme—couplet 3—*rondeau* theme—couplet 4—
rondeau theme—couplet 5—*rondeau* theme

Such a scheme can be abbreviated as: *A B A C A D A E A F A.*

This *rondeau*—a relatively short composition—reveals only a moderate degree of contrast between the *rondeau* theme and the succeeding couplets. In this case four of the five couplets are distinguished by varying degrees of tonal variety, whereas their rhythms and textures show only minimal change (except for couplet 4). As we shall learn in our subsequent study, it was not until the eighteenth and nineteenth centuries that rondo compositions normally incorporated more pronounced and sharply contrasted digressions.

Ex. 2–2. Chambonnières: *Chaconne for Harpsichord.*

* ⨎ : repeat the *rondeau* theme, beginning in measure 3.
 ※ : repeat the *rondeau* theme, beginning in measure 2.
 𝄋 : repeat the full *rondeau* theme.

(Rondeau Theme)

27

Rondo

1er Couplet

2me Couplet

3me Couplet

Rondo

Modern Rondo Form

In a rondo composed during and after the eighteenth century, the rondo theme[1] is usually clearly defined as a melody and accompanimental texture, its importance emphasized by its early presentation within the movement. The theme is further stressed by its reappearances, often unaltered, following digressions involving contrasting materials.

The following patterns represent common rondo schemes, a few of which we shall discuss presently.

```
A   B   A   B   A
A   B   A   C   A
A   B   A   C   A   B   A
A   B   A   C   A   D   A
```

The term *rondo* designates not only a form type, as we have defined it, but also connotes a character type. Rondo movements are usually characterized by uncomplicated dance-like themes in animated tempo. Thus, they become jaunty vehicles for the expression of whimsy, gaiety, flippancy, and humor. No rondo would better justify this statement than that whose main theme appears in the next example.

Ex. 2–3. Haydn: *Symphony No. 88*, IV.

The movement partially illustrated in Ex. 2–4 is a simple rondo composed from minimum materials. The characteristic effect is achieved through the use of rondo theme *a*, variation *a'*, and contrasting theme *b*.

Ex. 2–4. Mozart: *Sonatina in C Major*, III.

---

[1] Sometimes called *ritornello* or *returning passage*.

.**Ex. 2–5.** Mozart: Ibid.

Ex. 2–6. Mozart: Ibid.

* (a + 1) indicates rondo theme plus first ending;
(a′ + 2), variation plus second ending, etc.

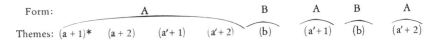

Form:		A			B	A	B	A
Themes:	(a + 1)*	(a + 2)	(a′ + 1)	(a′ + 2)	(b)	(a′ + 1)	(b)	(a′ + 2)

This five-part design illustrates certain important organizational features:

1. After its initial appearance, the rondo theme is immediately repeated with slight variation.
2. The primacy of the main theme is further established by its recurrences and proportionate duration. Twenty-four of the total thirty-four measures are devoted to (a) and (a′), while (b) encompasses only eight measures.
3. The modified version of the rondo theme adds a touch of variety, which relieves the monotony of literal repetition.

4. The subsidiary theme (four-measure phrase) differs markedly from the rondo theme because of its increased pitch-rhythm movement, the interruption of the Alberti accompaniment, and the change of harmonic rhythm.

To develop further the topic of rondo form, consider a more extended example by the same composer:

Ex. 2–7. Mozart: *Viennese Sonatinas*, the A rondo theme.

Ex. 2–8. Ibid., B theme.

Rondo

Ex. 2–9. Ibid., C theme.

Ex. 2–10. Ibid., Coda.

These thematic materials are arranged according to this scheme:

Section:	A	B	A	C	A	Coda
Tonality:	C	c	C	F	C	C
Meas.:	(1-32)	(33-64)	(65-96)	(97-128)	(129-160)	161-189)

In addition to the points previously made concerning rondo forms, the following additional features are exemplified by this Mozart piece:

1. The five-part form (plus coda) consists of an A section alternating with two contrasting sections, B and C.
2. The rondo theme consists of a contrasting double period. Note that the first period is parallel in that, except for the cadences, the phrases are identical.
3. Sections B and C are in the contrasting keys of c minor and F major.
4. Sections B and C contrast with each other and with the rondo theme, in accompaniment, theme, and key.
5. The various theme groups (double periods) follow with no intervening transitory or modulatory material.
6. A coda closes the movement. It is made of materials which are similar to, or derivative of, previous themes.

In the movement represented in Ex. 2–11, the technique of variation assumes importance; the rondo theme is constantly modified, never returning in its original form. Thus the basic repetitive character of the rondo (the unifying element) is maintained. The form here combines rondo characteristics with theme and variations. Only the main theme and the design of this movement are shown.

Ex. 2–11. Haydn: *Sonata No. 9*, III.

Form:

Another important factor in the study of rondo is that of *instrumentation* and its relation to form. Giuseppe Torelli, in his *Solo Concerto for Violin and Orchestra*, confines the repeated thematic materials (A sections) to *tutti* passages, while contrasting sections are performed by the solo violin and continuo.

Ex. 2–12. Torelli: *Solo Concerto for Violin and Orchestra*.

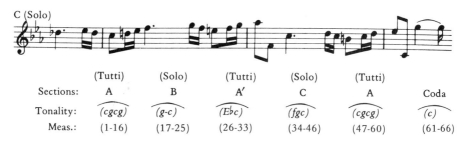

	(Tutti)	(Solo)	(Tutti)	(Solo)	(Tutti)	
Sections:	A	B	A′	C	A	Coda
Tonality:	(cgcg)	(g-c)	(E♭c)	(fgc)	(cgcg)	(c)
Meas.:	(1-16)	(17-25)	(26-33)	(34-46)	(47-60)	(61-66)

A different technique is employed in the third movement of Beethoven's *Violin Concerto in D major* (A B A C A B A-Coda), whose rondo theme appears in Ex. 2–13. In the rondo sections of this movement, the theme is stated first by the solo violin and then by the orchestra; in the episodic sections, the solo instrument predominates, with the orchestra generally functioning as accompaniment.

Ex. 2–13. Beethoven: *Violin Concerto in D Major*, III.

Beethoven, seldom content to conform to a stereotyped pattern, constantly sought to inject new elements of variety into his works. He enlarged the formal dimensions, exploited new key relationships, and treated thematic materials with greater freedom than did his predecessors. In the fourth movement of his *Piano Sonata in B-flat Major*, Op. 22, he alters the seven-section rondo pattern in that the sixth section consists of a return of both the first and second contrasting materials transposed to the tonic key.

Sections:	A	B	A	C	A	(CB′)	A	Coda
Tonality:	*B-flat*	*F*	*B-flat*	*b-flat*	*B-flat*	*B-flat*	*B-flat*	*B-flat*

In the third movement of his *Symphony No. 7*, Op. 92, Beethoven extends the form through repetition and arrives at the following five-section arrangement:

	Scherzo*		Trio		Scherzo		Trio		Scherzo
Sections:	A B A		C(c1-c2)		A B A		C(c1-c2)		A B A
Tonality:	*FA-FF*		*D*		*FA-FF*		*D*		*FA-FF*

Note that the trio sections (rounded binary forms) are used to balance the ternary grouping of A B A, and also observe the key relations (chromatic third) *F–A* and *F–D*. The thematic materials are shown in Ex. 2–14.

---

* For Beethoven, the scherzo at times replaces the *minuet*. While it, too, is in triple meter, its character is generally more vigorous and bustling than that of the *minuet*.

Rondo

Ex. 2–14. Beethoven: *Symphony No. 7*, Op. 92, III.

Our brief survey of the rondo [2] demonstrates that, although a composition may generally conform to a basic rondo scheme, composers frequently modify the basic pattern. One should recognize this fact and approach the study of each new work with the realization that the form plans are mere frames of reference. Furthermore, there are compositions whose forms are subject to multiple interpretations, while others conform to no particular stereotyped design.

Composers such as Schubert, Mendelssohn, Chopin, and Brahms, to name but a few, employed the rondo form in numerous works, two of which are partially illustrated in Ex. 2–15 and Ex. 2–16.

Ex. 2–15. Schubert: *Sonata for Piano in D Major*, Op. 53, Finale.

(Form: A B A'(var. A) C A" (var. A) Coda)

[2] A complete rondo movement appears in the Workbook, *Materials and Structure of Music* Vol. II.

Ex. 2–16. Chopin: *Mazurka in B-flat Major*, Op. 7, No. 1.

(Form: A B A C A)

Several works by contemporary composers exemplify more recent practices. The themes and attendant form patterns should be used as points of departure for the study of the complete scores and recorded performances.

Ex. 2–17. Barber: *Sonata for Piano*, Op. 26, II. Reprinted by permission of the copyright owner, G. Schirmer, Inc.

(Form: A B A C A Coda)

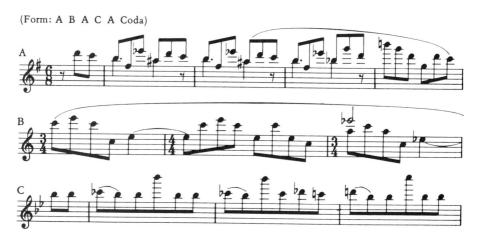

Ex. 2–18. Bartók: *Music for Strings, Percussion, and Celesta,* IV. Copyright 1937 by Universal Edition; Renewed 1964. Copyright and Renewal assigned to Boosey & Hawkes, Inc., for U.S.A. and to Universal Edition for all other countries of the world. Reprinted by permission.

Ex. 2–19 illustrates a work of particular interest because its sections *B, D,* and *Coda* are made up of developed fragments of *A.* Section *C* contains new materials that are not derived from the *A* theme. The result is a highly unified movement that suggests a ternary form, yet possesses characteristics of the rondo. Note how *B* and *D* are actual variants of *A.*

Ex. 2–19. Hindemith: *Third Sonata for Piano,* II. © 1936 by B. Schott's Soehne, Mainz. Renewed 1963. Reprinted by permission.

The next two examples illustrate less ambiguous schemes.

Ex. 2–20. Milhaud: *Suite Française,* V. © Copyright MCMXLV, MCMXLVI, MCML by Leeds Music Corporation, New York, N.Y. Used by permission. All rights reserved.

(Form: **A B A C A B A**)

Ex. 2–21. Prokofiev: *Violin Concerto No. 2,* Op. 63, III. By permission of the International Music Company, New York.

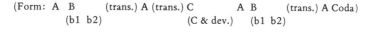

(Form: A B   (trans.) A (trans.) C   A B   (trans.) A Coda)
           (b1 b2)   (C & dev.)   (b1 b2)

From a more thorough study of recent music, it will become apparent that traditional practices have been modified considerably to fit the needs of twentieth-century composers. For example, literal repetition frequently is avoided, and tonality, once an obvious agent of formal organization, has become tenuous or irrelevant as a determinant of form. For an earlier composer, such as Mozart, one of the primary unifying features of form was the return to tonic key, variety effected by departure from it. Obviously, if the initial tonality is obscure or ambiguous, its strength as a unifying element is diminished. Although clearly established tonalities are found in many contemporary works, abrupt key changes are common and thus the need for extensive transitory (modulatory) materials no longer exists.

Exercises

For more detailed assignments see *Materials and Structure of Music II, Workbook*, Chapter 2.

1. For a detailed analysis of forms, see the following list. Outline the form, indicating themes, sections, keys, and measure numbers. Make a summary of the prominent features not apparent from the outline.
   Haydn: *Piano Sonata in C major*, III.
   Mozart: *Sonata in E-flat major for Violin and Piano*, K. 380, Rondo.
   Beethoven: *Piano Sonata*, Op. 13, III.
   Mendelssohn: *Midsummer Night's Dream*, Scherzo (the C section is developmental in character).
   Brahms: *Symphony No. 1*, III.
   Mahler: *Symphony No. 4*, II.
   Piston: *String Quartet No. 1*, III.
   Sessions: *Symphony No. 2*, IV.
   Barber: *Capricorn Concerto*, III.
2. Compose two rondo themes of two to three phrases in length, using at least one form of each of the following: V_7/V, V_7/iv, V_7/VI, V_7/ii.
3. Select one of the themes and make a setting for string quartet.
4. Compose a contrasting section to follow the rondo theme (Ex. 3–3), experimenting with changes of texture, thematic character, and key.
5. Arrange the material of Exercises 3 and 4 to create a rondo form as follows: A B A B A (Coda). For the sake of variety, use different dynamic levels and ranges for the repeated sections. Append a short coda made of materials derived from the rondo theme.
6. Copy score and parts for class performance.

Chapter Three

Diatonic Seventh Chords (Non-dominant)

To this point, our discussion of chords has been limited generally to diatonic triads, the dominant seventh, and secondary dominants. Let us now consider another group of tertian structures, commonly called *diatonic seventh chords*.

Diatonic Seventh Chords (Nondominant)

Diatonic seventh chords have as their roots (or primes) any of the degrees of the major or minor scales. They contain the intervals of 3rd, 5th, and 7th. Our present concern is with chords that are not of the major-minor seventh chord types, and thus do not function as primary or as secondary dominants.

Ex. 3–1. Mozart: *Piano Sonata*, K. 332, I.

Ex. 3–2. Bacharach: *What the World Needs Now Is Love.*

The following chart shows the chord types that occur most frequently in the music of the eighteenth and nineteenth centuries; they are arranged according to chord quality, which is indicated by a series of symbols: MM, mm, and so on. The first letter represents the triad type, the second the size of the interval of the 7th.[1] The terms *dimin-*

---

[1] Other types of seventh chords occur, often in a minor mode, as a result of chromatic inflection, such as *minor-major* and *augmented-major*. See measures 1 and 3 of Ex. 3-3b.

ished-minor and *diminished-diminished* are not commonly used, being replaced by half-diminished ($^{\varnothing}_7$) and diminished ($^{\circ}_7$), respectively.

QUALITY	MAJOR MODE	MINOR MODE
Major-Major (MM)	I₇, IV₇	III₇, VI₇
Major-Minor (Mm)	V₇	.V₇
Minor-Minor (mm)	ii₇, iii₇, vi₇	I₇, iv₇, (V₇)
Half-Diminished ($^{\varnothing}_7$) (Diminished-Minor)	vii$^{\varnothing}_7$	ii$^{\varnothing}_7$
Diminished ($^{\circ}_7$) (Diminished-Diminished)		vii$^{\circ}_7$ (harmonic and melodic minor scales)

Although the chords in the above chart are listed as in root position, all occur in 1st, 2nd, and 3rd inversions as well. Inversions are indicated as follows: 1st inversion— $^6_5$; 2nd inversion— $^4_3$; and 3rd inversion— $^4_2$. The complete set of diatonic seventh chords in major is shown in Ex. 3–3a. A few additional types are found in minor, and these appear in Ex. 3–3b, where the various alternatives are shown for the three forms of the minor scale.

Ex. 3–3a. Diatonic seventh chords.

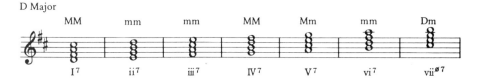

Ex. 3–3b. Ibid.

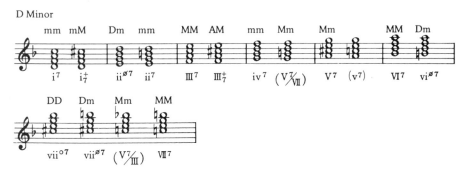

Treatment of the Dissonance

The seventh forms an unstable element and thus merits special attention. It often results from a purely melodic function, as a passing tone, appoggiatura, or suspension.

Ex. 3–4a. Palestrina: Motet, *Dies Sanctificatus.*

Chords
(Nondominant)
Diatonic Seventh

Ex. 3–4b. Ibid.

When no such melodic explanation is possible, as in Ex. 3–5, the 7th is a harmonic member of the chord.

Ex. 3–5. Schubert: *Der Greise Kopf.*

It is often impossible to distinguish between a seventh chord and a triad with an attendant nonchord tone. Thus the first two measures of Ex. 3–6 may be described as a basic harmonic movement from vi through I $^6_4$ to iii, being embellished by the escape tones *c-sharp* and *b*. If these pitches are considered as chord tones, the analysis is slightly different.

Ex. 3–6. Puccini: *La Boheme*, Act I, "Si, mi chiamano Mimi."

We will call a collection of pitches a *seventh chord* when the duration of the 7th is equal to that of other chord members. Remember, however, that many chords are subject to multiple interpretations, depending upon the particular circumstances.

Composers of different styles have used various means of approaching the 7th of the chord. In much music, the 7th occurs as a suspension. Note the following example, in which this occurs.

Ex. 3–7. Handel: *Suite No. 12 for Harpsichord, Gigue.*

Sometimes the 7th functions as a passing tone, even when its duration makes it fit our definition of *harmonic*. When the seventh chord follows its triadic form, as in the next example, the passing tone effect is rather clear.

Ex. 3–8. Beethoven: *Symphony No. 4 in B-flat Major, Op. 60, II.*

Ex. 3–9 has features in common with Ex. 3–8; the 7th in each seventh chord is part of a descending step-progression. In Ex. 3–9, however, the nondominant seventh chords are not preceded by their triadic forms. Here each member of the three-tone arpeggiation acts as a passing tone, thereby linking the parallel members of the preceding and succeeding patterns. In this sense the whole chord is a *passing chord*.

Ex. 3–9. Beethoven: *Piano Sonata*, Op. 14, No. 1, III.

A leap to the 7th emphasizes its dissonance. Note that both seventh chords in the following example have 7ths approached in this way.

Ex. 3–10. Monteverdi: *Ariana*, "Lasciatemi morire!"

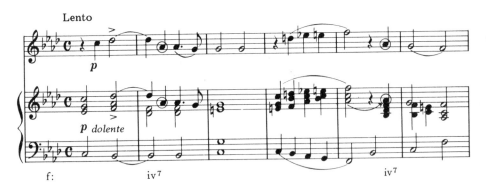

Composers have been consistent in their resolution of the chord's 7th, at least until the beginning of the twentieth century; the *seventh usually resolves down by step*, and if it does not, it is most frequently held over, continuing as a member of the next chord (as in Ex. 3–11b).

Ex. 3–11. Resolution of chord sevenths.

Chords
(Nondominant)
Diatonic Seventh

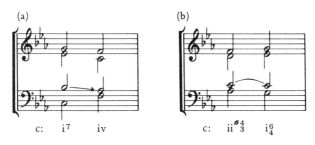

Seventh chords are used in progressions similar to those of their triadic counterparts. The usual resolution of such chords (except the subdominant and leading tone seventh chords) is to a chord with a root a perfect fifth below (or perfect fourth above) the root of the seventh chord.

Ex. 3–12. Usual resolutions.

Usual resolutions

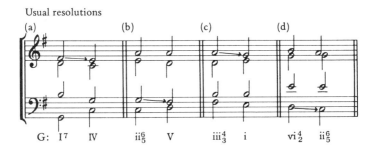

In other resolutions (a few of which appear in Ex. 3–13), the seventh is often held over. Four different root relations are represented by the progressions: (a)—step up; (b)—step down; (c)—third down, and (d)—third up.

Ex. 3–13. Other resolutions.

Other resolutions

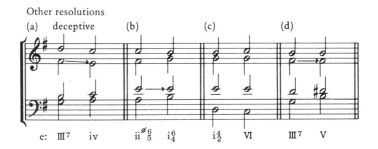

Subdominant seventh chords (IV$_7$, iv$_7$) usually progress to the dominant chord. Leading tone seventh chords (vii°$_7$, vii°$_7$) usually progress to the tonic chord. But they too may resolve in less predictable ways.

Ex. 3–14. Resolutions of subdominant and leading tone seventh chords.

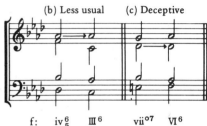

The following chart of common progressions (reproduced from Vol. I) will be helpful in planning progressions of diatonic seventh chords. Note how the chord resolutions cited in Ex. 3–11 through Ex. 3–14 relate to this general scheme.

TONIC		PRE-DOMINANT (subdominant)	DOMINANT	TONIC
I, i	vi, VI	IV, iv	V, V$_7$	I, i
	iii, III, III$^+$	ii, ii°	vii°$_6$	(vi, VI)
			(iii$_6$, iii	
			III)	

The harmonic cycle may begin at any point.
Any step in the cycle may be omitted.
Any step or steps may be retraced before normal direction is resumed.

As a rule, secondary seventh chords contain all four members. Exceptions may be found in progressions of four-part textures (sequential passages, for example) in which the chord of resolution is another seventh chord. In such cases, the 5th (or more rarely, the 3rd) may be omitted and the root doubled. Because of its pronounced resolution tendency, the 7th of the chord usually is not doubled.

Ex. 3–15.

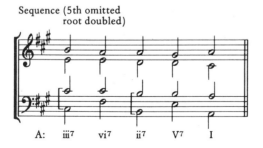

Let us now turn our attention to a few of the *roles* diatonic seventh chords play in music. As previously stated, they may appear singly or in series as do triads. In addition, they often appear at important structural points, such as at the beginning of a phrase, or at the point of climax as illustrated in measure 4 of Ex. 3–16. Note that the ii $\frac{6}{5}$ is preceded by another nondominant seventh chord, a IV₇.

Ex. 3–16. Mendelssohn: *Elijah*, "Behold God the Lord" (last 6 measures).

Seventh chords frequently function in connection with a cadence, both in the approach and in the cadence proper. The final cadence pattern in Ex. 3–17 consists of a series of triads appearing in conjunction with an *e-flat* pedal. Two of the resulting sonorities are seventh chords.

Ex. 3–17. Hindemith: *Mathis der Mahler* (last 6 measures). © 1934 by B. Schott's Soehne, Mainz. Renewed 1963. Reprinted by permission.

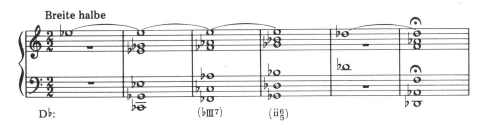

The MM7th chord in the next excerpt (Ex. 3–18) is actually the final-chord of the composition.

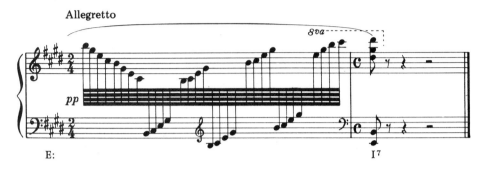

Chains of seventh chords provide the harmonic basis for sequences in the same way as triads. Ex. 3–19, containing five nondominant diatonic seventh chords, appears between two main thematic groups. It serves to dramatize the appearance of a new theme.

Ex. 3–19. Brahms: *Requiem,* Section VI.

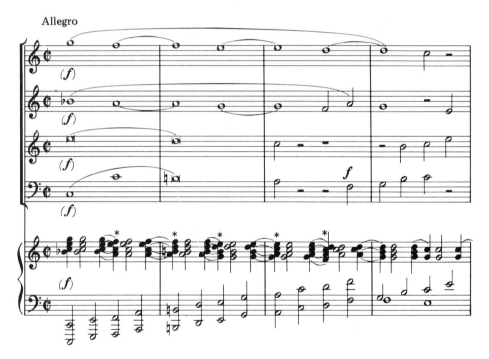

Seventh chords frequently serve as pivots in modulatory passages. In Ex. 3–20, a mm $\frac{4}{2}$ chord functions in this capacity, performing the dual role of iv $\frac{4}{2}$ in *G* and ii $\frac{4}{2}$ in *B-flat*.

Ex. 3–20. Beethoven: *String Quartet*, Op. 18, No. 6, IV.

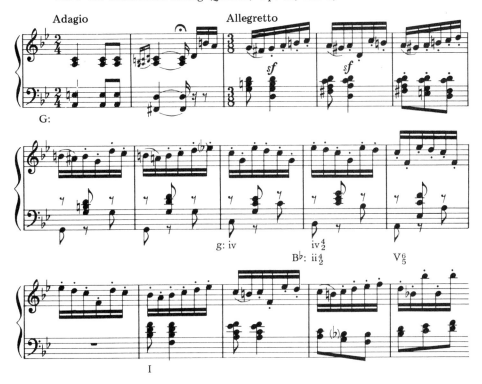

The Supertonic Seventh Chord

The supertonic seventh chord appears in two diatonic forms: ii$_7$ in major, and ii°$_7$ in minor. The ii$_7$ contains one unstable interval, the seventh between root and seventh; the ii°$_7$ contains two, the seventh and diminished fifth. The common resolution of both ii$_7$ and ii°$_7$ is to V. This progression is characterized by downward step resolution of the chord seventh, which moves in parallel thirds or sixths with another voice.

In the resolution to V and to I, the supertonic $^6_5$ bears a marked resemblance to the subdominant. For example, the *subdominant* character of the supertonic $^6_5$ chord in (a) and in (c) of Ex. 3–21 is intensified by the bass movement, which is a rise by step to V in the former, a drop to i in the latter.

Ex. 3–21. Comparison of ii $^6_5$ and IV.

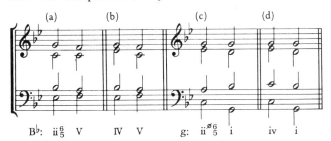

Because of these characteristics, and because this particular chord plays an important role in harmonic patterns (such as cadences), the supertonic 7th chord is often regarded as a subdominant with the added sixth. Since two perfect 5ths are present in the mm$^6_5$, there is the possibility of two different root interpretations. But in the $^6_5$, only one perfect 5th is present (between bass and chord 7th), and thus the bass pitch is the most probable root.

Ex. 3–22. ii$_7$ and ii°$_7$.

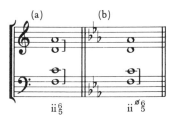

As subsequent examples will reveal, the supertonic chord usually is preceded by I or vi and resolves to V.

Uses of the Supertonic Seventh Chord

Since the root of the supertonic seventh chord forms a fifth relation with the root of the dominant chord, it frequently precedes the dominant, as in Ex. 3–23. Note here how the unstable chord members are treated in a conventional manner.

Ex. 3–23. Verdi: Requiem, *Ingemisco*.

The first inversion is used in a similar fashion with a bass line that moves 4-5-1, as in Ex. 3–24. Here the ii $^6_5$ is preceded by the submediant chord.

Ex. 3–24. Schubert: *Symphony No. 5 in B-flat Major*, I.

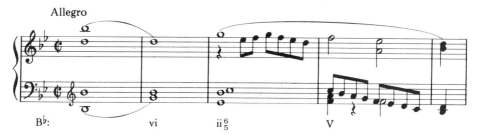

Resolution to the dominant chord may be delayed, the tonic $^6_4$ intervening between ii and V, as in the next excerpt.

Ex. 3–25. Verdi: Requiem, *Libera Me.*

Example 3–26 illustrates ii $^6_5$ followed by its mutated form, V$^6_5$/V. This secondary dominant links ii$_7$ to V, the cadence chord. The motion of the bass line from *f* to *g* is strengthened by the *f-sharp* inflection.

Ex. 3–26. Mozart: *Marriage of Figaro*, Act. III, Sextette.

Within a phrase, the ii₇ (or ii°₇) often embellishes the tonic chord through a kind of pedal point. This progression is almost the same as the i—iv $^6_4$—i relationship we saw earlier.

Ex. 3–27. Schubert: *Gute Nacht.*

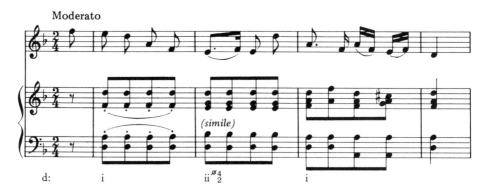

The supertonic seventh chord figures prominently in the approach to the authentic cadence of Ex. 3–28. Here the cadential i $^6_4$ is prolonged by the interpolation of a ii $^6_5$ chord.

Ex. 3–28. Leoncavallo: *Pagliacci*, Act I, "Recitar."

The next example contains the ii°₇ in a passage that shifts from an initial minor key to its relative major. In this instance, the ii°₇ serves as pivot chord for the modulation.

Ex. 3–29. Schubert: Quartet No. 14 in D Minor, *Death and the Maiden.*

Leading-Tone Seventh Chord

The leading-tone seventh chord is a half-diminished seventh chord (vii°₇) in major, and a diminished seventh chord (vii°₇) in minor. Both sonorities share common features as well as differences. The vii°₇ contains two dissonant intervals, a diminished fifth and a minor seventh, whereas the vii°₇ contains two diminished fifths. While the former in root position contains both major and minor thirds, the latter contains only minor thirds.

Ex. 3–30. vii°₇ and vii°₇.

Within an established tonality, both chords have strong resolution tendencies. They usually resolve to tonic, with augmented and diminished intervals resolving as noted in an earlier discussion.

Ex. 3–31. Resolutions of vii°$_7$ and vii°$_7$.

No special resolution problems arise in the inversions of these chords. The most significant feature of both chord forms is the usual resolution of the chord's *prime* (which is the leading tone of the key) to the tonic pitch.

The vii°$_7$ chord (and its inversions as well) frequently appears where a V$_7$ chord might otherwise precede tonic, and it also frequently occurs in conjunction with that chord. Note the exchanges of the two chords in Ex. 3–32.

Ex. 3–32. Chopin: *Nocturne*, Op. 37.

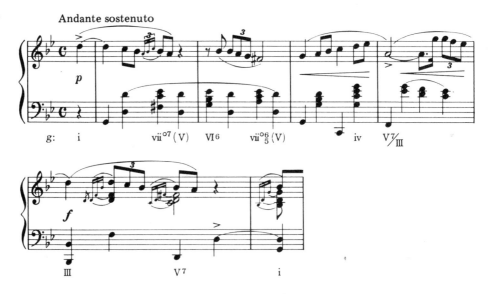

Example 3–33 shows other harmonic relationships formed by the vii°$_7$ and vii°$_7$.

Ex. 3–33. Other resolutions of °$_7$ and °$_7$.

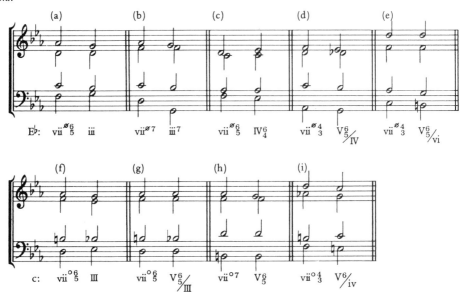

The vii°$_7$ plays an important role in the next two passages (Ex. 3–34).

Ex. 3–34. Beethoven: *Piano Sonata*, Op. 10, No. 1, I.

A vii° $\frac{4}{3}$ provides the harmonic opening for the second phrase of the following excerpt.

Ex. 3–35. Schubert: *Symphony No. 5 in B-flat Major,* III.

In Ex. 3–36, the leading tone seventh chord fills in between two tonic chords.

Ex. 3–36. Schubert: *Symphony No. 5 in B-flat Major,* I.

Embellishment of the dominant is the function of the vii° $\frac{4}{2}$ appearing in measures 1–6 of Ex. 3–37. This dominant elaboration dramatizes the reappearance of the movement's main theme in measure 9.

Ex. 3–37. Mozart: *Piano Sonata*, K. 457, III.

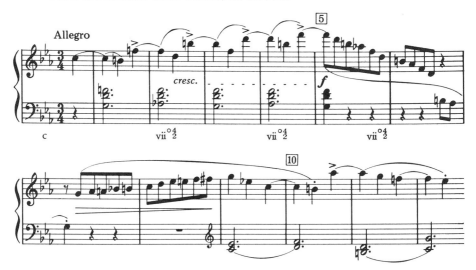

Although the leading tone seventh chord customarily resolves to tonic, it often resolves to other triads or seventh chords too. Note the less common resolutions in the following three excerpts.

Ex. 3–38. Bizet: *Carmen*, Act II, "Faites-Lui Mes Aveux."

Ex. 3–39. Mendelssohn: *Andante con Variazioni*, Op. 82.

Ex. 3–40. Bartók: *Little Pieces for Children,* Vol. I, No. 7. Reprinted by permission of the copyright owner, Edwin F. Kalmus.

C: vii$^{o6}_{5}$ V   V^{7}/IV   IV   V^{7} I

The Tonic Seventh Chord

Ex. 3–41. Stravinsky: *Petrouchka,* Third part. Copyright by Edition Rusee de Musique. All rights assigned to Boosey & Hawkes, Inc. Revised Edition Copyright 1947 by Boosey & Hawkes, Inc. Reprinted by permission.

The melody of Ex. 3–41 is a cornet solo. It outlines the seventh chord that is the topic for this section. As study of the example reveals, the constituent intervals above its root (*G*) are: major third, perfect fifth, and major seventh.

In the minor mode i$_7$ is a mm$_7$ chord, which is identical in structure to the ii$_7$ (major mode) previously discussed. The i$_7$ usually employs the unaltered seventh degree (subtonic) of the minor scale rather than the leading tone.

Ex. 3–42. i$_7$ chord.

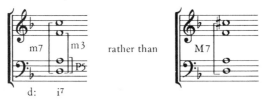

The tonic seventh chord generally moves to the subdominant, thus permitting the downward resolution of the chord's seventh. When the tonic seventh is a MM$_7$ chord (thus containing the leading tone), this resolution is contrary to the usual ascent of this scale member. In the

progression to the subdominant, the inversions generally follow the resolution patterns described for inversions of other seventh chords. That is, the bass of the first inversion generally moves up by step; that of third inversion, down by step; and that of second inversion, up or down by step.

In one typical occurrence, the tonic seventh chord appears early in a phrase as an elaboration of the basic progression I–IV, as illustrated in Ex. 3–43. Here the chord's seventh results from the passing motion between 8 and 6, the root and third of the chords in measures 1 and 3.

Ex. 3–43. Puccini: *La Bohème*, Act II, "Quando me'n vo."

In other passages, the MM₇ chord may serve as a cadence chord, as in the next example.

Ex. 3–44. Krenek: "The Moon Rises." Reprinted by permission of the copyright owner, G. Schirmer, Inc.

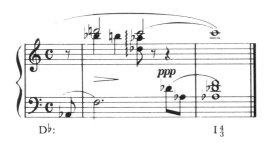

In Ex. 3–45, the seventh of I_7 appears as an unresolved suspension, prepared as the 3rd of the preceding V_7. The I_7 moves to vi_6, following which the I_7 appears again.

Ex. 3–45. Mendelssohn: *Elijah*, "Behold God the Lord."

Subdominant Seventh Chord

The two unaltered forms of the subdominant seventh chord are MM_7 in major and mm_7 in minor, as illustrated in Ex. 3–46.

Ex. 3–46. Copland: *Appalachian Spring*. Copyright 1945 by Aaron Copland. Reprinted by permission of Aaron Copland, Copyright Owner, and Boosey & Hawkes, Inc., Sole Licensees.

As you know, seventh chords often resolve to a chord whose root is a perfect fifth below. This is not the case with the IV_7; it more often resolves directly to V, or indirectly to V through I_4^6 or ii_7.

Inverted forms often occur when the bass moves by step. Less commonly, the subdominant seventh chord progresses to other chords, such as tonic, supertonic, or various secondary dominants. But the movement to tonic and to supertonic is most usual.

The subdominant seventh chord often appears near the end of a phrase, either just before a cadence or as a member of the cadence pattern itself. In the next excerpt (Ex. 3–47), IV₇ appears following vi, just before the V chord in a progressive cadence.

Ex. 3–47. Bartók: *Concerto for Piano*, No. 3, II. Copyright 1947 by Boosey & Hawkes, Ltd. Reprinted by permission of Boosey & Hawkes, Inc.

A plagal cadence closes Ex. 3–48. Here IV₇ resolves to I, which is embellished by a 6–5 suspension.

Ex. 3–48. Chopin: *Nocturne*, Op. 62, No. 2.

Noncadential occurrences of the subdominant seventh chord are common.

Ex. 3–49. Chopin: *Nocturne*, Op. 48, No. 1.

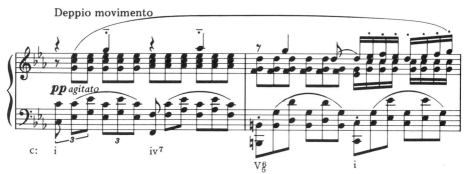

Ex. 3–50. Puccini: *Tosca*, Act II, "Vissi d'arte."

At times the IV$^4_3$ functions as a tonic embellishment. This is especially true in passages that feature a tonic pedal, as in the next example.

Ex. 3–51. Chopin: *Nocturne*, Op. 37, No. 2.

The progression from IV$_7$ to V$^6_5$/V often accompanies a bass line that moves chromatically up to the V chord. Observe the strong motion to E♭ (which is the fifth scale degree) in Ex. 3–52.

Ex. 3–52. Chopin: *Waltz*, Op. 69, No. 1.

The submediant seventh chord usually is found in one of two forms: as a mm₇ chord in major or as a MM₇ chord in minor. Its usual resolution is to a supertonic chord. Ex. 3–53 illustrates several common resolutions, to IV, V, V/V, and directly to I.

Ex. 3–53. Resolutions of vi₇ and VI₇ and inversions.

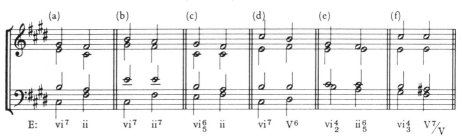

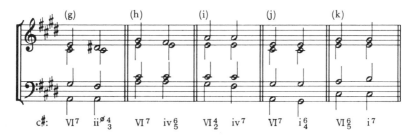

In Ex. 3–54, vi₇ precedes ii₇ in the approach to a terminal cadence, forming a strong root progression by fifths (D—G—C—F).

Ex. 3–54. Chopin: *Ballade in F*, Op. 37, Andantino.

Frequently, the submediant seventh chord is followed by its mutation, the V₇/ii. This relationship forms chromatic motion toward the II, which in turn prepares the cadence.

Ex. 3–55. Offenbach: *Les Contes d'Hoffman,* "Elle a fui, La tourterelle."

B♭:   vi⁶₅   vi⁶₅/ii   ii   I⁶₄   V⁷   I

The Mediant Seventh Chord (iii₇ or III₇)

The mediant seventh chord usually appears as mm₇ in major, MM₇ in minor. It regularly resolves to the IV chord, whose root is a fifth below, or to a mutation of that chord, such as V₇/ii.

In Ex. 3–56, the mediant seventh chord appears twice. First it involves a passing bass tone that follows the mediant triad, creating the third inversion (iii⁴₂). It next appears in a sequential stream of diatonic seventh chords. Note that every diatonic nondominant seventh chord appears in this passage.

Ex. 3–56. Debussy: *The Blessed Damozel.*

A: iii   iii⁴₂   I⁷   IV⁷   viii⁰⁷iii⁷   vi⁷   ii⁷

Every diatonic seventh chord is also used within the first four measures of Ex. 3–57, and in each instance the seventh resolves regularly. The alternation between accompaniment and vocal line creates an interesting sequence.

Ex. 3–57. Grieg: *An der Bahre einer Jungen Frau.*

E♭:   iii⁶₅

The mediant seventh chord sometimes progresses to the subdominant, as in Ex. 3–58, in which the subdominant seventh also occurs.

Ex. 3–58. Copland: *Appalachian Spring.* Copyright 1945 by Aaron Copland. Reprinted by permission of Aaron Copland, Copyright Owner, and Boosey & Hawkes, Inc., Sole Licensees.

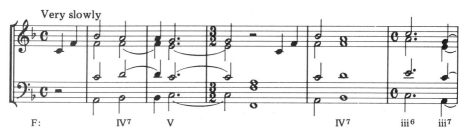

Exercises

For more detailed assignments see *Materials and Structure of Music II, Workbook,* Chapter 3.

1. Spell various types of seventh chords (nondominant) from the bass up, and identify them as to chord type and function in various major and minor keys.
2. Considering *d* as the root, third, fifth, and seventh, respectively, of different nondominant seventh chords, spell various types (mm⁷, MM⁶₅, °⁴₃, °₇, etc.) and indicate the function of each of the major and/or minor keys in which they might appear as diatonic chords.
3. Indicate the chord quality and function of each of the *seventh* chords appearing in Ex. 3–16, Ex. 3–19, Ex. 3–37 and Ex. 3–56.
4. Sing (from the bass up) various types of nondominant seventh chords (root position and inverted).
5. Using the following harmonic progressions, create a number of different phrases in both choral and instrumental styles. Vary the harmonic rhythm, texture, and keys in the different settings. Perform them at the piano to test their effectiveness.
    a. I—iii⁴₃—vi⁷—V⁶₅/V—I⁶₄—V⁴₂—I⁶—IV⁴₂—ii⁷—V—I
    b. i—V⁴₃—vii°⁶₅—i⁶—iv—ii°⁶₅—V—i⁶₄—iv⁷—ii°⁶₅—V
6. Compose a phrase for piano characterized by a sequential treatment in which all of the diatonic seventh chords appear.
7. Analyze a number of the following, indicating keys, chords, and nonchord tones.

a. Bach: *Prelude in C-sharp minor* (Well-tempered Clavier, Bk. I) (1–10)
b. Beethoven: *Symphony No. 3 in E-flat Major*, Op. 55, II (83–86)
c. Chopin: *Nocturne*, Op. 48, No. 1 (65–71)
d. Debussy: *Prelude VII*, Book I (24–27)
e. Gluck: *Orfeo*, Act I, "Ah! se intorno" (16–23)
f. Grieg: *Mein Ziel* (76–84)
g. Handel: *Rinaldo*, "Leave Me in Sorrow" (1–8)
h. Menotti: *Amahl and the Night Visitors*, "Shepherds' Chorus" (1–7)
i. Ravel: *Pavane* (1–12)
j. Rubinstein: *Ich Fuhle deinem Oden* (3–6)
k. Schubert: *Die Schöne Müllerin*, "Mit Dem Grunen Lautembande" (1–3)
l. Schumann: *Symphony No. 5 in B-flat Major*, I (11–14)
   Symphony No. 1, III, trio (1–3)
m. Scriabin: *Prelude in E-flat Major*, Op. 11, No. (5–8)

8. Find examples of nondominant seventh chords in the music composed for your own instrument.

Chapter Four

Embellishing Diminished Chords

We turn now to a chord type whose basic sonority is the diminished triad and whose usual harmonic function is to embellish a diatonic chord. In Chapter Twenty of Vol. I, we discussed the way a collection of diatonic chords can be enriched by secondary dominants. Embellishing diminished chords are chromatic chords whose main link with a diatonic chord is that of *secondary leading tone*. The diminished triad ($^{\circ}{}^{5}_{3}$) and the fully diminished seventh chord ($^{\circ}7$) perform this function in the music of the eighteenth and nineteenth centuries more frequently than any other chord types.

The structures of these chords make them well-suited for their embellishing roles; they are not stable chords as compared to major and minor triads. Since they lack the simple intervals that in other chords can make a root effect, we shall call the bottom note of their fundamental position the *prime*.

Ex. 4–1. Intervals of diminished chords.

It is the secondary leading tone relation that forms the link between this chord and the chord it embellishes. In this instance, the embellishing chord performs the same harmonic role as a secondary dominant, and it should be clear that this chord type shares pitches with the Mm7th chord type.[1]

Ex. 4–2. Similar structure of Mm₇ and diminished chords.

Because of this strong identity between secondary diminished chords and secondary dominants, a separation of the two types in terms of *harmonic function* is misleading. It is only the absence of the root relation by a fifth, in the progression of the secondary diminished chord to its successor chord, that warrants separate identification.

Embellishing Diminished Triads

The only difference between the diminished triad and the diminished seventh chord is that of sonority; the triad lacks the richer sound of the four-note structure. One could replace the other in any musical context, except in passages where limitation of voices or characteristic melodic patterns preclude the use of the four-note chord.

Secondary diminished chords usually are preceded by a diatonic chord. In Ex. 4–3, the usual °₇ chord relates directly to diatonic chords within a given key.

---

[1] We shall refer to the secondary diminished function in a way that is consistent with our analysis of the secondary dominant function. Thus °/V represents a secondary diminished embellishment of the dominant, while °6, °⁶₄, etc., refer to inversions of this chord.

Ex. 4–3. $°_7$ chords as embellishing chords.

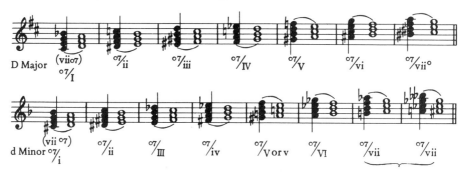

Notice that the $°_7$ chord built on the leading tone of the minor scale (vii$°_7$) is a diatonic chord. In major, it contains a mutation (flatted sixth degree) of the diatonic vii$°_7$ (which in D major would be *c-sharp—e—g —b*). All the other chords are nondiatonic.

In Ex. 4–4, the dominant chord is embellished by the $°_6$/V that immediately precedes it in a weak metric position. The diminished chord is further subordinated by the pedal on the dominant pitch, C.

Ex. 4–4. Beethoven: *Symphony No. 6*, I.

Further typical embellishing roles are shown in Ex. 4–5, where the ii and V chords are preceded by their secondary diminished triads. Notice that I$^6_4$ separates the V chord from its diminished embellishment.

Ex. 4–5. Mozart: *Piano Sonata*, K. 330, III.

71

The basic harmonic structure of this passage would not be altered if the texture were thickened by the addition of sevenths to each of the embellishing triads. Mozart might well have done this had he not preferred the thinner three-voice texture that typifies the passage. But in terms of *function,* the four-note chords could replace the simpler triads.

Because of this identical function of the two sonorities, we shall regard the two as interchangeable, the only difference being that of sonority. Everything said about secondary $°_7$ chords in terms of harmonic function is equally true of the diminished embellishing triad.

Embellishing $°_7$ **Chords**

Lacking a root tone, the diminished triad and the diminished seventh chord are indeterminate. They lack the stability that is required to create a definite sense of pitch focus. And yet, it is just this instability that makes them two of the most interesting chords in music, particularly music in which diatonic chords dominate the harmony.

It is significant that the $°_7$ chord depends upon notation for its functional identity. The same set of actual pitches that constitutes the fully diminished sonority can be spelled in many different ways and still form a notationally *correct* $°_7$ chord. Ex. 4–6 shows the three basic sets of notes that form all available diminished seventh chords within the twelve-note scale system. Notice that each basic chord is subject to at least the four other notated versions shown, not to mention the many other enharmonic possibilities.

Ex. 4–6. $°_7$ chords, enharmonic spellings.

Unlike major and minor triads and Mm7th chords, the *sound* of the isolated $°_7$ chord cannot imply inversion. If chord *x* of Ex. 4–7 is played at the piano, listeners have no reason to assume that they are not hearing the "inverted" forms of *y* or *z*.

Ex. 4–7. Ibid.

The most common secondary $^\circ_7$ chord embellishes the dominant, usually as a lower leading tone resolving up to the root of the V chord.

Ex. 4–8. Schumann: Op. 15, No. 1.

G: I $^{\circ 7}\!/_\text{V}$ V   V$^6_5$

In Ex. 4–8, the arrival of the V chord in measure 2 is made more imminent by the appearance of the $^\circ_7$ on the second beat of measure 1. Aside from the rootlessness of the diminished chord, the linear tensions suggested by the voices are compelling: the *g—c sharp* tritone of the bass line (following the stable G major triad) suggests a resolution to *d* of the bass line; and the *b—b-flat* step-progression of the middle voice clearly sets up the logical chromatic continuation to *a* (the fifth of the V chord).

This Schumann passage (Ex. 4–8) also demonstrates the usual voice leading in the resolution of the $^\circ_7$ chord; the notation clearly shows the secondary leading-tone function and resolves as such.

Ex. 4–9. Resolution of $^\circ_7$.

Since the $^\circ_7$ chord includes two tritones, both do not always resolve in the way prescribed for the single tritone. One of these intervals frequently bypasses the usual expansion or contraction resolution; this usually is the tritone that *does not* form the secondary leading-tone relation with the subsequent chord. In Ex. 4–10, the (a) resolution is more typical than the (b) or (c).

Ex. 4–10. Resolutions of $°_7$.

	L.T.	L.T.	L.T.
		(Direct 5ths in outer voices)	(No L.T. Resolution)

However, when the leading-tone member is not the bass tone and the resolution is to a V_7 chord, the leading tone frequently resolves down by step to the seventh of the V_7. As the next example shows, the third of the $°_7$ varies in resolution, moving up or down by step as demanded by the particular melodic pattern of the context.

Ex. 4–11. Resolutions of $°_7$.

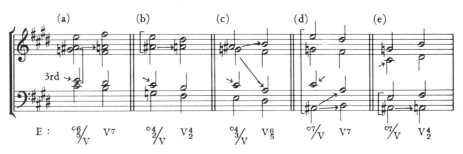

The resolutions of (c) and (d) are problematic because of the cross-relations formed when the secondary leading tone does not step down to the seventh of the subsequent chord.

We can extend the notion of leading-tone relation to other degrees of the major or minor scales so that *any* chord within a diatonic set might be embellished by a $°_7$ chord. Ex. 4–12 contains four such chords, each bearing a leading-tone relation to a diatonic chord of the *F* major scale.

Ex. 4–12. Schumann: *Nachtstücke*, Op. 23, No. 2.

It is important to pause here and concentrate on the aural effect of this rapid succession of mixed chromatic and diatonic chords. Although every eighth note in some of these measures carries a different complete chord, the total result is more that of interesting harmonic motion *between* some structurally important tonal landmarks.

The tonality of the passage is not vague; if anything, the embellishing $°_7$ chords have strengthened the resolution chords, heightening their functions *within* the tonality of F. The upper line's contour from f^2 down to f^1 and the bass motion within f^1—C both establish the structural framework of the passage.

In contrast, the embellishing $°_7$ chord can momentarily wrench our attention to its resolution chord as a potential tonic if its duration and phrase location (such as at a cadence) make it more prominent. In Ex. 4–13, the two-measure units of the phrase structure focus our attention on the $°_7$/vi—vi cadence, creating a fleeting emphasis on the relative minor tonic.

Ex. 4–13. Beethoven: Setting of "God Save the King."

The embellishing diminished sonority is not always relegated to a position of rhythmic insignificance by virtue of its "secondary" harmonic role. In subsequent examples we shall see the embellishing function manifested by chords whose durations are as great as those of their chord of resolution. As a matter of fact, musical styles that emphasize appoggiatura patterns often contain embellishing chords whose durations are relatively great. For instance, the durational relations in measure 2 of Ex. 4–14 are typical of this reversal of durational stress; here the $°_7$ chord occurs on a strong beat, and its duration is four times greater than its resolution chord.

Ex. 4–14. Reger: *String Quartet,* Op. 109, I.

Our discussion thus far has dealt exclusively with the diminished chord as a secondary *lower* leading-tone embellishment of diatonic chords, but the $°_7$ and $°$ triad sometimes appear as *upper* leading-tone embellishments.

Ex. 4–15. $°_7$ as lower and upper leading-tone embellishment.

A: V   Lower L.T.   Upper L.T.

Within a musical passage, the dual embellishment by $°_7$ chords can represent a prolonged linking of two diatonic chords within a clear tonality. Note the linking of IV and V in this way in Ex. 4–16.

Ex. 4–16. Bach: *Well-tempered Clavier*, Book I, Prelude No. 1 in C Major.

It is important to recognize that although the chords of measures 2 and 3 in Ex. 4–16 are formed by different tones, they are both examplars of the same sonority ($°_7$), and they both perform the same function: chromatic embellishment of the dominant. For this reason, they are represented by the same analytical symbol, $°_7/V$, with the addition of directional arrows to indicate leading-tone direction ($\uparrow°_7/V$ and $\downarrow°_7/V$). A similar condition is shown in the next excerpt.

Ex. 4–17. Mozart: *String Quartet in B-flat*, K. 458, III.

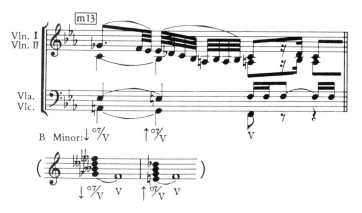

In making harmonic analyses it is not essential to employ arrows (denoting upper or lower leading-tone embellishments), as we have seen here, although precision and clarity would in some cases justify this additional indication.

**Irregular
Resolutions
of °₇ Chords**

In accordance with the leading-tone function of the secondary °₇, its "regular" resolution entails that the leading-tone relation, above or below, progress by semitone to the root of the next chord. According to this procedure, the (a) resolution in Ex. 4–18 is regular, while (b) is irregular.

Ex. 4–18. Resolutions of °₇ chords.

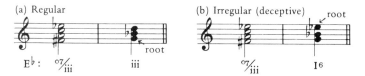

When the °₇ resolves as in Ex. 4–18b, it no longer functions as a secondary leading-tone chord in the usual sense. Rather, its embellishing role is fulfilled as a *collection of tendency tones*, some of which are not diatonic; it frequently operates as such between two positions of the same chord (see Ex. 4–19). Since the subsequent chord in this progression is I rather than V, it is a kind of *deceptive* resolution.

Ex. 4–19. Brahms: *Symphony No. 3,* I.

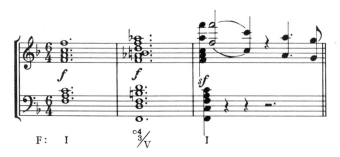

In this irregular resolution the common note between the $^{\circ}_7$ and the following chord represents a point of stability; the remaining notes are unstable members which move by step to members of the resolution chord. The usual tritone resolution is still operative in such a scheme, $^{\circ}5$ contracting, $+4$ expanding.

Ex. 4–20. Irregular resolutions of $^{\circ}_7$ chords.

The same irregular resolution can be found where the $^{\circ}_7$ does not link different distributions of the same chord. Again, the common note and attendant linear tendencies represent the most salient features of this relation. In Ex. 4–21 the $^{\circ}_7$/V stands between the ii$^6_5$—I$^6_4$ cadence. The *g-flats* of the $^{\circ}_7$ could also be notated as *f-sharps,* thereby revealing more clearly the obvious parallel sixth progression that frames the outer voices of the passage.

Ex. 4–21. Beethoven: *Piano Sonata,* Op. 31, No. 3, I.

The same type of irregular resolution occurs in Ex. 4–22, but here the embellished chord is VI (in *b* minor) rather than tonic. Since the °₇ formed on the first beat of the second measure is the diatonic vii°₇ (as vii $\frac{4}{2}$), the progression is similar to the deceptive cadence, V—vi in minor.

Ex. 4–22. Chopin: *Prelude*, Op. 28, No. 6.

Our next example shows the vii°₇ in *g* minor functioning as °$\frac{4}{2}$/III. The *a* of the °₇ here represents the leading-tone link between the two chords.

Ex. 4–23. Rameau: *La Poule.*

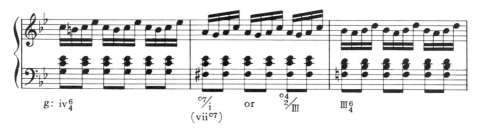

The °₇ Chord as an Agent of Tonal Instability

Our discussion thus far has centered on the °₇ chord as a chromatic sonority, whose functional identity is determined by the chord that follows. This is not its only role. Its instability makes it an effective modulatory pivot chord, and this same ambiguity also makes it a useful source of tonal instability within any passage.

The passage illustrated in Ex. 4–24 contains a vii $\overset{\circ}{3}$ that moves directly to another °₇ chord. Obviously, no immediate resolution occurs, and the lack of stability created by the succession heightens the listener's anticipation of resolution with some forthcoming chord. This return to stability does not occur until the eighth measure, when i $\frac{6}{4}$ appears as part of a cadential pattern.

Ex. 4–24. Schubert: *Symphony in B-flat*, III.

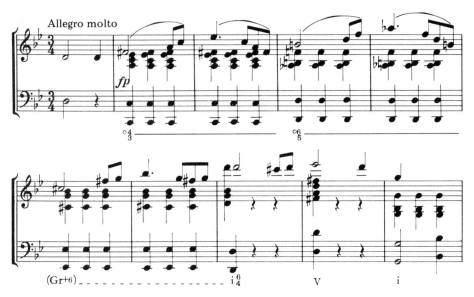

A similar passage, marked by ambiguity but again bounded by clear tonality, is shown in Ex. 4–25. F major is established at the beginning and end of the passage, but the harmonic progression from measure 6 through measure 8 unfolds a quite foreign set of harmonies. Both $^{\circ}_7$ chords resolve irregularly, forming the same linear resolutions shown in Ex. 4–18b.

Ex. 4–25. Mozart: *Piano Sonata*, K. 533, II.

In the next example, a rearticulated suspension adds harmonic color to the passage. A diminished 7th chord of measure 2 is linked with what appears to be °$^6_5$/V but never resolves as such. If the section immediately preceding this passage had not already established *E-flat* as tonic, the first 2½ measures of the excerpt would be tonally vague. Within the passage, a sense of key is suggested only in the third and fourth measures with the *e-flat* minor triad and the cadence that suggests V$_7$.

Ex. 4–26. Franck: *Praeludium, Chorale and Fugue for Organ.*

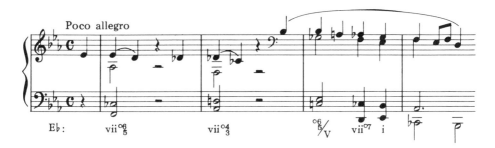

Since the °$_7$ chord is inherently unstable, the composer's desire to create a passage of vague tonality can be easily realized by using a string of such sonorities, none of which provides a sense of harmonic stability. This procedure is followed by many late nineteenth-century composers for exactly this purpose, as illustrated in Ex. 4–27. Example 4–28 reveals that this practice was well-known by at least one composer of much earlier times as well.

Ex. 4–27. Liszt: *Piano Concerto in E-flat*, I.

Embellishing
Diminished Chords

Ex. 4–28. J. S. Bach: *Well-tempered Clavier*, Book I, Prelude No. 6 in D Minor.

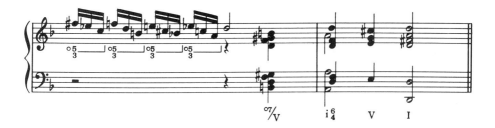

The ° ₇ Chord as Modulatory Pivot

The potential leading-tone function of the °₇ chord and its inherent lack of tonal stability make it an obvious choice as a linking chord wtihin a modulation. Since any °₇ chord can be spelled enharmonically in many different ways (see Ex. 4–6), any of its forms can be accommodated easily into any key. This potential for different spellings of the same chord increases its number of potentially logical resolutions as well, as illustrated in Ex. 4–29.

Ex. 4–29. Four resolutions of a single °₇ chord.

This kind of enharmonic shift is illustrated in the next example. Here the pivotal °₇ chord is immediately spelled within the new key rather than the old. Parentheses set off the "correct" spelling as it could have functioned within the former key of *d* minor (presumably as ° ⁴₃ / V).

Ex. 4–30. Mozart: *Piano Sonata*, K. 332, I.

Composers of the eighteenth and nineteenth centuries capitalized on this ambiguity of the $^{\circ}_{7}$ within schemes of rapidly shifting keys. Example 4–31 announces shifts of tonic by unexpected appearances of $^{\circ}_{7}$, each of which progresses to one of the alternative chords of resolution. In each brief section, the listener accommodates the particular $^{\circ}_{7}$ chord within the established key, realizing that a new tonic probably is forthcoming, but never knowing exactly *which tonic* it might turn out to be next.[2]

Ex. 4–31. Schubert: *String Quartet in A Minor*, I.

A similar effect is induced by the passage shown in Ex. 4–32. Here, successions of secondary $^{\circ}_{7}$ chords, secondary dominants, and their respective resolutions establish a passage of kaleidoscopic change. After the beginning in *C* major, the section passes through a series of temporary points of stability, each embellished by its attendant $^{\circ}_{7}$ or secondary dominant. The passage reaches a more settled area of tonal focus in the *b* minor statement where the excerpt ends.

[2] The chords enclosed in parentheses in the example show an enharmonic spelling of the $^{\circ}_{7}$ chord that relates it more readily to the next chord.

Ex. 4–32. Haydn: *Piano Sonata in E Minor*, I.

Passages such as this paved the way for the more fluid, less definite tonal focus of late nineteenth- and early twentieth-century music. Similar passages, in which relatively unstable sonorities follow one another in extended progression, made chromaticism an end within itself for some composers, so that tonality sometimes resulted more as a fortuitous *by-product* of chords than as a *basis* for total pitch organization.

The °₇ Chord   Like the °₇ chord, the °₇ (or dm₇ or *half-diminished* seventh chord) frequently appears as an embellishment of a diatonic chord, but it also
occurs in some contexts solely for its contribution to the overall harmonic color, devoid of strong relationship to the prevailing tonality. As
discussed in Chapter 2, the °₇ sonority occurs as a diatonic chord within
the minor scale as ii°₇, in major as vii°₇.

As an isolated sonority, the °₇ presents a fascinating case study of
harmonic root, for its notational spelling does not reveal its important
structural characteristics. If we reduce the chord to its simplest notation
of stacked thirds, the bottom note appears to be the root. However, the
pitch in this position suffers the same intervallic weakness as the lowest
member of the notated °₇ chord, for it is a member of a tritone. We shall
refer to this member as the *prime* rather than the *root*.

Ex. 4–33. °₇.

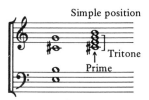

The simplest interval in the °₇ is formed between the third and the
seventh (represented by *e—b* in Ex. 4–33). It is a perfect fifth or, when
inverted, a perfect fourth. This interval is the most stable unit of the
whole sonority, and its root is the root—albeit a tenuous one—for the
whole chord.

It is interesting to note, that as a collection of intervals, the °₇ has
a strong similarity to the Mm7th chord; its interval complement is the
exact inversion of that sonority.

Ex. 4–34. Comparison of °₇ and Mm₇.

Since the presence of the perfect fifth (or fourth) lends an element
of stability to the °₇, one arrangement of the chord appears in rare instances as a tonic sonority. This function is the same as that performed
by the Mm- chord in first inversion—the "added sixth chord"—that we
discussed in Chapter 2. The °⁶₅ version gives the effect of a major sixth
added to a basic minor triad.

Ex. 4–35.

Both of the excerpts in Ex. 4–37 contain the $^\circ\overset{6}{5}$ enacting the tonic function.

Ex. 4–36. Debussy: *Danse.*

Ex. 4–37. Gershwin: *Prelude for Piano,* No. 3. Copyright 1927 by New World Music Corporation. Used by permission.

mands a much less imposing structural role. It is shown here at the beginning of our discussion to accentuate this somewhat improbable use of a slightly ambiguous chord functioning as a structural unit of harmony—even as tonic.

In its role as an embellishing chord, the $^\circ_7$ contains the chromatic tendency tones that are typical of the secondary $^\circ_7$. It is found frequently as a chromatic embellishment of V in a major key. In Ex. 4–38 its embellishing role is clarified by its appearance above a *dominant pedal* as well as preceding the *dominant* chord. (Note also the embellishment of the dominant from above (*A-flat*) in the previous measure.)

Ex. **4–38.** Schubert: *Die Schöne Müllerin, "Morgengrüss."*

C: I6   ii6   V   °⁷⁄ᵥ V

More typically, the °₇/V in Ex. 4–39 occurs on a weak beat followed by the dominant. This particular passage contains suspensions
which delay the full realization of dominant sonority; in some instances
the tonic ⁶₄ separates the °₇ and the full dominant chord.

Ex. **4–39.** Wagner: *Die Meistersinger*, Act I.

C: iii   °⁷⁄ᵥ   V

The cross-relation present between the °₇/V and i in a minor key
makes this relationship most improbable.

Ex. **4–40.** Cross-relation between °₇/V and minor tonic.

c: °⁷⁄ᵥ   V   i

As with the fully diminished seventh chord, the function of the °₇
as an embellishing sonority is not determined by its root; on the contrary, it is usually established by reference to a member of the tritone
that serves as a secondary leading tone (above or below) to the root of
the chord of resolution. Even though the third member of the °₇ must be
regarded as its *acoustical root*, the secondary leading-tone action defines
the chord's harmonic role.

Ex. 4–41. The leading tone in $^\circ_7$ chords.

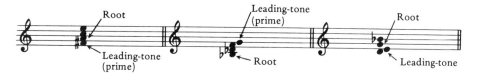

In Ex. 4–42, the first chord is not a diatonic member of the *A-flat* tonality. But its prime, *d*, bears a leading-tone relation to the root (*e-flat*) of the dominant chord that follows, so the $^\circ_7$ is an embellishment of the diatonic V chord.

Ex. 4–42. Wagner: *Siegfried*, Act III.

Since melodic progression frequently affects a composer's notation, the spellings of the $^\circ_7$ (as with the $^\circ_7$) are not always trustworthy guides to harmonic function. Ex. 4–43 contains three different $^\circ_7$ chords, each of which embellishes a brief dominant. But these chords are not *notated* as if they were of the same type, nor do they each bear the same leading-tone relationship with the chord they embellish. In (a) and (b) it is the prime of the chord that serves as the leading-tone link, but in (c) it is the seventh. In all three cases the composer's notation reveals more concern for linear motion than for chord spelling.

Ex. 4–43. Wagner: *Tristan und Isolde*, Prelude to Act I.

If we respell these chords in order to make their identity as $°_7$ chords more clear, the following result:

Ex. 4–44. Enharmonic respellings of $°_7$ chords of Ex. 4–43.

In Wagner's passage, the three $°_7$ chords are not parallel in structure, for in (c) the chord's seventh is in the bass. It is significant, however, that the semitone step down to the root of each of the temporary dominants does project a pattern of harmonic sequence.

Ex. 4–45. Embellishing functions of three $°_7$ chords.

Embellishing E   Embellishing G   Embellishing B

The Wagner excerpt reveals more clearly than any other single passage how the grip of diatonic notation, as it had evolved from the major-minor key schemes, was loosened by many late nineteenth-century composers. The chromatic melodies that bear much of the organizing burden in such music demanded notational procedures that were free from the traditional spellings.

Some composers of the late nineteenth and early twentieth centuries, whose music still maintained strong ties to a functional system of harmonic relationships, adopted the $°_7$ as a sonority useful primarily for its own sound, aside from its immediate relation to a diatonic scheme. Its rich sound became a frequent sonorous image within the harmonic palettes of those composers who, like Strauss, Debussy, and Ravel, occasionally strived for an effect of *suspended tonality* in order to achieve dramatic musical ends.

Ex. 4–46. Debussy, *Pelléas et Melisande*, Act IV.

Ex. 4–47 contains a passage in which °$_7$ and °$_7$ chords, almost to the exclusion of any other sonority types, make the harmonic image a striking contrast to the sharply delineated tonal schemes of most earlier music.

Ex. 4–47. Debussy: *Blessed Damozel.*

Later in the same score a °$_7$ acts as the cadential chord for the entire section, in this case the final utterance of the principal soloist of the composition.

Ex. 4–48. Ibid.

We have seen the $°_7$ as a diatonic chord (as ii$°_7$ and as vii$°_7$); in other contexts as a secondary embellishing chord (as $°_7$/V); again as the most important harmonic function within the pitch structure (as tonic in the form of $°_5^6$); as a chromatic chord related by leading tone (upper or lower) to a member of the subsequent chord; and finally as a purely coloristic sonority whose slight ambiguity adds harmonic spice. It should not surprise us to find a single chord type acting in such different ways; many words in our language derive their meanings exclusively from the contexts in which they occur, and some—such as the word "to" ("two," "too") retain the same spoken sound but derive both meaning and spelling from functional relations within written speech. In this sense, the $°_7$ chord, more than any other sonority type, is a "tonal homonym," its musical meaning derived exclusively from the relation it bears to its harmonic neighborhood.

Exercises

For more detailed assignments see *Materials and Structure of Music II, Workbook*, Chapter 4.

1. Mentally trace through the notes of any major or minor scale. For each scale degree, spell the $°_7$ chords whose primes are related as upper and lower leading tones. Write out each chord for SATB voices and resolve to its regular chord of resolution.
2. Write a passage for solo instrument and piano based on the following chord scheme. (Use a simple block chord style for the piano part.)

G major, $\frac{3}{4}$:

$^{\circ}{}^{6}_{5}\!\!\diagup\!\!_{vi}$ vi6 $^{\circ}7\!\!\diagup\!\!_{ii}$ ii $^{\circ}7\!\!\diagup\!\!_{iii}$ iii   IV6   I$^{6}_{4}$ V7   I

3. Plot a chord progression that modulates to a distant-related key through a diminished seventh chord that is enharmonically relatable to the second key. Write a texture for SATB (using the syllable "ah" as text) based on this progression.

4. Play a note at the piano that is in comfortable voice range. Immediately sing the $^{\circ}_{7}$ chord whose prime is the leading tone for this pitch.

Example

Play: Sing:

5. Explore the embellishing possibilities for the $^{\circ}_{7}$ chord *d—f—a—c* in several different major and minor keys. Keep in mind the possibility of any of its four members as a potential "leading-tone" relationship to a diatonic chord.

6. Write a simple work for piano that utilizes the $^{\circ}_{7}$ as an embellishment of V, as in the following chord scheme:

I $^{\varnothing 7}\!\!\diagup\!\!_{V}$ V7   I   I $^{\varnothing 7}\!\!\diagup\!\!_{V}$ V7   I   I $^{\circ 4}_{3}\!\!\diagup\!\!_{V}$ I $^{\varnothing 4}_{3}\!\!\diagup\!\!_{V}$ I $^{\circ 7}\!\!\diagup\!\!_{V}$ V7   I

7. At the piano, establish a key with I—V—I. Then play a $^{\circ}_{7}$ or $^{\circ}_{7}$ and immediately resolve to a logical chord that is diatonic to the established key.

Example

                         $\varnothing7$ V   or $\varnothing7$ V

Chapter Five

Neapolitan and Augmented Sixth Chords

All the chromatic chords we discussed in earlier chapters have resembled dominant harmony in some way. In fact, they are described as *secondary* since their roles are defined by the relationship they bear to a *primary* chord. In most cases, this relationship consists of a chord embellishing a diatonic scale step. One of their common characteristics is the presence of a leading tone, which the chords discussed in this chapter share.

But now a dual leading tone relationship is involved. The Neapolitan chord[1] exploits an upper and a lower leading tone melodically; augmented sixth chords exploit these harmonically. Study the two examples of these relationships shown in Ex. 5–1.

Ex. 5–1. Leading tone relationships, upper and lower.

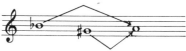

Realized melodically

Neapolitan and augmented sixth chords both occur most frequently as approach chords to the dominant or tonic chord. Originating in the late Renaissance, both chord types became part of harmonic practice by the mid-seventeenth century, appearing in minor keys at first, but later (especially in the earlier nineteenth century) in major keys as well.

The Neapolitan Chord

The Neapolitan chord is a major triad based on $^\flat$II of the scale. It appears most often in first inversion (hence the common use of the term Neapolitan *sixth*, N_6). Note how the tonic (here *a*) is in effect surrounded by its lower and upper leading tones.

Ex. 5–2. Melodic evolution of the N_6.

The same diminished third (*b-flat* to *g-sharp*) appears in Ex. 5–3. It also focuses attention on the tonic through the converging of the two leading tones.

Ex. 5–3. Beethoven: *Bagatelle,* Op. 119, No. 9.

---

[1] The name most likely comes from the chord's use in the music of eighteenth-century composers from Naples, but the chord can be found in many works composed before that time.

This pattern usually occurs in a less direct way, as in Ex. 5–4. Here the strong downward pull of the upper leading tone (*a-flat*) is not resolved until a full measure later.

Ex. 5–4. Schubert: "Der Müller and der Bach" (*Die Schone Müllerin*).

The following illustrations show typical doublings and voice motion in progressions involving N_6: characteristic are the doubling of the fourth scale degree, the descending melodic motion of the line with the chromatic tone, and the *stepwise voice motion* throughout.

Ex. 5–5. Typical doubling and voice motion in progressions with N_6.

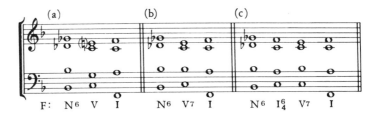

Uses of the Neapolitan "Sixth"

In cadences, the N_6 frequently moves to V or V_7. The colorful tritone root relation is formed when the Neapolitan moves to the dominant, and a cross-relation may occur between the Neapolitan's root and the fifth of the dominant chord.

Often, in an effort to avoid such cross-relations, composers have resolved N_6 to a tonic six–four, as in Ex. 5–6. This progression also avoids the characteristic melodic diminished third (such as g^b–e) and results in smooth stepwise motion in all voices.

Ex. 5–6. Beethoven: *Sonata in C-sharp Minor*, Op. 27, No. 2, III.

Neapolitan and
Augmented Sixth
Chords

A similar N_6 appears in Ex. 5–7, although here it is within a major key.

Ex. 5–7. Brahms: *Ein deutsches Requiem*, Op. 45, "Denn alles Fleisch."

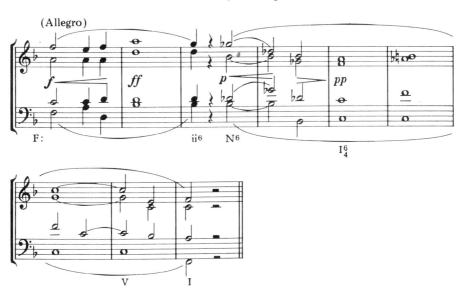

Ex. 5–8 shows a striking N_6 in a kind of plagal cadence, resolving directly to tonic.

Ex. 5–8. Brahms: *Quartet*, Op. 51, No. 1, I.

Turning to other harmonic uses, we find the N_6 in passages of extended parallel motion, as in the two following examples. In Ex. 5–10 N_6 is combined with extensive chromaticism in a particularly striking setting.

Ex. 5–9. Haydn: *Sonata in E Minor*, I.

Ex. 5–10. Beethoven: *Sonata in D Minor*, Op. 31, No. 2, I.

The Root Position Neapolitan Chord

Although less frequent than the N_6, the Neapolitan triad is effectively used in root position. When resolving to dominant, as in Ex. 5–11, the tritone root relationship is dramatically exposed in the bass line.

Ex. 5–11. Chopin: *Prelude in C Minor*, Op. 28, No. 20.

In Ex. 5–12, the tonic and Neapolitan triads alternate as the content of an extended cadence. The contrary motion in the outer voices conceals the basically parallel nature of the progression.

Ex. 5–12. Kabalevsky: "Novelette" from *Fifteen Children's Pieces*, Op. 27, Book 1. © Copyright MCMXLVI by Leeds Music Corporation, New York, N.Y. Used by permission. All rights reserved.

Other Forms and Uses of the Neapolitan

The Neapolitan triad in second inversion is rare. One such passage is quoted in Ex. 5–13, in which the progression N_4^6–V_7 resembles a Phrygian cadence.

Ex. 5–13. Handel: *Messiah*, "Rejoice Greatly."

Ex. 5–14 presents a more complex situation: the N $^6_4$ embellishes a mutated submediant (^{b}VI) and sounds more like a subdominant chord in the region of *B-flat* major. This harmonic activity is part of an elaborate preparation for the half-cadence that concludes the excerpt.

Ex. 5–14. Schubert: Mass in G, *Sanctus.*

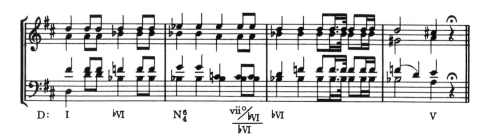

Ex. 5–15 contains an effective resolution of N$_6$, using the bass note as preparation for the 7th of the dominant seventh chord.

Ex. 5–15. Bach: *Prelude in E-flat Minor,* W.T.C., Book I.

The Neapolitan triad can also function as a pivot chord in modulations. Since it originates as a chromatic chord in the original key, two possibilities for pivot chord relationships exist: (1) becoming a *diatonic* chord in the new key, or (2) becoming a *chromatic* chord in the new key.

The first of these possibilities is illustrated in Ex. 5–16: N$_6$ is the pivot connecting *c* minor and *A-flat* major; i.e., the N$_6$ becomes the IV$_6$ in the new key.

Ex. 5–16. Schubert: *Quartet in C Minor*, I.

In the modulation of Ex. 5–17 (from *A* major to *D* major), *both* roles of the pivot triad are as chromatic chords, resulting in a temporary tonal ambiguity.

Ex. 5–17. Wagner: *Lohengrin*, Prelude to Act I.

At times the Neapolitan is preceded by its own dominant, as in the next examples.

Ex. 5–18. Chopin: *Mazurka*, Op. 7, No. 2.

When this harmonic relationship is emphasized or prolonged, the lowered second scale degree is established as the tonic of a Neapolitan region. The Neapolitan is established even more firmly as a temporary tonic in Ex. 5–19, first in measures 4 and 5, and later in measures 7 and 8. Secondary diminished seventh chords focus attention to the Neapolitan scale degree.

Ex. 5–19. Schumann: *Symphony No. 2,* III.

The Neapolitan Key Relationship

The Neapolitan relationship may be an integral part of the key scheme of a composition. We have seen how the Neapolitan chord might be the tonic of a tonal region. On a larger scale, the key a semitone higher (a *Neapolitan relation*) than the original key might be used for variety, as well as to mark off formal units.

Ex. 5–20 contains such a Neapolitan relationship, providing dramatic tonal contrast to the initial thematic statement. Such use of the Neapolitan key in sequence following the tonic is a characteristic of Beethoven's style.

Ex. 5–20. Beethoven: *Quartet in E Minor*, Op. 59, No. 2, 1.

Nineteenth-century composers expanded large formal divisions of their compositions by using Neapolitan key relationships. Rather than connect keys through a diatonic pivot chord, composers turned to more chromatic modulatory procedures and enharmonicism. Ex. 5–51 contains a passage in which a Neapolitan region (*E* major) is set within the context of a larger section in *E-flat* major. Both modulations involve the use of an enharmonic pivot chord.

Ex. 5–21. Wagner: *Lohengrin*, Act II, Scene 4, Procession.

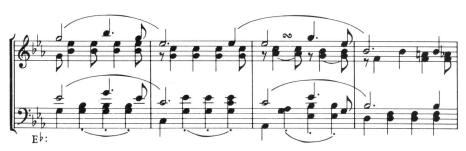

The Neapolitan key relationship may extend to the various movements of a multimovement work, as in Ex. 5–22. The E major (enharmonically *F-flat* major) forms the Neapolitan of *E-flat*, the tonic of the first and third movements. The relationship, uncommon in composers of Haydn's generation, became more frequent in the nineteenth century.

Ex. 5–22. Haydn: *Sonata in E-flat Major.*

The identifying characteristic of these chord types is the augmented sixth (or its inversion, the diminished third) as a *vertical interval*. This pair of complementary intervals, illustrated below, embodies the leading tone relationships (upper and lower) shown in Ex. 5–1. The augmented sixth gives this entire family of chords a unique harmonic color and sense of melodic urgency.

Ex. 5–23. The augmented sixth and diminished third.

The chords that arise from this interval are seen in subsequent examples as approach chords to cadences or other important structural points. Furthermore, they possess a high potential effectiveness for modulation, a potential that became fully realized by nineteenth-century composers.

The linear origin and interval structure of augmented sixth chords is best shown through an examination of the two-voice cadence. Of the various two-voice cadential patterns, perhaps the most frequent is the $^{7-8}_{2-1}$ form, approaching the final octave in contrary motion by step, both from above and below.

Ex. 5–24. Cadence resolution to the octave $^{7-8}_{2-1}$.

The size of the melodic seconds (which constitute the $^{7-8}_{2-1}$ pattern) is variable, depending upon the prevailing mode. Three cadence possibilities are illustrated in Ex. 5–25: Dorian, Lydian, and Phrygian. Note that in the Dorian cadence only major seconds occur; in each of the others, one voice moves by a major second, the other by a minor second. We might say that each of the latter demonstrates the leading tone—tonic relationship (Lydian featuring the *lower* leading tone, Phrygian the *upper* leading tone).

Ex. 5–25. Resolution in Dorian, Lydian, and Phrygian modes.

In the fourteenth, fifteenth, and sixteenth centuries, it was customary for performers to insert leading tones in cadences whether indicated in the music or not. Such a practice may have led to the emergence of the augmented sixth interval in the two-voice cadence. Ex. 5–26 illustrates the same cadences with leading tones added.

Ex. 5–26. Cadences with leading tones added.

This characteristic upper/lower leading tone motion to an octave is the most important feature of augmented sixth chords. Ex. 5–27 illustrates various forms of the augmented sixth in three and four voices.

Ex. 5–27. Augmented sixth chords.

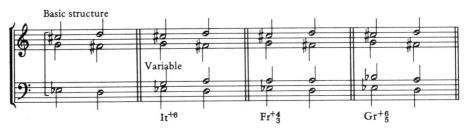

All the common types of augmented sixth chords share the same basic three-voice structure: to the augmented sixth interval a third voice is added, a major third above the bass. In thicker textures other tones are often added, as in Ex. 5–27. Note the step motion of all members of these chords in their resolutions.

The fourth member added to this basic three-part structure is variable in that it can form a major third, a tritone, or a perfect fifth above the bass. These chords are traditionally identified with the geographical labels Italian, French, or German, for reasons that remain obscure. Since the use of this terminology is widespread, we shall retain it, but we shall indicate the intervallic structure of the chords with abbreviated symbols such as It$_{+6}$ (Italian sixth); Fr $^{+6}_{\,4\,3}$ (French six-four-three); and Gr $^{+6}_{\,5}$ (German six-five).

There is disagreement regarding the roots of these chords. If we follow the traditional means of determining roots, we arrive at the following fundamental tones for the chords in Ex. 5–27. *C-sharp* for both It$_{+6}$ and Gr $^{+6}_{\,5}$; A for the Fr $^{+6}_{\,4\,3}$. Aurally, however, these seem questionable choices, since to many ears the lowest tone (*E-flat*) of each of these is a more stable tonal foundation. This apparent contradiction between notation and sound makes the question of root determination in augmented sixth chords problematic. For the moment, it is more profitable to measure the intervals solely from the bass. The figured bass symbols are used to indicate these.

The tonal placement of augmented sixth chords is significant, since they are clearly embellishing or ornamental chords that are closely tied to a diatonic resolution chord. In almost all cases, the augmented sixth interval expands by steps to the octave (root) of the following chord, usually the dominant. Since they usually function as approach chords to the dominant, their role is similar to that of ii and IV. Ex. 5–28 illustrates the It$_{+6}$ in g minor resolving to V.

Ex. 5–28. Haydn: *Quartet*, Op. 74, No. 3, III.

Several points should be kept in mind when employing augmented sixth chords:

1. The augmented sixth interval is formed by the upper and lower leading tones of the dominant (the raised fourth and lowered sixth scale degrees in major, the raised fourth and diatonic sixth scale degrees in minor).
2. This interval resolves in contrary motion to the octave on the dominant.
3. A major third appears above the bass.
4. Another voice may appear either as a major third, tritone, or perfect fifth above the bass.
5. Each chord member resolves by step to the nearest tone of the chord of resolution.

When augmented sixth chords appear within a strongly defined tonality, their resolution possibilities are few and, thus predictable. Approach possibilities, though, are more numerous; any chord that might appropriately precede ii or iv serves well. The context of the augmented sixth chords in Ex. 5–29 (two obvious augmented sixth chords and one that is implied) illustrates several possible approaches—from i_4^6, ii_3^4, and iv. Dominant and submediant chords are equally effective in such a context.

Ex. 5–29. Beethoven: *Quartet in C Minor*, Op. 18, No. 4, IV.

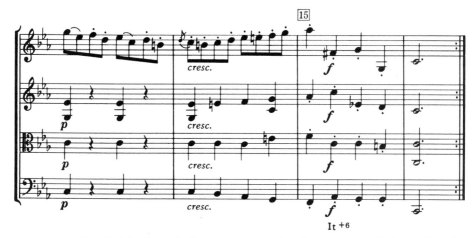

It +6

Ex. 5–30 through Ex. 5–32 contain characteristic Italian, French, and German augmented sixth chords in various contexts and in combinations with different nonchord tones.

Ex. 5–30. Mozart: *Piano Concerto in D Minor*, K. 466, III.

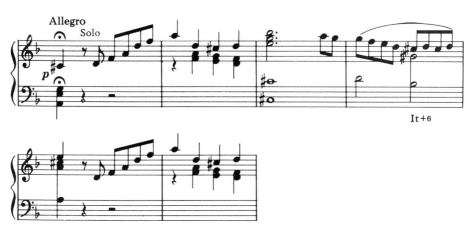

It +6

Ex. 5–31. Bruckner: Mass in F Minor, *Crucifixus*.

Ex. 5–32. Chopin: *Sonata in C Minor,* IV.

Augmented sixth chords resolve to the tonic six-four almost as frequently as to V. Compare Ex. 5–33 (which illustrates this procedure) with Ex. 5–27. The motion in each voice is generally by step, and the resolution still emphasizes the octave of the dominant (although it is now the fifth instead of the root of the resolution chord).

Ex. 5–33. Resolution to i_4^6.

Ex. 5–34 and Ex. 5–35 illustrate the Gr $^{+6}_5$ in typical resolutions to V and i_4^6. In the first of these examples, Haydn has avoided the parallel fifths that frequently result from this progression (Ex. 5–27). The Schubert example is particularly striking with its prolonging of the Gr $^{+6}_5$ over several measures.

Ex. 5–34. Haydn: *Quartet in E-flat Major, Op. 76, No. 6, I.*

Ex. 5–35. Schubert: *Die Winterreise,* "Rast."

"Inverted" Augmented Sixth Chords

The effect of augmented sixth chords is not altered when the lower note of the characteristic interval is no longer in the bass. Ex. 5–36 contains a sampling of some of the possibilities, many of which will appear in subsequent examples. In the first of these chords, the interval of the augmented sixth has been inverted to a diminished third.

Ex. 5–36. Inverted augmented sixth chords.

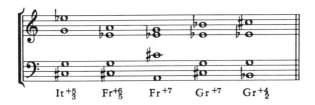

Ex. 5–37 is particularly rich in inverted augmented sixth chords, their role basic to the harmonic vocabulary. Observe the tendency for voice motion to become more and more conjunct; as chromaticism increases in music, the part motion narrows until most or all voices move primarily by semitones.

Ex. 5–37. Mussorgsky: *Songs and Dances of Death,* IV.

Still another inversion of the French type appears in Ex. 5–38. Again the characteristic interval has become a diminished third, which converges upon the root of the resolution chord.

Ex. 5–38. Bruckner: Mass in F Minor, *Sanctus.*

The Gr $^{+6}_{5}$ sonority is often inverted, as in the following examples. The first, in Ex. 5–39, clearly displays the resolution of the Gr$_{+7}$ (compare its resolution to that of the $°_7$ built on the same pitch). In Ex. 5–40, the Gr$_{+7}$ in measure 3 evolves gradually through linear activity in all four parts, emphasizing the chord's contrapuntal origins: each of the four parts progresses by half-step, culminating in the B major six-four chord, which is the apparent goal of the progression.

Ex. 5–39. Chopin: *Sonata in B-flat Minor,* I.

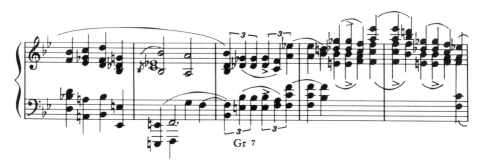

Ex. 5–40. Liszt: *Sonata in B Minor.*

Neapolitan and
Augmented Sixth
Chords

The GR$^{+6}_5$ and Enharmonic Uses

The Gr$^{+6}_5$ displays some peculiar properties. Its common notational spelling obscures the fact that its structure is the same as that of the major-minor seventh chord. Out of context it might well be heard as this more familiar chord; only within a context can its identity as an augmented sixth chord become apparent. Because of this ambiguity, its possibilities are numerous. As Ex. 5–41 illustrates, the It$_{+6}$ shares this enharmonic potentiality with the German type, since it is indistinguishable (as an isolated sonority) from an incomplete major-minor seventh chord.

Ex. 5–41. Enharmonic forms of German and Italian sixths.

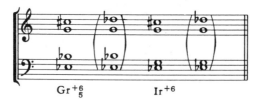

The enharmonic resolution of the Gr$^{+6}_5$ has been exploited by composers in the last 200 years. The possibility of a sudden shift of key coupled with smooth melodic progressions made this an attractive modulatory device for composers who were seeking chromatic tone relations. The procedure is simple; any major-minor seventh chord can be interpreted enharmonically as a Gr $^{+6}_{5}$ and resolved accordingly.

Ex. 5–42. Enharmonic resolution of augmented sixth chord.

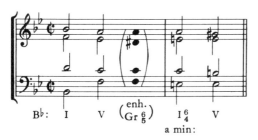

This process can, of course, be reversed. When we consider that any dominant seventh or secondary dominant seventh can assume this tonal guise, we see how varied the possibilities are.

This extended type of "common chord" modulatory technique occurs in Ex. 5–43. For several measures, Beethoven has prepared the tonic "arrival" in *G* major by a dominant pedal point. In the measures before the fermata, the It$_{+6}$ is used as a neighboring chord to V. At the fermata, however, another member is added, and the chord is here notated as a major-minor seventh chord. Nonetheless, the previous context leads the listener to expect a resolution to a structural chord in *G*, as if the chord in question were a Gr $^{+6}_{5}$. Considerable surprise results when the chord resolves as V$_7$ of *A-flat* major. (A few measures later the key of *G* major is restored.)

Ex. 5–43. Beethoven: *Quartet*, Op. 18, No. 2, Finale.

Occasionally the Gr $^{+6}_{5}$ is spelled with a doubly-augmented fourth, the usual perfect fifth above the bass replaced by its enharmonic equivalent. Ex. 5–44 contains a progression that illustrates this deviation. In major keys, the enharmonic spelling more clearly suggests the resolution of the upper note of this interval.

Ex. 5–44. Schubert: *Am Meer.*

Many composers have remained indifferent to this linear aspect, spelling the chord as the common Gr$^{+6}_5$, regardless of its resolution. In Ex. 5–45, the composer used the spelling *D* in preference to *C-double sharp*—even though the latter would have revealed more clearly the leading-tone relation to its *D-sharp* resolution.

Ex. 5–45. Verdi: *Otello,* Act III.

In the harmonic analysis of nineteenth-century music, every seemingly remote chordal succession involving a major-minor seventh chord should be considered potentially as a Gr$^{+6}_5$ or V$_7$. Composers (especially Schubert) frequently used this means of modulation when moving up or down a minor second.

Spelling reveals the enharmonic dual relationship in Ex. 5–46. The fourth measure contains a chord with the dual function of V$_7$/IV in *E-flat* major and Gr$^{+6}_5$ in *G* major.

Ex. 5–46. Haydn: *Quartet,* Op. 76, No. 3, I.

Augmented Sixth Chord as Related to Tonic

Since the interval of the augmented sixth, as a dual set of leading tones, imparts great emphasis to its resolution tones, it is inevitable that the chords characterized by this interval should embellish the tonic as well as the dominant. The resolution of the augmented sixth to the tonic octave establishes a relationship similar to that of dominant-to-tonic, but somewhat more intense in resolution because of the greater number of leading tones.

Ex. 5–47, which we have seen earlier in this chapter, contains a typical progression from It$_{+6}$ to I.

Ex. 5–47. Schumann: *Symphony No. 2*, III.

The $\frac{7-8}{2-1}$ progression of the outer voices clearly indicates the lines of progression from the two-voice cadence formula illustrated earlier. If we compare this cadence to its diatonic equivalent, we see that it differs by only one note from the progression, viiø^6—I. It is interesting to observe that the *D-flat* is prepared earlier in the measure as the root of the Neapolitan chord, demonstrating the obvious identity of function of these chords. The entire measure is characterized by its harmonic relation as a chord whose root is the *upper* leading tone of tonic.

The Fr $^{+6}_{3}$ appears more frequently in this context than either of the two other augmented sixth chords, possibly because it contains the dominant pitch. Most examples of augmented sixth chords related directly to tonic resolve to the major tonic triad rather than the minor, although this is not essential. Ex. 5–48 illustrates the Fr $^{+6}_{3}$ in this role.

Ex. 5–48. Brahms: *Symphony No. 4*, Finale (Theme).

Augmented Sixth Chords in Other Relationships

Augmented sixth chords sometimes resolve to chords other than the dominant and tonic. In Ex. 5–49, an It$_{+6}$ serves as an embellishment of the supertonic, resolving to V/V.

Ex. 5–49. Brahms: *Symphony No. 1,* I.

In Ex. 5–50 and Ex. 5–51, the relation of the augmented sixth chord to the prevailing tonality again is not completely clear at the moment it occurs. Ex. 5–50 contains a prolonged Fr $^{+6}_{3}$ in a context that is eventually confirmed as *E-flat* major.

Ex. 5–50. Mahler: *Symphony No. 8,* Finale.

Even more remote is the augmented sixth in Ex. 5–51, built on the subdominant and resolving to V/vi. Despite this apparent remoteness from the tonic, the tonal center is never really in doubt.

Ex. 5–51. Beethoven: *Quartet,* Op. 18, No. 5, III.

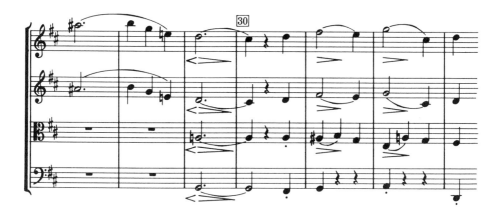

Although twentieth-century composers have generally discarded the traditional augmented sixth sonorities, as they are described in this chapter, they have retained one of their characteristic features—the cadence on a unison or octave approached in contrary motion by double leading tones, as in Ex. 5–52.

Ex. 5–52. Diminished third as double leading-tone cadence.

But, despite the appearance of isolated examples of the above, augmented sixth sonorities are of little significance in twentieth-century harmonic practice. They are, at best, peripheral features even in the harmonic idiom of the eighteenth and nineteenth centuries. As fashions of dress change, so do fashions in sonority. In many respects the emergence of these chords as significant harmonic elements in late nineteenth-century syles was symptomatic of the growing chromaticism that elaborated a diatonic system.

Exercises

For more detailed assignments see *Materials and Structure of Music II, Workbook,* Chapter 5.

1. Practice spelling the Neapolitan chord in all major and minor keys.
2. Practice spelling drills related to augmented sixth chords as follows:
   a. Locate rapidly both the upper and lower leading tones of:
      F-sharp, A, D, G-flat, B, E-flat, C-sharp, A-flat, F.
   b. Spell augment sixths on the following pitches:
      G-flat, F, B, D-flat, A-flat, C, E-flat, G.

c. Spell, from the bass note, the following:

an It$_{+6}$ on *B-flat*

a Gr $^{+6}_{5}$ on *G*

a Fr $^{+6}_{3}$ on *D-flat*

an It$_{+6}$ in the key of *e-flat* minor

a Gr $^{+6}_{5}$ in the key of *c-sharp* minor

a Fr $^{+6}_{3}$ in the key of *f* minor

3. Make an analysis of the first movement of Beethoven's *Sonata*, Op. 31, No. 2. Locate as many different Neapolitan chords as possible, note how they are approached and left, and state how the Neapolitan participates in modulation.

4. Spell a Gr $^{+6}_{5}$ in any major or minor key, then convert enharmonically into a dominant seventh chord and resolve accordingly. Write a short melody that utilizes this harmonic scheme for modulation.

5. Write melodies using the following sequential harmonic pattern: a phrase clearly delineating the tonic key followed by a sequential phrase in the region of the Neapolitan (see Ex. 5-20 for a model).

6. Experiment with short passages using the N$_6$ (or N) and augmented sixth chords as the basis for modulation. Then study the second movement of Schubert's *Unfinished Symphony* (Exposition, second theme group) as a brilliant example of enharmonic modulation using Gr$_{+6}$ chords.

7. Spell:

a. three different Gr $^{+6}_{5}$'s in each of the following keys:

D major, *A-flat* major, *f* minor (and spell the resolution chord of each).

b. the tonic-embellishing Fr in each of the following keys:

c-sharp minor, *a* minor, *f* minor.

c. an It$_{+6}$ resolving to vi in *E* major; in *D-flat* major.

d. the Gr$_{+7}$ in *d* minor; in *f-sharp* minor; in *A* major.

e. the Fr$_{+7}$ in *f-sharp* minor that embellishes the tonic.

Chapter Six

Variation
and Cantus Firmus
Forms

Variation is one of music's fundamental processes. It has been throughout music's long history. No other technique can as efficiently promote
the simultaneous achievement of music's twin goals, *unity* and *variety*.
Even the simplest folk song can be used to demonstrate how variation
operates in music. In Ex. 6–1, a series of variants of a brief motive forms
the entire basis for the song.

Ex. 6–1. Spanish Folk Song.

In the continuing variation of a given pattern, we see one of the most powerful ways of achieving a sense of musical motion and continuity. The given pattern provides the unifying element, giving a feeling of *oneness* to a piece, and making its progress seem logical and inevitable. The variations—as the name implies—provide the variety that keeps our interest alive and a sense of change.

Variation is, simply, an enhancement or enrichment of a musical idea. The idea itself can be anything that qualifies as a musical idea— a melody, a succession of chords, a rhythmic pattern. The enhancement may be either *simultaneous* or *successive:* one basic type of simultaneous variation occurs when a musical idea remains intact throughout a composition, forming the unchanging basis for the changing musical texture, similar to the string that runs through a necklace of pearls. This is called the *cantus-firmus* principle (literally "fixed chant"). The term derives from the application of this technique in Medieval music, when a Gregorian chant melody was used (often in very long notes) as the structural foundation of a composition.

When the underlying musical idea itself (again a tune, a rhythmic pattern, etc.) undergoes a series of transformations or enhancements, we see the process of *successive* variations at work. One commonly-accepted term for these is *independent variations*. We can note another important point of difference between the two types: cantus-firmus variations tend to be continuous; independent variations, on the other hand, tend to be sectional.

The Cantus Firmus Principle

Ex. 6–2 illustrates cantus-firmus technique in a way. The tune *L'Homme armé* ("The Armed Man") was a popular song in Medieval Europe and well-known in Dufay's day. The tune appears in the tenor, and around it is built an elaborate contrapuntal texture.

Ex. 6–2a. *L'Homme Armé.*

Ex. 6–2b. Dufay: Mass based on *L'Homme Armé*, Kyrie I.

(L'homme armé tune in tenor voice)

Later tunes also served as foundation melodies for larger compositions, especially the German chorale tunes used by Lutheran composers
of the Baroque era. *Chorale prelude* is the most general term used to
describe works built on such tunes; this term is even applied loosely
to any kind of piece built on a cantus firmus, whether the melody is a
folk song, a religious hymn, or a patriotic song. Although many of our
examples will be for organ, this type of writing is found frequently in
vocal music as well.

Although there are many possible subtypes of chorale preludes,
our discussion will concentrate upon two of the most important—the
imitative chorale prelude and the embellished chorale. Still other appli-
cations of *cantus-firmus* technique will follow later in this chapter.

The Imitative (or "Fugal") Chorale Prelude

One of the most interesting treatments combines a contrapuntal
texture with the successive phrases of the selected tune. This type begins with an exposition section much like the *invention,* to which is

added, at an appropriate moment, the basic tune in relatively long note values. The previous texture continues as an accompanying web, thus forming continuity with the imitative opening. Ex. 6–3 shows the chorale tune "Vater Unser im Himmelreich" ("Our Father in Heaven") and the opening section of a chorale prelude based on it.

Ex. 6–3a. German Chorale, *Vater Unser im Himmelreich.*

Ex. 6–3b. Telemann: Chorale Prelude, *Vater Unser im Himmelreich.*

The initial motive is derived by diminution from the first few notes of the *cantus firmus*, thereby creating a "preview" of the melody. This preview section is called (in German) *vorimitation*, literally *fore-imitation*, and a similar procedure introduces each new section of the chorale prelude, always anticipating the next phrase of the melody.

Ex. 6–4 begins where Ex. 6–3b ended. Note that the pitch interval of imitation between the first and second voices is different in this phrase —a sixth instead of a fourth.

Ex. **6–4.** Continuation, *Vater unser im Himmelreich.*

The successive phrases of the *cantus firmus* (C.F.) form the sectional organization of the complete chorale prelude. The length of the work is related, then, to the number of phrases of the melodic basis and their respective lengths. Since the chorale illustrated in Ex. 6–3 contains six phrases, this particular chorale prelude is organized into six sections, each of which begins with a brief section of vorimitation.

The total composition could be expanded considerably if the sections of vorimitation were developed to greater lengths. Obviously, the composer plans these bridge sections to fit the scale of the composition he wishes to create, so aside from the phrase structure of the original tune, this variability of length can be controlled by other means.

Although the listener expects important melodic utterances to appear in the higher parts of a texture, the *C.F.* appears in the lowest part in some examples, in the middle in others. In the work whose beginning section appears in Ex. 6–5, the *C.F.* is placed at the bottom.

Ex. **6–5.** Telemann: Chorale Prelude, *Herzlich thut mich verlangen.*

In many chorale preludes, the melodic pattern introduced at the beginning of the piece is not derived from the *C.F.*; it is used as the motivic basis for each bridge section, thus forming a monothematic basis, as in the invention. This technique creates a more tightly unified composition, but it sacrifices the advantage of phrase-by-phrase variety that results from the use of vorimitation.

Ex. 6–6 shows two excerpts from a chorale prelude in which a single pattern is the motivic accompaniment for all statements of the *C.F.* This pattern is not derived from the *C.F.* (except for its first three pitches: *e, f-sharp, g*), and thus the various interludes are not heard as related to the underlying melody.

Ex. 6–6. Bach: Chorale Prelude, *Wo soll ich fliehen hin.*

C.F. (sounding *8va* higher than written)

2nd phrase

27

1st phrase, C.F.

Some Baroque chorale preludes have the chorale tune itself ornamented. This technique is effective only insofar as the listener knows
the *C.F.* and can thus follow its variation. One such chorale and a prelude built on it are illustrated in Ex. 6–7. Notice that the motive used in
the imitative accompaniment in measures 3 and 4 is derived from the
first five notes of the chorale.

Ex. 6–7a. Chorale Melody, *Nun komm, der Heiden Heiland.*

Ex. 6–7b. Bach: Chorale Prelude, *Nun komm, der Heiden Heiland.*

Although the exact relationship between the accompanying voices
and the *C.F.* may vary to a considerable degree, the form of the chorale
prelude is determined by the phrase structure of the original tune. The
contrapuntal texture built around this tune serves the same function as
the frame around a painting; it establishes an appropriate context, and
it focuses attention on the primary element, the *cantus firmus* itself.

Another notable setting composers have developed for the presentation of a preexistent melody is essentially more homophonic than the imitative chorale prelude. By fusing several voices into a tonal fabric that weaves through the chords implied by a given melody, an activated harmonic accompaniment can be created that sets the main line in relief and adds a dimension of interest that is not present in a bare *harmonization*.

It is impossible to draw a precise line of distinction between the embellished setting and the simple harmonic—or "familiar style"—setting of a chorale tune. However, the examples that follow in this section reveal the gist of what constitutes the embellished type. Again, the chorale preludes of Baroque composers are ideal examples; many of them served as models for later composers who have utilized this *cantus firmus* organizational plan for brief works.

Ex. 6–8 shows excerpts from two settings by J. S. Bach of the chorale *Christ lag in Todesbanden* ("Christ lay in the bonds of death"). The first is a straightforward *harmonization;* the second shows the more active voices that characterize the *embellished chorale prelude.*

Ex. 6–8a. Bach: *Christ lag in Todesbanden,* harmonized version.

Ex. 6–8b. Ibid., embellished version.

These two settings of the same melody make an apt comparison, for their harmonic progressions are almost duplicates. The basic difference lies in the more active nature of the participating voices in the embellished version. In this respect, note that a subdivision of the basic duration, the quarter note, occurs on each beat in the embellished setting, except at the cadence on *d* of the second phrase. (The only other slackening of motion occurs at the final cadence.)

In at least one respect, the embellished chorale prelude is similar to the fugal chorale prelude: it also frequently contains a motivic unit that functions as a thread of continuity. In the setting of Ex. 6–8b, this motive is the sixteenth-note group (). It usually appears with a pitch contour similar to its first statement, in the tenor voice,

When a motive is used as a common feature, the composer's problem is to weave this motive into each voice at one location or another to create thematic units. This procedure usually leads to imitative relations between voices, but without the vorimitation of phrases that is a feature of the fugal chorale prelude. In some of Bach's embellished settings, the motive lends itself to a predominantly imitative style, the overlapping of "active-passive" patterns between voices creating a forward propulsion in a texture that otherwise could be rhythmically static.

Ex. 6–9. Bach: *Christ ist Erstanden.*

The same continuous motivic imitation persists in Ex. 6–10, which is an excerpt of an embellished setting of *Christ lag in Todesbanden*. Another setting of the same kind appeared earlier in Ex. 6–8.

Ex. 6–10. Dupré: Chorale Prelude, Op. 28, *Christ lag in Todesbanden*. Copyright 1932 by The H. W. Gray Co., Inc. Used by permission.

An unusual example of a two-voice embellished setting, also illustrative of motivic organization, was made by Bach's contemporary, Telemann. Compare the harmonic progression of Ex. 6–11 with the first two phrases of Ex. 6–8b and Ex. 6–10.

Ex. 6–11. Telemann: Chorale Prelude, *Christ lag in Todesbanden*.

Ex. 6–12a uses a single rhythmic motive. A powerful monorhythmic piano accompaniment has been added to the simple chorale melody played by the trumpet, which lies within the middle and upper regions of the piano texture. A more contrapuntal setting by Bach of the same tune is shown for a comparison of techniques.

Variation and
Cantus-Firmus
Forms

Ex. 6–12a. Hindemith: *Trumpet Sonata*, III. © 1936 by B. Schott's Soehne, Mainz. Renewed 1963. Reprinted by permission.

Ex. 12b. Bach: Chorale Prelude, *Alle Menschen müssen sterben*.

Some examples of the embellished type contain episodic fragments between phrases of the cantus. These extend the composition beyond what its length could be if strict adherence to phrases of the original tune were maintained. Ex. 6–13 shows episodes in the form of double echoes of preceding cadence patterns.

Ex. 6–13. Brahms: Chorale Prelude, *O Welt, Ich muss dich lassen.*

A quite different setting, but of the same type, makes use of an obbligato line that is more prominent than the other parts. In Ex. 6–14, the hymn-tune *C.F.* is presented in midtexture, then with an obbligato line above, these two voices supported by a very simple bass line.

Ex. 6–14. Barber: Variations on the hymn *Wondrous Love*, Variation No. 3. Reprinted by permission of the copyright owner, G. Schirmer, Inc.

Some tunes can be set against themselves in canon, so that the embellished type is further enhanced by canonic statements of the melody. This procedure was often used by Bach when the chorale melody was amenable to such treatment. Ex. 6–15 is an excerpt in which the top and bottom voices state the tune at a measure's separation, the two inner parts filling out the harmonic structure with characteristic patterns.

Ex. 6–15. Bach: Chorale Prelude, *Gotte, durch deine Güte.*

An even more unified composition results when a double canon is created from *C.F.* and accompanying line, as illustrated in Ex. 6–16.

Ex. 6–16. Bach: Chorale Prelude, *In Dulci Jubilo.*

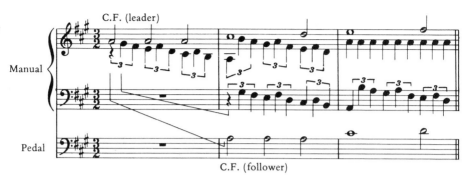

Cantus-Firmus Variation Types

We now return to our main theme—*variation*—and the ways in which the *cantus-firmus* principle can be used within the context of variation technique. We defined *cantus-firmus* variations earlier in this chapter as variations in which *the underlying musical idea remains intact throughout the composition.* Once again, this idea may consist of a melody, a chord progression, or even a rhythmic pattern.

But first, one must distinguish between *C.F.* variations and the form of the chorale prelude; the following are the major points of difference:

1. *C.F.* variations are built around repetitions of the same pattern; chorale preludes are usually built over successive phrases of the melody.
2. *C.F.* variations are therefore constructed on brief patterns, normally not more than eight measures; chorale preludes often contain longer sections.
3. *C.F.* variations are often based on a series of chords; chorale preludes are based on melodies.

Because of the shortness of the pattern used for *C.F.* variations, many variations are necessary if the piece is of any great length. The typical *cantus-firmus* variation forms are the *ground*, the *passacaglia*, and the *chaconne*. Despite efforts to standardize the names for these types, composers have persisted in using the terms very loosely; *chaconne* and *passacaglia* are used almost synonymously in the Baroque period. We shall follow current general practice in defining these forms as follows:

1. *ground*—variations over a *short* melodic pattern in the bass.
2. *passacaglia*—a more highly developed composition over a longer

melody, appearing first in the bass but later capable of migrating into the upper parts.

3. *chaconne*—variations over a series of chords, *i.e.*, the basis is harmonic rather than melodic.

Ex. 6–17 shows parts of a composition based on a ground: a four-measure pattern serves as the melodic substructure for each of the twenty-one variations. Notice how the melodic phrases overlap the statements of the ground, creating a smooth melodic continuity.

Ex. 6–17. Purcell: *Dido and Aeneas*, "Ah! Belinda." Copyright 1961 by Hawkes & Son (London) Ltd. Realization by Britten. Reprinted by permission of Boosey & Hawkes, Inc.

In contrast to the *ground,* the *passacaglia* is usually a more highly developed composition based on a longer, more tunefully "melodic" pattern, usually from six to eight measures long. As in the ground, the passacaglia cantus (*C.F.*) is first stated in the bass voice, where it remains during most of the composition. However, the pattern frequently is moved up into the middle and top regions of the texture at some point during the variations, normally around the middle portion.

The passacaglia is in a triple meter, either written in a triple-simple notation such as $\frac{3}{4}$ or $\frac{3}{2}$, or in some instances, as the compound meter of $\frac{6}{8}$ or $\frac{12}{8}$. This affinity for triple meter is apparently a vestige of the form's origins as a dance.

The three variations appearing in Ex. 6–18 have been extracted from a powerful work for organ. A study of the entire work through listening, combined with a careful reading of the score, will give a more accurate picture of the magnificent structure created around this simple eight-measure theme.

Ex. 6–18. Bach: Passacaglia for Organ in C Minor.

Variation and
Cantus-Firmus
Forms

The *chaconne* has come to be regarded as a series of variations based on a recurrent harmonic scheme, as opposed to the purely melodic C.F. of the ground and the passacaglia. It is not restricted to triple meters, appearing frequently in duple-simple schemes.

In the chaconne, a set of chords (or a linear pattern too simple to be termed *melodic*) forms a harmonic substructure above which a series of variations is woven. A clear example of the whole process can be heard in the series of instrumental variations played by a group of jazz performers when no preestablished melody (such as a popular tune) is the point of departure for their improvisations. In this sense, the innumerable jazz renditions of the basic "blues" progression could all be regarded as chaconnes. Each makes use of a series of chords—the *cantus firmus* as a harmonic scheme—to which are appended free melodic variations. In the blues progression, a pattern of slow harmonic rhythm runs through a twelve-measure phrase-form.

Ex. 6–19. Basic "blues" progression.

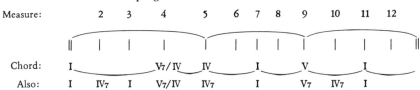

A more classic example of the chaconne uses a shorter chord series for its harmonic foundation, usually a four- or six-measure unit.

As we mentioned earlier, a lack of conformity persisted in the application of names for these *cantus firmus* types during the Baroque period, and one of the clearest, simplest examples of what we now call *chaconne* was titled *passacaille* by its composer, Handel. Ex. 6–20 contains the four-measure C.F. of this piece, followed by excerpts from five of the fifteen variations.

Ex. 6–20. Handel: *Passacaille* ("Chaconne").

The alterations of harmony that occur within the later variants (only in number 11 here) are negligible changes made for the sake of variety once the basic pattern has been thoroughly established (as it certainly has been). Following deviations of this kind, the progression usually resumes its original form, as is the case in this composition.

A modern adaptation of the same principle forms the basis for the chaconne illustrated in Ex. 6–21. In this piece, the *C.F.* is a pattern devoid of the motion necessary to be called "melodic"; it consists of a series of three chromatic steps upward in a static rhythm of four dotted half notes. This unyielding little pattern pervades the whole movement, giving rise to thirty statements of the four-measure sequence, all clothed in rich orchestral textures. As an example of *cantus firmus* variation, the almost constant reiteration of the four-measure figure makes a rigid basis for the varied instrumental tracings built around it. Note that the pattern is transposed to different pitch levels in later variations.

Ex. 6–21. Dello Joio: Variations, Chaconne, and Finale, Chaconne. Copyright 1950 by Carl Fischer, Inc. Reprinted by permission.

**Independent
Variations**

The freer technique of independent variation grew up alongside *cantus-firmus* variations in the seventeenth and eighteenth centuries and ultimately became more popular with Haydn, Mozart, Beethoven, and their contemporaries. Their term for this formal type was *theme and variations*.

In this type, the theme takes on greater dimensions than in cantus-firmus variations, becoming in effect a complete, short composition. This *theme* is followed by a series of separate variations, each retaining some characteristic(s) of the parent theme: formal structure, harmonic pattern, and/or melody. Each variation becomes an individual statement, modelled upon the theme but possessing its own distinctive texture, rhythmic figuration, etc. Again, *unity* and *variety* are achieved in an attractive synthesis—unity is produced by the kinship of the variations with the theme, variety by the pleasantly changing aspects of the successive variations.

Many sets of *theme and variations* are similar to the *cantus-firmus* type in that they retain the thematic element in a relatively unaltered state through each section. Most Baroque variations illustrate this type. However, they differ from the *cantus-firmus* variation procedure in at least two important respects: (1) each separate variation is a self-sufficient part of the overall design; and/or (2) the basic pattern is never continued to the bass of the texture. (This latter does not mean, of course, that the theme cannot appear in the bass within one or more variations.)

The variations from which the excerpts in Ex. 6–22 were taken illustrate in simple terms the textural, harmonic, and rhythmic changes that might be applied in this kind of variation procedure.

Ex. 6–22. Scheidt: Variations on a German song, "Ei, du feiner Reiter."

VARIATION IV (meter change, imitative texture)

In other theme and variation compositions, the variation procedure is rooted in elaborations or distillations of the melody, creating a decorative technique that ushers in all manner of melodic variety. One distinguishing element, then, is the degree of transformation undergone by the theme. In many such variations, the original pitch line is so camouflaged that the probability of immediate recognition is reduced. Ex. 6–23a follows its melodic prototype in a uniform way, while Ex. 6–23b departs from its parent drastically, utilizing only its basic pitches as a framework.

Ex. 6–23a. Handel: *Klavier Suite No. 5*, "Air with Variations."

THEME

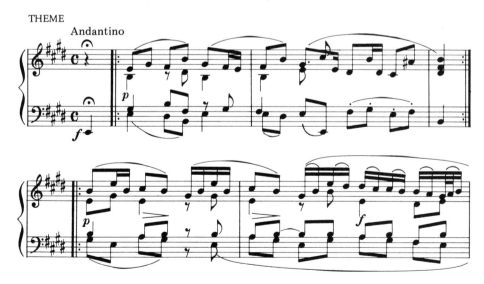

VARIATION I
Un poco più animato

Ex. 6–23b. Dello Joio: *Piano Sonata No. 3*, I. Copyright 1948 by Carl Fischer, Inc. Reprinted by permission.

THEME

VARIATION I ($\quad$ = 80)

Composers of the Classical period evolved a successful plan for the theme and variations that has been adopted by many later composers. The following outline summarizes their treatment:

1. Theme—usually a complete binary or rounded binary structure.
2. Several variations—each with a different figuration and rhythmic structure, but following closely the harmonic and formal plan of the theme, and in the same mode. Variations are frequently paired, especially in keyboard variations, so that one variation may feature the right hand, the next the left hand.
3. A variation in the relative or parallel minor or major key—often slower and with considerable chromaticism.
4. Return to the original mode—the next-to-the-last variation is generally an *adagio* with a very free, *fantasia*-like texture; the final variation returns to strict organization and a faster tempo.

While not all Classical variations follow this pattern exactly, its generalizations are valid for most independent variations written between 1750 and 1850. Ex. 6–24, for example, lacks the *adagio* variation but is otherwise an excellent example of the pattern we have described. Each of the variations is a replica of the form of the theme, each incorporating its rounded binary design (A A B A).

Ex. 6–24. Mozart: *Piano Sonata*, K. 331, I.

Andante grazioso

Variation and
Cantus-Firmus
Forms

Var. 1
Section A beginning

Section B

Section A return

Maggiore

151

Variation and
Cantus-Firmus
Forms

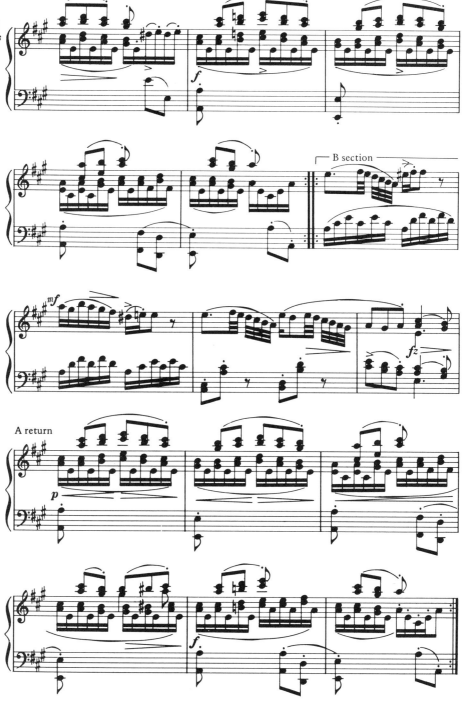

In most melodic variations the pitch line is preserved in a way that clearly reveals its origins. But it is possible to organize a variation that, although derived exclusively from the theme, is so drastically changed in other ways that even the original theme's pitch line is not apparent to the listener. Ex. 6–25 contains excerpts from a work in which the original melody of the theme is entrenched as a *cantus firmus* in the truest sense of the term, but the octave displacements and rhythmic shifts have hidden the original from all but the most perceptive ears.

Ex. 6–25. Hindemith: Theme and Four Variations. © 1947 by B. Schott's Soehne, Mainz. Reprinted by permission.

Still another approach to the variation procedure depends less rigidly upon pitch-line duplications by using the theme as a kind of melodic springboard. Each of the variations' patterns is derived from some unique characteristic of the theme, rather than from wholesale pitch repetitions.

Ex. 6–26 shows this method as it occurs in two variations from a large work. In the first variation, an imitative texture is built out of the first fragment of the theme's melody, this texture leading to a cadence that duplicates the original thematic organization. In the second variation, the first five pitches of the original theme are the melodic basis of an *antecedent-consequence* phrase grouping.

Ex. 6–26. Beethoven: *String Quartet,* Op. 18, No. 5, III.

Variation and
Cantus-Firmus
Forms

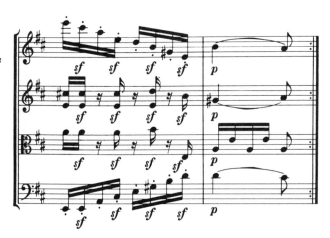

Variation 3, beginning section

A motive can be shaped from fragments of the original theme and the variation spun out by the developmental processes applied to these units. Ex. 6–27 shows an excerpt from a variation that has been created from the abbreviation and rhythmic reshaping of patterns from the original theme.

Ex. 6–27. Dello Joio: *Piano Sonata No. 3,* I. Copyright 1948 by Carl Fischer, Inc. Reprinted by permission.

The point of departure for any such variation might be a conspicuous rhythm, a unique pitch contour, or as in the chaconne, a series of chords that is typical in some way of the theme. Any (or several or all) could establish the link of continuity between theme and variant.

One of the distinguishing features of the theme in the *Variations* partially illustrated below is the after-beat beginning that veils the meter during the first few measures. Beethoven capitalizes on this feature by stressing after-beat patterns within each of the variations that follows.

Ex. 6–28. Beethoven: *String Quartet in C-sharp Minor,* Op. 131, IV.

Variation and
Cantus-Firmus
Forms

Variation 2

Variation 3

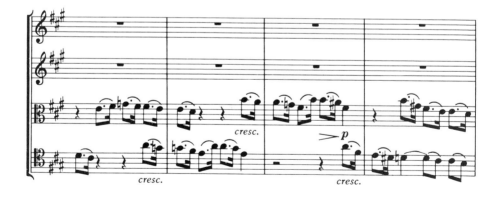

A rather obvious but significant stepchild of the classic theme and variations design incorporates more than a single melodic prototype within the theme. In its simplest manifestation, two themes of contrasting nature (but of comparable length and importance) appear successively within the theme section. The succeeding variations take both of these melodies as their points of departure, each serving as the basis for a separate variation section. In this schematic order it is natural that fewer variations of a single theme occur, since there are more themes to be varied.

Some of the simplest examples of this bithematic variation type can be found in works by Haydn, who was probably the first to develop the plan. Ex. 6–29 shows the first parts of two themes of a theme section, the first in G major, the second in parallel minor, that serves as the basis for only three variations, two of the "A" theme, one of the "B." The design of the total movement is diagrammed below the two themes.

Variation and
Cantus-Firmus
Forms

Ex. 6–29b. Formal plan of total movement.

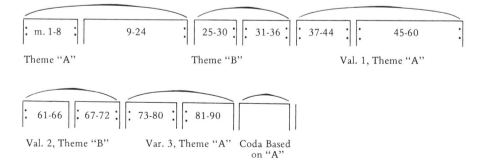

The excerpts in Ex. 6–30 can be matched with the organization illustrated in Ex. 6–29 to gain a more vivid idea of the process incorporated within this movement.

Ex. 6–30. Ibid., opening of Variation I, Variation II, and Variation III.

Beethoven wrote some variations that parallel rather faithfully this bithematic principle. A particularly interesting sample appears in the slow movement of his *Piano Trio in E-flat*, Op. 70, No. 2. It is perhaps through Beethoven that the idea was passed on to contemporary composers, particularly Paul Hindemith, whose *Theme and Four Variations* has a theme of three distinct sections—each of which contrasts in a marked way with its associates.

In Hindemith's work, each of the four variations [1] is also a three-part design, each separate section of which is derived from its respective "theme." Ex. 6–31 illustrates the three themes and their incorporation into the first two variations of the work.

---

[1] The subtitles of the Variations are drawn from the medieval classification of the bodily humors, which establish the *affection*, or mood, as it shifts from one variation to the next. In order, they are: *melancholic, sanguine, phlegmatic,* and *choleric.*

Ex. 6–31. Hindemith: *Theme and Four Variations,* Three Themes. © 1947 by
B. Schott's Soehne, Mainz. Reprinted by permission.

(strgs. tutti)

Variation 2
Theme A
Waltz
Piano

Strgs

Theme B

ff　*mf*

Theme C

ff

This tri-thematic basis results in a total plan that is considerably more complex than the theme-variations title normally implies. Here each variation is in reality a set of three sections, all of which total twelve variation-parts. The principle is remarkably sound. The composer has at his disposal the element of unity, through each variant's common bond with its respective theme; but variety is an inherent feature as well, through the contrasts afforded by the succession of three themes as they are couched within each variation.

An even more fascinating accommodation of the theme and variations format can be heard in a number of works by living composers in which melody and harmony, in the traditional sense, play no part. In György Ligeti's *Atmospheres*, for example, the *theme* is a brief sound event whose main characteristic is a sense of motionlessness. This static blob of complex sound provides the point of departure for a set of twenty-one *variations*, all of which—in twenty-one different ways—replicate a sense of stasis, or "nonmotion." In works such as this a *musical condition or state* is the theme rather than a single musical property such as harmony or melody or form.

Exercises

For more detailed assignments see *Materials and Structure of Music II, Workbook*, Chapter 6.

1. In class or in private, play through several chorale preludes, directing your attention to the following:
   a. thematic elements and general type of chorale prelude
   b. *vorimitation* sections (if present) and their thematic basis
   c. key scheme, deviations from the tonic if present
   d. relation of C.F. to original tune: phrase structure, alterations of rhythm or meter, pitch alterations, decorative patterns
2. Write a fugal chorale prelude for three voices, based on a selected C.F. Derive vorimitative episodes from the C.F. for each section.
3. Write an embellished chorale prelude for four voices, basing it on a chosen C.F. Begin by making a simple harmonization of the melody, and then decorate the accompanying lines to create a more contrapuntal texture.
4. Study one or more of the following works, following a recording with the score in hand. Note the following points:
   a. Type: *cantus firmus* or independent
   b. Techniques: What is the theme or elemental unit? How is variation accomplished? How is unity incorporated within each variation?
   c. Structure: What is the overall plan of the work?
   [Works]:
   Beethoven: *Thirty-two Variations in c Minor*
   Brahms: *Variations on a Theme by Handel*

Haydn: *Quartet, Op. 55, No. 2,* I
Bach: *B Minor Mass,* Crucifixus
Vaughan-Williams: *Symphony No. 5,* Finale
Hindemith: *Quartet in E-flat, III*
Beethoven: *Symphony No. 5,* II and *Symphony No. 9,* III
Schubert: *Quartet in D Minor,* II ("Death and the Maiden")
Reger: *Variations on a Theme by Mozart* (compare to Ex. 6–24)
Hindemith: *Nobilissima Visione,* "Passacaglia"
Schuman, Wm.: *Symphony No. 3,* "Passacaglia" (first section of Part I)
Ligeti: *Atmospheres*
(Or any of the works cited in this chapter)

5. Add a series of four variations to a short *ground* pattern.
6. Write three variations on a chosen theme that are in a consistent harmonic and melodic style with that theme.
7. Plan a chord progression of from six to eight measures, then write a series of simple textures elaborating this progression to form a short *chaconne*.

Chapter Seven

Thematic Development in Two-Voice Counterpoint

How do composers achieve musical coherence and continuity in extended forms? This chapter, by focussing upon one type of composition —the *invention*—will provide some answers to this question. In our models, the two-part inventions of J. S. Bach, we find both tonal and rhythmic coherence and continuity as a result of Bach's developmental/ imitative style.

A broad description of what might occur in an invention might include any process in which a musical idea is stated, then progressively developed in a series of imitative combinations. The musical idea conceivably could be a rhythmic pattern, a series of chords, a melodic pattern, or even a single tonality. Inventions have been written in which each of these has served as the nucleus of a musical creation.

As an introduction to this study, listen to performances of several of Bach's inventions, either from recordings or played by a fellow student. Or best, play them yourself.

General Characteristics

The invention is a brief contrapuntal work in any tempo, usually lasting no more than forty to sixty seconds. In terms of actual measures, an invention might run twenty or fifty measures, depending upon the meter notation: a $\frac{12}{8}$ work might consist of only twenty measures, while one notated in $\frac{3}{8}$ might well consume considerably more.

The invention is a sectional piece in which key is one of the main formal determinants.[1] Generally, each section has a tonic different from its immediate predecessor, but all are grouped in relation to a common tonic that begins and ends the form. Each section contains a reworking of the basic melodic material, the *subject*, in a variety of melodic and harmonic environments.

The Two-part Invention in *d* minor of Bach, reproduced as Ex. 7–1, is a clear example of the features that normally appear in the whole invention.

Ex. 7–1. Bach: Two-part Invention in D Minor.

---

[1] An invention could very well be atonal, in which case key would not be a relevant structural factor.

Thematic
Development
in Two-Voice
Counterpoint

The most obvious characteristic of this piece (and of other inventions as well) is its total incorporation of the melodic subject first announced at the beginning. With the exception of measures 17, 37, 48, 51, and 52, every measure of the piece is in some way devoted to the continued exploitation of this simple scalar pattern. And even these exceptional measures consist of a common cadential formula that, by its repetition, adds unity to the whole design.

The key scheme of this Invention is as follows: *d* minor—*F* major —*a* minor—*d* minor. Thus each main section is marked by a separate tonic and, in two cases, a change from minor to major (or *vice versa*).

Four primary techniques of development are applied to the restatements of the subject:

1. inversion, as at measure 22
2. pitch alteration, as at measure 7
3. shift to a new position within the tonality, as in measure 30 where the subject begins on the third scale degree of *a* minor, not the tonic
4. change of key

A detailed formal outline follows:

Measures	1– 6	Announcement of subject in each voice
"	7–17	Slight change in contour of motive, sequential repetitions, and cadence confirming *F* major

Other unifying elements are present within the parts which contain the subject. For example, the simple rhythm in the top voice of measures 3 and 4 (♩♫♩) plays a prominent accompanying role throughout the whole work. It can be called a *countersubject* because of its major role as a melodic foil to the statements of the subject.

Further accompanimental patterns are derived from the subject itself. The figure of the top voice in measure 11 is constructed from fragments of the subject, as illustrated in Ex. 7–2.

Ex. 7–2. Bach: Two-part Invention in D Minor, original motive.

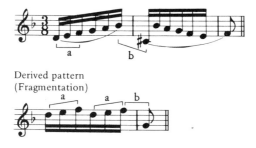

Derived pattern
(Fragmentation)

This derivative method represents still another way Bach has taken material from his original melodic pattern. The technique of *fragmentation* is, then, a fifth means of subject development incorporated in this one invention.

It is important to recognize the equal significance of each of the two voices in this invention, for here lies one of the main characteristics. The whole texture is permeated by a give-and-take contrapuntal relation between the two participants, each contributing to the development of the material at hand, and both outlining simple harmonic progressions which create a unified counterpoint.

The Subject

Since the single subject dominates the entire invention, it must be a pattern that is definite in contour, clear in tonality, and generally worth hearing repeatedly. The Bach examples fulfill each of these requirements.

Each subject delineates the tonic chord of the whole piece, and each is a "catchy" melodic utterance that makes a definite, forthright impression on the listener.

With few exceptions, subjects of predominantly conjunct motion adhere to the mode of the piece, thus establishing immediately the pitch basis for what is to follow. When disjunct patterns form the subject, its skips almost always outline the tonic triad. The rudimentary analyses that accompany Ex. 7–3 reveal the structural causes of clear tonality.

Ex. 7–3. Tonal frameworks of invention subjects.

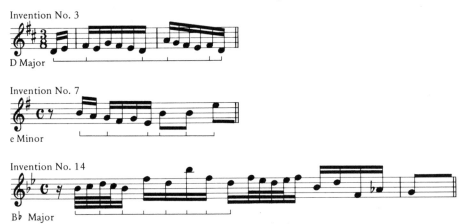

Similarly, the subject establishes its metric framework with clear articulations of basic beats. A majority of the Bach examples begin with an upbeat figure that propels the subject forward. An accompanying pattern can establish clearly the metric structure, as Ex. 7–4 illustrates.

Ex. 7–4. Bach: Two-part Invention in B Minor, No. 15.

Most inventions have a brief subject. (Most of the Bach examples begin with a subject no longer than two measures.) Imitative entries between parts are generally more forceful if the leading voice does not run for a long time before it is answered by the follower. If the subject is longer, the total pattern consists of smaller units which are repeated to fill in the whole. For instance, the opening subject of the Invention in ƒ minor (No. 9) consists of one measure repeated sequentially, thus reducing the actual number of motive patterns.

Ex. 7–5. Bach: Two-part Invention in F Minor, No. 9.

Most of the subjects are more succinct than that of Ex. 7–5, many lasting no more than a few beats.

Ex. 7–6. Subjects of Inventions No. 10, No. 13, and No. 1.

Beginning Section of the Invention

The opening statements of the subject present the melodic material for the whole composition. At the same time certain other fundamental things occur: the basic key is introduced, the important rhythmic patterns are established, and accompaniment patterns are combined with the subject. This takes longer to describe than it does to happen; all these goals are met by the successive imitative statements in the participating voices. After the first statements, the two parts are usually heard together for the rest of the piece.

In most of the Bach Inventions both voices make their first statements in the tonic key. The second part thus repeats the subject an octave lower than the first. The *D* major Invention, No. 3, illustrates this normal arrangement of entrances.

Ex. 7–7. Bach: Two-part Invention in D Major, No. 3.

In some inventions the subject is stated more than once by each voice during the opening section. It is heard twice in each part during the first two measures of Invention No. 13, after which derivations of the subject are pitted one against another in imitative fashion.

Ex. 7–8. Bach: Two-part Invention in A Minor, No. 13.

The leader-follower plan of the opening section presents the possibility of a canonic relationship between voices—the follower duplicating the leader exactly. Although none of the Bach Inventions maintains this exact duplication throughout, some do contain sections that are *canonic*. Invention No. 8 is strictly canonic through its first seven measures, and then a shift of harmony disrupts the exact duplication in measure 8. At that point, the lower voice duplicates the upper at the interval of a ninth below.

Ex. 7–9. Bach: Two-part Invention in F Major, No. 8.

Invention No. 2 contains a canonic relationship to the first beat of measure 11, and then another long section of exact duplication begins when, in measure 13, the top voice states an answer to the pattern that began in the bottom voice at measure 11. Only the first two notes of the subject are not duplicated exactly.

Ex. 7–10. Bach: Two-part Invention in C Minor, No. 2.

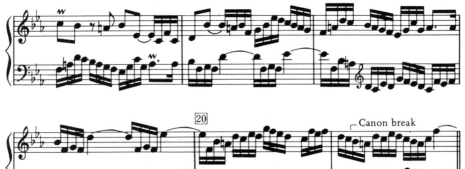

This section of canonic relation continues for eight measures, breaking off into free counterpoint at measure 21.

The invention usually is less rigidly controlled by part-duplications; inexact imitations are found even in the initial statements. For example, Invention No. 10 is exceptional in that its lower part sounds the answer at the dominant scale level and, in so doing, presents a pitch alteration that keeps this first section solidly entrenched in the tonic key. (This minor change is not enough to change the character of the subject.)

Ex. 7–11. Bach: Two-part Invention in G Major, No. 10.

Although the lower voice commonly answers the upper immediately, some inventions reveal a wider separation of entries. Invention No. 14 begins with three statements of the subject (at different pitch levels) followed by a two-measure episode that bridges the gap between this introductory statement and the complete version of the subject in the second voice. This particular episode is built from the imitative echoes of a fragment of the subject.

Ex. 7–12. Bach: Two-part Invention in B-flat Major, No. 14.

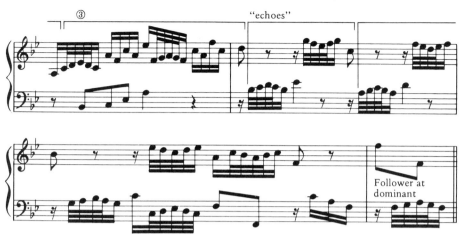

One of the most interesting of all the Bach Inventions, No. 6, makes extended use of textural inversion or *double counterpoint*. In this passage a section is turned upside down so that an original upper part now becomes the lower, and vice versa. The first eight measures of this invention are derived from this simple but effective process. Note that this kind of inversion of parts *in relation to each other* is not the same as *melodic inversion*.

Ex. 7–13. Bach: Two-part Invention in E Major, No. 6.

Textural inversion is so successful here that Bach incorporates it as the main developmental procedure throughout the remaining sections of this invention.

Developmental Sections

The heart of the invention lies in those sections which follow the expository statements, in which the subject is developed through several keys and combined with new contrapuntal associations.

We noted earlier how Bach used *contrary motion, pitch alterations, sequential tonal shifts within a single key, fragmentation, modal change,* and *changes of key* in shaping the many variants of the basic subject. All of these procedures and a few more play an important role in the sections of the invention that follow the opening.

For a composition no longer than the invention, the developmental sections cannot be extensive. The Bach examples generally fall into a division of four units of approximately equal length. The key scheme for such a plan is relatively flexible, and it is dependent upon the structure of the subject and upon whether it is in major or minor. The following diagrams show usual characteristics of key outlines in the Bach Inventions.

Section:	1	2	3	4
Key:	I (major)	V (major)	vi (minor)	I (major)
		or		
	i	V	VII	i
		or		
	i	III	V	i
		or		
	I	V	ii	I

All such key schemes must be thought of as generalizations, since the developmental character of the middle sections often makes it difficult to identify a single clear tonality. In some cases it is quite impossible.

The section following the exposition usually begins like a reexposition in the new key that has been established by a strong cadence. In some inventions the voice that acted as *follower* in the exposition now assumes the role of *leader,* as Ex. 7–14 illustrates.

Ex. 7–14. Bach: Two-part Invention in C Major, No. 1.

The peculiarities of a subject may require rhythm or pitch changes to sustain the forward motion at the junction between sections. To fulfill this need, the subject might be given a decorative addition such as Bach made at the beginning of the second section of Invention No. 3.

Ex. 7–15. Bach: Two-part Invention in D Major, No. 3.

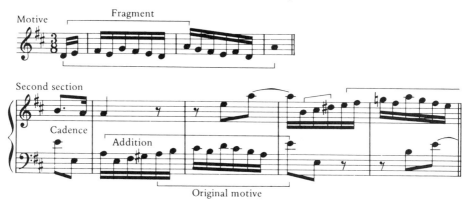

In this Invention Bach added three notes at the beginning of the subject, causing it to span the two-beat vacuum that otherwise would lie between the first-beat cadence and the third-beat pickup of the subject. He retains this revised version of the subject through the remainder of the Invention.

The invention's second section normally is imitative, each voice tossing the subject or variants of the subject back and forth in successive statements. This is also the logical location for the appearance of developmental alterations of the subject, although these might have figured prominently in the earlier expository statements.

Variation of the subject can occur within the first few measures of an invention. It appears in the first four measures of Invention No. 1 and Invention No. 13, but such examples are rare.

Ex. 7–16. Bach: Inventions No. 1 and No. 13, subject variants.

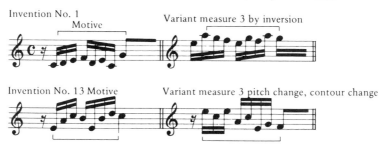

A different kind of developmental technique appears in No. 7. Here successive fragmentations of the subject are spun out in a modulation that leads to a reexposition in both voices beginning in the relative major key.

Ex. 7–17. Bach: Two-part Invention in E Minor, No. 7.

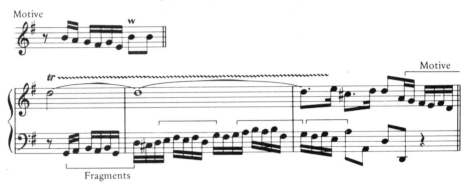

Still another kind of development is used in No. 6. Here the second large section (following a repetition of the exposition) forms the second part of a *binary* form. The initial eight measures in the key of the dominant (*B* major) are a textural inversion of the first eight measures of the exposition section.

Ex. 7–18. Bach: Two-part Invention No. 6, double counterpoint.

A final illustration of developmental procedures can be seen in Invention No. 5. The top voice states the main pattern of the subject three times in a modulatory sequence. This is answered by a full statement of the subject in the bottom voice. The accompanying line for the subject appearances in the top voice is derived from the *countersubject* carried by the lower voice at the beginning of the exposition.

Ex. 7–19. Bach: Two-part Invention in E-flat Major, No. 5.

Whatever the particular departure made within the interior sections of the invention, their common function is to carry the subject through a series of developmental stages that are interestingly varied, but are always linked by rhythmic and harmonic relations with what has gone before. This linkage is effected by a careful planning of large sections, returning always to the tonic key as an aspect of formal close. In this sense the invention can be regarded as a form that begins with a statement of an idea in a particular key, then runs through a series of transformations—thematic and tonal and textural—and then returns to the original tonality for its eventual resolution.

Closing Section

None of Bach's Inventions ends with a subject statement that exactly parallels the initial statement of the exposition. However, most of the Inventions do imply a return to something akin to the first thematic statements. This kinship is brought about by similarities of texture, range, harmony, and rhythm with the opening section, as well as by the return to tonic key. A glance at some of the final sections of the Bach models should make clear how this effect of return separates the final statements from the preceding developmental sections.

A clear *reprise* occurs in Invention No. 3. In measure 43 there is a complete contrast of texture in a return to the single voice that began the Invention. This sets into relief the return of the subject in the original tonic key and at the original pitch level. Only the duplet anacrusis has been altered in order to continue the descending scale line that leads into this section.

Ex. 7–20. Bach: Two-part Invention in D Major, No. 3, last section.

The final section of Invention No. 2 is forcefully signaled by a strong V—I cadence to the original tonic in measures 22–23. The entire subject is stated by the upper voice in measures 23–24 for the first time in the tonic key since the exposition of measures 1–4. The bass voice counters with the last statement that ends the Invention, measures 25–26. The combination of original key (and pitch level) and the accompanying figure in the bass that served as a counterpart within the exposition are strong indications that the formal circle is closing.

Ex. 7–21. Bach: Two-part Invention in C Minor, No. 2, beginning of the reprise.

Stretto (the close overlapping of imitative voices) marks the beginning of the final section in Invention No. 14. This dramatic device is of particular significance in fugue writing and will be discussed further in Chapter 8.

Ex. 7–22. Bach: Two-part Invention in B-flat Major, No. 14, stretto imitation.

It is interesting to see in this excerpt how Bach alters the subject in the top voice at the third beat of measure 2 so that the two parts will join as effective counterpoint.

The element of return in simple A　B　A fashion is not essential to the invention, and it does not occur as a clear aspect of the design in some of the Bach models. Invention No. 8 ends without a strong restatement of the original subject, although the pattern is present *at different pitch levels* within the tonic key toward the end.

Ex. 7–23. Bach: Two-part Invention in F Major, No. 8, final section.

Contrapuntal Association

The Inventions are tightly knit, incorporating a bare minimum of melodic patterns. A glance at any page of the Bach collection will show that the same rhythmic units are used repeatedly in the sections directly based on the respective subject and those free of the subject proper.

Invention No. 1 is a masterpiece of thematic unity since every pattern can be traced back to the initial subject. Even the most prominent accompanimental pattern is itself the rhythmic augmentation of the first four notes of the motive. Ex. 7–24 shows the way Bach combined the original subject in contrary motion with the rhythmic magnification of the same pattern in its original ascending contour.

Ex. 7–24. Bach: Two-part Invention No. 1, augmentation in contrary motion.

When the first statement of the subject is accompanied, the same associative pattern is normally used in later passages as a countersubject. These later appearances occasionally appear slightly altered or elaborated; at other times they are exact duplications of the original pattern. The motive of Invention No. 9 is constantly combined with its countersubject.

Ex. 7–25. Bach: Two-part Invention in F Minor, No. 9, contrapuntal association.

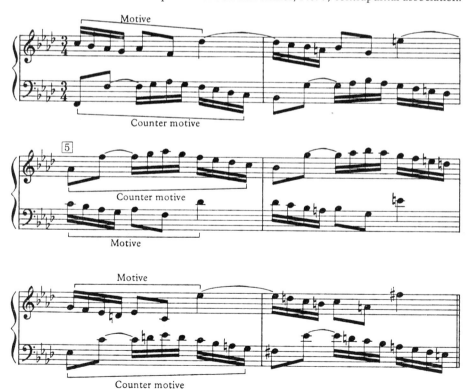

The countersubject of Invention No. 13 appears first in measure 1 as the logical continuation of the subject line in the top voice. It returns in a variety of pitch modifications with every subsequent statement, both as a contrapuntal foil for the subject proper, and combined (in fragmented form) with parts of the subject.

Ex. 7–26. Bach: Two-part Invention in A Minor, No. 13, subject variants.

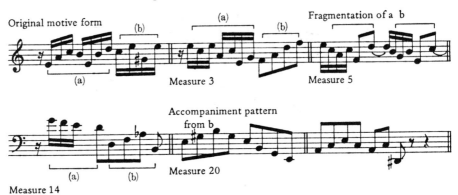

In spite of these numerous instances of extreme thematic homogeneity, the invention can effectively introduce patterns that are unrelated to the main subject—material that serves as episodic "filler" between successive treatments of the subject proper. The sequential chordal patterns of Invention No. 8—first introduced as an accompaniment to the subject—serve this function.

Ex. 7–27. Bach: Two-part Invention in F Major, No. 8, episode.

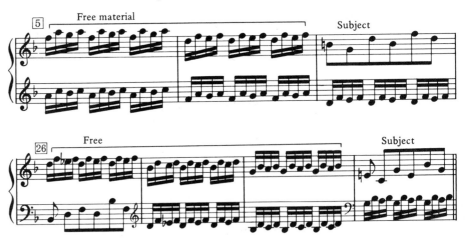

Use of a pedal note (usually trilled in the Bach Inventions to sustain the keyboard tone) is an obvious accompanimental pattern that is unrelated to the subject of the Invention. Its use in the Bach examples is restricted to developmental sections in which the motive goes through sequential patterns in one voice.

Ex. 7–28. Bach: Two-part Invention No. 7, trilled pedal.

The texture that contains the pedal figure is frequently inverted, so that the formerly static voice becomes the active partner. In Ex. 7–29, the "answer" version to Ex. 7–28 is shown, the upper voice now providing the melodic interest.

Ex. 7–29. Ibid., trilled pedal inverted.

The same static accompanying technique occurs in Invention No. 3, but in this case the pedal figure is a rearticulated octave pattern rather than the more common trill.

Ex. 7–30. Bach: Two-part Invention No. 3, activated pedal.

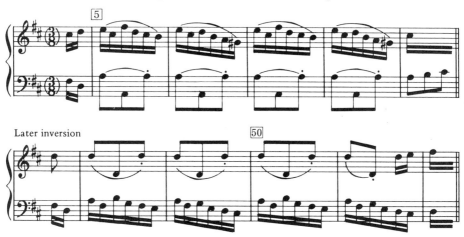

These figures that are unrelated to the main subject and independent of the countermotive are less common than those connected with motive material. This rigid single-mindedness of melodic organization is more in keeping with the compositional "inventiveness" implied within the very name *invention*.

More Recent Inventions

While there are virtually no inventions written by later eighteenth- or nineteenth-century composers, this miniature form has been resurrected by many twentieth-century composers—particularly because of its usefulness as a teaching piece. The twentieth-century invention is as diverse in style as the composers who write them. What it inherited from the Baroque invention is its strict texture, relative simplicity, and rigorous exploitation of a single musical idea. These features are clearly displayed in Ex. 7–31.

Ex. 7–31. Bartók: Chromatic Invention (*Mikrokosmos*, Vol. III).

Exercises

For more detailed exercises see *Materials and Structure of Music II, Workbook*, Chapter 7.

1. Make a detailed study of the use of the subject in Invention No. 1 in C Major. Note all developmental techniques applied throughout this Invention.
2. Write a subject that would be suitable for an invention. Apply every one of the developmental techniques discussed in this chapter to a separate section that develops this subject.
3. As a listening project, play recordings of the Inventions (or have a friend play them for you) and mark on a premeasured slip of paper the following information:
   a. Locations of strong formal junctions;
   b. Location of any significant contrapuntal features such as stretto or inverted textures;
   c. Location of a reprise section if present, or return of a hint of reprise and the original tonality; then
   d. Trace the key relations in the Invention without checking with the score.
4. Make an analysis of the chord relations outlined or implied by the voices in any of the Bach Two-part Inventions.
5. Write an invention (of about the same length as the Bach examples) in which the subject is developed mainly through sequential passages of its original form and its inversion.

Chapter Eight

Fugue

Imitative counterpoint reached its peak of development in the fugues composed by J. S. Bach during the first half of the eighteenth century. In fact, the fugue itself is a musical process developed (during Bach's time and just before) to provide a formal musical capsule within which imitative counterpoint is the exclusive texture. The two-voiced works we discussed in Chapter 7—especially the invention—exhibit most of the characteristics of the fugue. It would be accurate to describe Bach's *Inventions* as fugues for a keyboard instrument. The developmental techniques applied to motives, the play of one voice against another, and the constant counterpoint are the same in both kinds of works.

You may find it helpful to distinguish between several words that are similar: *fugal, fugue, fugato,* and *fughetta.* Remember *fugal* as the key term; it describes the kind of imitative texture that is common to works identified by the other three terms.

For example, a *fugue* is a complete single-movement work that follows broadly predictable procedures, the most important of which is a contrapuntal texture of a rather formalized imitative style. As a distinction, *fughetta* refers to any relatively brief fugue, implying a diminutive example of the bigger, more highly developed form.

On the other hand, a *fugato* is a fugal section within a larger work that, as a whole, is not a fugue. It is an extended passage that incorporates fugal procedures as a means of thematic statement or development. As an illustration of this interpolated fugal texture, Ex. 8–1 shows a passage from a composition that is not a fugue. Since the imitative theme statements set it apart from its immediate context as *fugal,* the entire section (all of which is not quoted) is a *fugato.*

Ex. 8–1. Bernhard Heiden: *Sonata for Piano,* Four Hands, I. © 1953 by Associated Music Publishers, Inc., New York. Reprinted by permission.

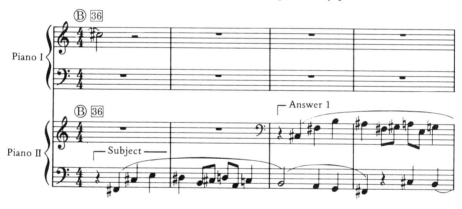

Since the fugue is the principal form incorporating all the procedures that characterize these other related imitative styles, our attention will focus on its features.

There is no such thing as "the fugue form." The fugue is, rather, a composition that embraces a combination of usual ingredients. These ingredients are blended into a contrapuntal texture whose chief aim is the development of a single melodic idea and subsidiary patterns associated with that idea.

Exposition

The core element that most clearly stamps a composition as *fugal* is the imitative principle. A fugue contains a series of sections in which the topic melodic idea, the *subject*, is stated by each participating voice in a series of imitative statements. The first of these sections is called the *exposition*; as in the invention, this section contains the first presentation of the melodic strands that will form the basis of all subsequent sections.

Ex. 8–2. Bach: *Well-tempered Clavier*, Book I, Fugue No. 19 in A Major.

Ex. 8–3. Giannini: *A Canticle of Christmas* (Fugue section based on "Come all ye faithful"). © 1959 by G. Ricordi & Co., New York. By permission of Franco Colombo, Inc., New York.

The number of statements in the exposition is usually limited to the number of participating voices in the whole fugue.[1] Thus a "four-voice

---

[1] This isn't always true for orchestral or keyboard fugues.

fugue" begins with an exposition of the subject by each of four parts, a cumulative texture gradually being built up by their successive entrances. The exposition proper is finished with the end of the statement made by the final voice.

Ex. 8–4. Bach: *Well-tempered Clavier*, Book I, Fugue No. 10 (two-voice exposition).

Ex. 8–5. Hindemith: *Ludus Tonalis*, Fuga Secunda in G (three-voice exposition). © 1943 by Schott & Co., Ltd., London. Reprinted by permission.

As Ex. 8–5 illustrates, the exposition does not always consist of successive statements of the subject in a strict additive order. In this particular exposition, a three-measure bridge stands between the second and third statements. Here, as in most bridges of fugue expositions, the total subject is not present.

Similar bridge passages appear in the three- and four-voice expositions quoted earlier in Ex. 8–1, Ex. 8–2, and Ex. 8–3. These "nonsubject"
passages serve a twofold purpose: they help to avoid the monotony of
strictly successive entries, and they also prepare for subsequent statements in terms of key, rhythmic contrast, and textural emphasis. Each of
these three factors is utilized in the bridge (or "episode") passage of
Ex. 8–6 that spotlights the entrance of the subject in the bass voice.

Ex. 8–6. Bach: Three-part Invention in F Minor.

A fundamental characteristic of the fugue exposition is the tonal
contrast projected by the successive subject statements. In fugues written before the twentieth century, tonic-dominant interplay is usually
established between the entrances of the separate voices. When applied
to a four-voice exposition this arrangement would yield the scheme of
tonic-dominant–tonic-dominant, or in some less common examples,
tonic-dominant–dominant-tonic. Many fugues written during the present
century also follow one of these tonal plans, but the less restrictive key
schemes of recent music have led to more flexible arrangements of
entrances.[2]

[2] The distinction between "real" and "tonal" answers will be discussed subsequently.

The tonality contrasts typical of the second and fourth voice statements led to the common application of the names *subject–answer* to the relation of the successive statements. But this distinction is not altogether helpful in fugues that do not maintain the simple two-level order of *tonic-dominant–tonic-dominant*, etc. The fugue exposition from which Ex. 8–7 is taken contains a succession of seven subject statements, each a semitone higher than its predecessor. The first three appear in this excerpt.

Ex. 8–7. William Schuman: *Symphony No. 3*, Fugue. Reprinted by permission of the copyright owner, G. Schirmer, Inc.

Developmental Sections

It is dangerous to generalize about what happens in fugues after the exposition section. As stated earlier, the fugue is more a set of probable ingredients than it is a defined formal design. However, the basic ingredients, as well as some elemental procedures, can be established for all fugues, even though none can be expected to follow a pat formula.

In most fugues the postexposition sections are similar to the initial exposition in that they are molded from imitative restatements of the subject. But the composer's goal following the exposition is to create thematic, textural, and harmonic transformations of the original subject. In a restricted sense, the unfolding of the fugue consists of continuous variations of the initial exposition.

We can illustrate this developmental nature of subsequent sections by quoting an entire fugue here. It should be performed at the keyboard or heard in a recorded performance several times before reading the discussion that follows.

Ex. 8–8. Bach: *Well-tempered Clavier*, Book I, Fugue No. 11 in F Major.

196

Fugue

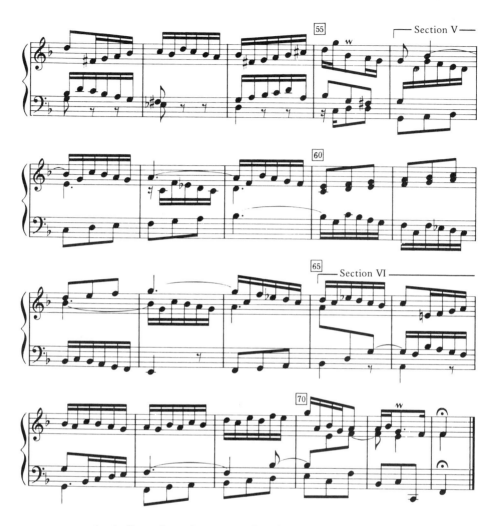

As indicated in the score, this fugue falls into six large sections, some of which can be divided into still smaller groups as noted. We can itemize the most salient features of each section.

Section	Description
I	Exposition of subject, voice order 2 (middle), 1 (top), and 3 (bottom). Last statement ends at measure 13, the subsequent four measures bridge this section to the next, II.
II	Essentially another exposition containing the same order of keys (*F-C-F*) but with the different voice order of 1–2–3. Because of this basic similarity of technique and tonality arrangement, this section is called a *counterexposition*. Ends with slightly abbreviated statement in the middle voice that is in stretto with the bass (measures 27–30).

III   Section is marked by change of mode to minor and by stretto statements of subject, voice order 1–2–3.

IV   Divided from Section III by decisive V-I cadence in measure 45. Section is a kind of "answer" in that same stretto relations are formed, but now in *g* minor and following opposing orders of entries, 3–2–1.

V   Punctuated by same cadential form as measure 45, this section leads back to original tonality of *F* major. Similar to bridge passage in section II (measures 31–35). Again, thematic material derived from subject's first measure (in contrary motion) in patterns of rising eighth notes.

VI   Camouflaged return to subject in top voice, imposed on continuation of pattern that dominated section V. As reprise, most obvious feature is reestablishment of initial key, *F* major.

A summary of the resources used in the organization of the total fugue follows: (1) dominance of the subject as melodic source; (2) key change as element of variety (*F*, *d*, *g*, *F*), (3) modal variation of subject (in this fugue from major to minor); (4) fragmentation as a developmental procedure; (5) stretto as a developmental procedure; and (6) melodic elaboration as a developmental procedure (as applied to the subject in measures 64–68).

Later we shall be concerned with a more thorough investigation of some of these fugal ingredients. For the present we must observe some of the developmental procedures that are commonly applied to the subject in the developmental sections.

Ex. 8–8 illustrated three techniques prominent in the inventions discussed in Chapter 7: *fragmentation, melodic elaboration,* and *change of mode.* The full roster of procedures used in the invention can be found in fugues, with the addition of a few others which we shall discuss presently.

Inversion is one of the most common variants of the fugue subject. It is an effective means of thematic variation because rhythm is preserved and the conjunct-disjunct nature of the subject remains, even though the directions of pitch movement are reversed. Ex. 8–9 and Ex. 8–10 each show a fugue subject and accompanying passages that draw upon contrary motion as a source of development.

Ex. 8–9. Hindemith: *Ludus Tonalis,* Fuga Quarta in A Major. © 1943 by Schott & Co., Ltd., London. Reprinted by permission.

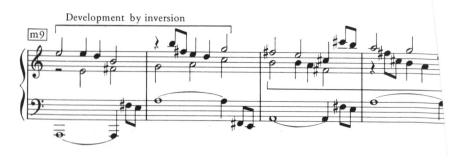

Development by inversion

Ex. 8–10. Shostakovitch: Twenty-four Preludes and Fugues, Fugue No.

An interesting texture results from a combination of the subject i its original form and in its contrary motion version. In Ex. 8–11 the tw appear in a stretto.

Ex. 8–11. Bach: *Well-tempered Clavier*, Book I, Fugue No. 6 in D Minor.

Modifications of pitches within a subject usually retain the contoural features of the original, skips and steps duplicated in the variant. Amplifying a characteristic skip by means of a wider interval plays a prominent role in the development of a motive fragment of the Invention shown in Ex. 8–12. Here the skip-step pattern is preserved intact, even though the exact interval sizes of this relation are altered considerably.

Ex. 8–12. Bach: Three-part Invention in F Minor.

Three other developmental procedures that occur, though infrequently, in the fugue are *augmentation*, *diminution*, and *retrogression*. The first two are rhythmic alterations through which the durations of a subject can be proportionately stretched or shrunk. Both usually occur only within a two-level scheme, an original pattern made twice as long (by augmentation) or half as long (by diminution).

Ex. 8–13. Bach: *Well-tempered Clavier*, Book II, Fugue No. 2 in C Minor.

Ex. 8–14. Schönberg: *Suite for String Orchestra*, Fugue. Reprinted by permission of the copyright owner, G. Schirmer, Inc.

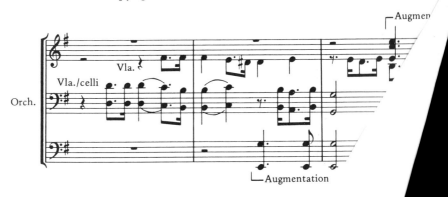

But greater scales of proportion have not been overlooked by composers.

Ex. 8–15. Bartók: *Concerto for Orchestra*, Finale. Copyright 1946 by Hawkes & Son (London) Ltd. Reprinted by permission of Boosey & Hawkes, Inc.

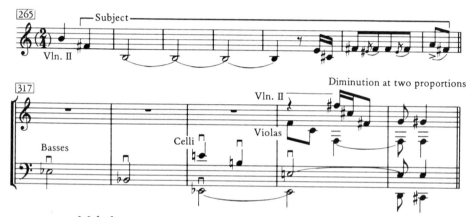

Melodic *retrogression* [3] consists of the total reversal of a pattern, so that its last pitch becomes its first and vice versa. This compositional "trick" appears within the developmental sections of some fugues, even though the effectiveness of the process is questionable as a means of thematic transformation. Its validity is relative to the structure of the subject so ordered; a short, rhythmically simple pattern might well be recognized in its retrograde version. Ex. 8–16 shows a subject and its reversal that seems to represent favorably the latter set of conditions.

Ex. 8–16. Hindemith: *Ludus Tonalis*, Fuga Tertia in F Major. © 1943 by Schott & Co., Ltd., London. Reprinted by permission.

[3] Also known as *cancrizans*.

The structure of Ex. 8–17 (which is not from a fugue) is less easy to recognize as a retrograde version of its original form.

Ex. 8–17. Honegger: *Symphony No. 5*, II. © 1951 by Editions Sallabert, Paris, by permission of Franco Colombo, Inc., New York.

Many composers have regarded the fugue as a vehicle for plying their "bag of contrapuntal tricks," so it is not surprising that the listener's recognition of retrogression has not been regarded as a crucial test of acceptability.

Another common developmental process within the fugue is *stretto*. This is not a technique of melodic variation, for the subject usually occurs in almost exact duplication within the stretto to achieve an effect of imitative compression.

As we noted in our discussion of the invention in Chapter 7, the composer might, by virtue of the structure of his motive, be able to use several different spans of imitation, thereby achieving greater and lesser degrees of compression within stretto sections. The fugue from which Ex. 8–18 is taken contains many different spans; the entire fugue is organized by means of successive sections of stretto among the four participating voices.

Ex. 8–18. Bach: *Well-tempered Clavier*, Book I, Fugue No. 1 in C Major.

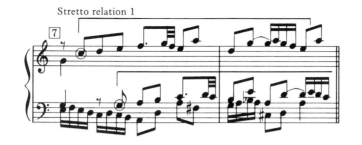

Stretto relation 1

Stretto relation 2,3, and 4

Most fugues do not exhibit such a wealth of stretto possibilities as this example, and most fugue subjects are not amenable to this multiplicity of overlapping combinations. One of the composer's chief problems in writing an effective fugue subject is to accommodate stretto relations in at least one span of imitation.

One flexibility inherent to stretto lies in the intervallic relation between the overlapped imitations. The usual relation is the octave, because without pitch modifications of the subject, this relation most readily avoids chromaticism that could undermine tonality. But granted the possibility of "tonal" imitations that produce pitch modifications, other interval relations may be accommodated into a simple key framework.

In more recent fugues of less restricted key schemes, stretto relations can be found at any interval gap. The goal of overlapping imitation is still paramount.

Ex. 8–19. Barber: *Piano Sonata, IV,* "Fuga." Reprinted by permission of the copyright owner, G. Schirmer, Inc.

Stretto 3rd below

Ex. 8–20. Hindemith: *Ludus Tonalis*, Fuga Sècunda in G Major. © 1943 by Schott & Co., Ltd., London. Reprinted by permission.

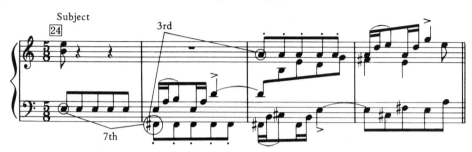

Sectional Linkage

The composer must so organize his work that it produces the effect of continuity from the outset until the final chord, without creating a feeling of choppy sectional groupings, of one section merely tacked on to another.

Earlier we noted the bridge sections that link parts of the exposition together into a continuous series of related parts. Similar bridge passages are used elsewhere in most fugues, both as temporary relief from the sections of imitative subject statements and as a procedure of modulation that leads to the key of the next subject statements. The melodic substance of these bridge sections frequently is derived from the subject by fragmentation. In many such passages two fragments are joined together in a contrapuntal association such as that shown in Ex. 8–21.

Ex. 8–21. Bach: *Well-tempered Clavier*, Book I, Fugue No. 2 in C Minor.

This episode bridges the exposition to a statement of the subject in a new key. The sequential pattern drops by steps until the new tonic, *E-flat*, becomes imminent in the last measure of the excerpt. Aside from this linking function between the two sections which contain the full subject, the passage reveals how development can occur in the bridge, here as a dialogue between two voices, each the manipulation of a subject fragment.

Such a fragmented portion of the subject might be taken from any of its parts, but usually favored is a pattern readily perceived as a derivative of the subject. In Ex. 8–22 the fragment is obviously related to the final turn of the subject.

Ex. 8–22. Bach: *Art of the Fugue,* Contrapunctus II.

In a particularly long fugue the bridging role may be expanded to become a section of considerable significance in the whole form. Ex. 8–23 shows the beginning of a ten-measure passage that lasts long enough to be recognized as somewhat more important than a mere bridge. This particular bridge is built from a pattern that first appeared in the exposition of the fugue.

Ex. 8–23. Barber: *Piano Sonata, IV,* "Fuga." Reprinted by permission of the copyright owner, G. Schirmer, Inc.

sost. Ped.

When materials not clearly related to the subject achieve a significant level of formal distinction, it is difficult to justify the usual term "bridge," for this designation implies lesser structural importance. However, this term remains as a way of distinguishing sections based upon imitative development of the subject from those which are independent of the subject.

Bridge sections are not always based on subject-derived materials. They must be similar in rhythm to the subject passages that surround them, but the contrast desired in some such sections may be best achieved by the absence of specific references to the subject. The passage shown in Ex. 8–24 forms a logical continuation of what has preceded, mainly because of the continuing sixteenth-note motion. But it bears no direct melodic relation to the subject as a whole, nor is it a fragmentary derivation. As usual, the organization is sequential.

Ex. 8–24. Bach: *Well-tempered Clavier*, Book I, Fugue No. 10 in E Minor.

Whatever the method of development in a particular fugue, the process always involves shifts of tonality, these shifts in themselves acting as an element of developmental variety. The brief tonality contrasts in the exposition represent an interior kind of shift; the fugue as a whole offers further tonal variety in the form of sectional key contrasts.

It is impossible to set down a prescribed order of keys for the fugue; such a generalization would be contradicted by too many particular fugues. However, most examples written before the present century maintain a set of key orders consistent with the definition of *near relationships* given in Book I. The general rule of "no more than one sharp or one flat removed from tonic key," based on the major-minor key signature system, is an adequate guide. The key schemes illustrated as typical on page 176 apply to the conventional fugue as well.

The important tonal convention of all fugues is the return to the tonic key for the final statement (or statements) of the subject. In most fugues it is this return to the initial key, usually in conjunction with a clear statement of the subject and a return to a simpler texture, that signals impending closure to the listener.

Space does not permit the quotation of entire fugues here to display the incorporation of all those elements that might produce a sense of formal reprise. However, the brief excerpts and attendant synopses of Ex. 8–25, Ex. 8–26, and Ex. 8–27 will provide a guide for a study of the fugues represented.

Ex. 8–25. Bach: *Well-tempered Clavier*, Book II, Fugue No. 6 in D Minor.

Ex. 8–26. Barber: *Piano Sonata IV*, Fuga. Reprinted by permission of the copyright owner, G. Schirmer, Inc.

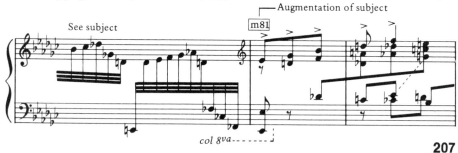

207

Ex. 8–27. Bach: *Well-tempered Clavier*, Book I, Fugue No. 6 in D Minor.

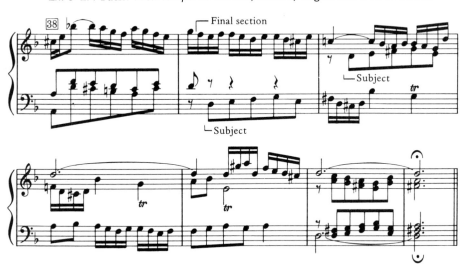

In some fugues, the return to tonic key does not coincide with the final return of the subject. It is when the two factors appear *combined*, of course, that a reprise is most strongly implied. In such examples, the beginning of the final section is reinforced by a strong cadence or a textural contrast that marks the junction between what has been developmental and what can be regarded as a closing section. In Ex. 8–28 the extreme contrast of texture that spotlights the bass entrance, in tonic key, forcefully emphasizes the return of the subject in something like its

expository form. In this fugue the statement quoted is also the first appearance of the subject in a lower voice since the exposition, thereby
reinforcing the formal significance of this statement in tonic.

Ex. 8–28. Bach: *Well-tempered Clavier*, Book I, Fugue No. 14 in F-sharp Minor.

In some fugues the return to tonic at the closing section is accompanied not by the more conventional simplification of texture, but by a
stretto that builds these final statements into a climactic fusion of all the
voices.

Ex. 8–29. Bach: *Well-tempered Clavier*, Book I, Fugue No. 22 in B-flat Minor.

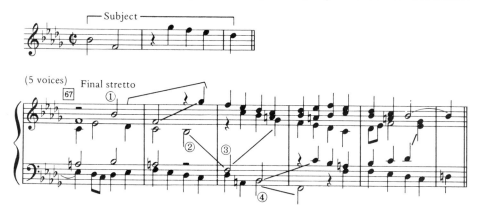

The composer's selection of the organizational methods used for
closing his fugue depends upon the formal order he wishes to establish.
If his composition is to move to a climax within an interior section,
driving to a pitch of greatest developmental tension there, then the
closing section might logically be a return to simple texture, as well as
the usual return to tonic and less modified versions of the complete
subject.

**Fugal
Exposition**

Any complete melodic figure could be used as the subject of a fugue;
there is no singular quality that makes one pattern intrinsically "fugal,"
another "nonfugal." Certain features, however, do make one melodic

pattern more workable within the fugal procedure than others. We can enumerate some significant traits which, when present in a melodic pattern, make it more readily adaptable to the usual fugal procedures.

1. *Closed form:* i.e., a pattern complete in itself rather than fragmentary. For this reason most fugue subjects are several measures long and usually can be divided into small motive fragments. Ex. 8–30a, Ex. 8–30b, and Ex. 8–30c illustrate this tendency toward melodic completeness as opposed to the fragment-like brevity of the usual invention motive.

Ex. 8–30a. Bach: *Well-tempered Clavier*, Book I, Fugue No. 16.

Ex. 8–30b. Schumann: *Fugue for Piano*, Op. 72.

Ex. 8–30c. Bartók: *Concerto for Orchestra*, IV. Copyright 1946 by Hawkes & Son (London) Ltd. Reprinted by permission of Boosey & Hawkes, Inc.

2. *Rhythmic vitality:* a unified rhythmic structure that is dynamic rather than static, projecting forward in a way that lends a propulsion to the fabric of the whole fugue. Many subjects begin with upbeat patterns for this reason.

Ex. 8–31a. Shostakovitch: *Fugue No. 2 for Piano*, Op. 87. © Copyright MCMLV by MCA Music, a division of MCA, Inc., New York. All rights reserved.

Ex. 8–31b. Harris: *Symphony No. 3*. Reprinted by permission of the copyright owner, G. Schirmer, Inc.

3. *Clear tonality and meter:* Since the subject is the nucleus from which the total form grows, it usually delineates a tonality from the beginning by emphasis on a single pitch by means of repetition, duration, or intervallic play. For the same reason, it usually establishes a meter from the outset.

The subject normally appears solo in its initial statement, although some fugues do begin with an accompanied subject. The effect of cumulative texture is best achieved by the gradual addition of voices, rendering the solo statement the most striking means of initiation. In addition, the uncluttered effect of the solo statement most clearly sets forth the subject for the listener's immediate comprehension.

The second voice usually enters at the end of the statement of the subject by the first voice, though there are exceptions to this rule. Some are interrupted by the answer of the second voice, thus creating a "stretto exposition." It is not always easy to pin down the exact note on which the subject proper ends, but answers that enter before the close of the subject usually produce the stretto effect.

Ex. 8–32a. Bach: *Well-tempered Clavier*, Book I, Fugue No. 22.

Ex. 8–32b. Bach: *Well-tempered Clavier*, Book II, Fugue No. 3.

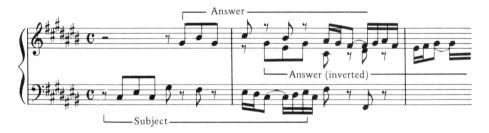

An opposite condition, the answer delayed after the subject appears to have run its full course, occurs in some expositions. It may happen if the subject seems to close on an interior beat while the answer is best stated beginning with the first beat of the following measure. Ex. 8–33 shows a subject that is actually completed two beats before its answer begins.

Ex. 8–33. Bach: *Well-tempered Clavier*, Book I, Fugue No. 7.

Under similar circumstances, many composers have not hesitated to place the answering voice in midmeasure, even though the preceding subject began at the beginning of a measure.

Ex. 8–34. Bach: *Well-tempered Clavier*, Book II, Fugue No. 9.

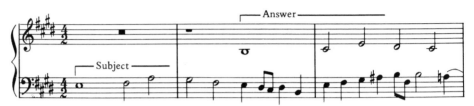

Ex. 8–35. Hindemith: *Ludus Tonalis*, Fugue No. 6. © 1943 by Schott & Co., Ltd., London. Reprinted by permission.

This notational offset occurs only when parallel stresses (strong answered by strong, weak answered by weak) are preserved. A subject that begins on a metric stress would not be followed by an answer that begins on a weak beat, for such a relation would obliterate the character of the subject.

Tonal and Real Answers

The answers of a fugue exposition are not always exact pitch duplications of the subject's first statement. The bridging of the initial tonality with the tonality of the second statement is frequently expanded by a *tonal* (inexact) as opposed to a *real* (exact) pitch version of the subject. In fugues of major or minor scale basis this *tonal* form of the subject usually entails only a slight alteration at the beginning of the answer, the remainder of the line coinciding with the exact transposition of the original pattern.

The tonal answer illustrated in Ex. 8–36 is typical of eighteenth-century fugue expositions; subjects whose first few notes dwell on *tonic-dominant* pitches are usually answered by the reverse order of *dominant-tonic*.

Ex. 8–36. Bach: *Well-tempered Clavier*, Book I, Fugue No. 8.

The same reversal is common when *dominant-tonic* is answered by *tonic-dominant*.

Ex. 8–37. Schumann: *Fugue for Piano,* Op. 72.

Notice particularly that the simple changes made in each of these subjects occur within the first few notes. The remainder of the answer is an exact transposition of the subject.

Similar changes occur in some answers after the first few notes, usually to avoid an abrupt change of tonality. The alteration that makes the answer of Ex. 8–38 *tonal* appears at the fourth pitch, to avoid an abrupt sounding of the leading tone of the new tonality of F.

Ex. 8–38. Hindemith: *Mathis der Maler,* I. © 1934 by B. Schott's Soehne, Mainz. Renewed 1961.

When the subject's length or pitch structure makes the key contrast of the answer less abrupt, the *real* answer form is as likely to be used as the *tonal.* The end of the subject shown in Ex. 8–39 prepares the listener for the dominant key, the *e-natural* implying the shift.

Ex. 8–39. Bach: *Fugue for Organ in G Minor.*

If this bridging function had not been an integral part of the subject, a tonal version, such as that shown in Ex. 8–40, would have been a logical answer for this subject.

Ex. 8–40. Ibid.

Bach provided this solution for a subject of similar pitch structure but of considerably lesser length.

Ex. 8–41. Bach: *Art of the Fugue.*

If an alteration of the answer is not required to make it fit into the initial tonality, a subject is usually answered by its exact transposition. Most fugues written with a freer tonal basis than the major-minor key system preserve the exact identity of the subject by building up the exposition from *real* answers after the initial subject statement.

Order of Voice Entries

The effect of gradual textural accumulation mentioned in several earlier discussions is frequently reinforced by the successive expansion of pitch range in the exposition. This is achieved by an order of entrances that follows a "rule of adjacent voices." That is, the first subject statement is usually answered by a voice adjacent in range above or below (such as alto answered by soprano or by tenor); it in turn is answered by its neighbor, and so on until the full complement of parts and total breadth of texture has been reached.

This neat rule of entrances is encountered more frequently in three-voice than in four- or five-voice fugues, for a consistent tiered ordering of so many statements could become monotonous. However, three-voice fugues whose subjects are introduced by the top or bottom voice normally follow the 1–2–3 or 3–2–1 scheme.

Ex. 8–42. Bach: *Well-tempered Clavier*, Book I, Fugue No. 6.

Ex. 8–43. Hindemith: *Ludus Tonalis,* Fugue No. 2. © 1943 by Schott's Co., Ltd., London. Reprinted by permission.

Less frequently, a fugue that begins in the lowest voice is answered by the highest, creating a vivid contrast of register that is interlocked when the middle voice joins.

Ex. 8–44. Bach: *Well-tempered Clavier,* Book I, Fugue No. 4.

The entry order in fugues of more than three voices usually follows some grouping by adjacent pairs, such as two upper-voice statements paralleled by a similar order in two lower voices (2–1, 4–3), or the two lower voices preceding the two upper voices (3–4, 1–2).

Fugue

Ex. 8–45. Bach: *Well-tempered Clavier*, Book I, Fugue No. 17.

Only in rare instances is the "rule of adjacency" followed for the entry order of four-voice fugues, producing a successive accumulation from low to high—or high to low—of all voices.

Ex. 8–46. Beethoven: String Quartet, Op. 131, I.

**Tonality
Contrasts
of Entries**

As we mentioned earlier, the tonic-dominant balance of entries in the traditional fugue exposition does not always govern the subject-answer relation of more recent fugues. The relaxation of this general rule reflects the broader tonal relationships that prevail in all aspects of twentieth-century music.

The tonic-dominant order represents a relationship that is consistent with the harmonic vocabulary of seventeenth-, eighteenth-, and nineteenth-century music, which, as a whole, operates within a diatonic pitch framework with emphasis on V—I as a harmonic basis. In the fugue, the answer's appearance a fifth above its predecessor retains enough tones that are common to both keys (such as E major–B major) that the change is readily heard as a smooth shift from one tonal plane to another. The usual brevity of these shifts in the fugue exposition might well be regarded as less than definite modulation, rather more like an elaboration of the dominant *tonal region* of the tonic key.

Ex. 8–47 shows a subject-answer in which this shift to the key of the dominant gives more emphasis to the dominant chord (supported by secondary dominant relations) than an actual modulation to the dominant key.

Ex. 8–47. Bach: *Well-tempered Clavier,* Book I, Fugue No. 9.

The *tonal* answer discussed earlier is another way the composer can minimize the key contrast of the successive statements, so that each answer is more closely allied to the original key.

As we have noted previously, some music that draws upon a richer set of tonal resources—chromatic scale, complex chords, and chord relations—nonetheless retains the simple tonic-dominant contrast as the basis for fugal entries of the exposition.

Ex. 8–48a. Wm. Schuman: *American Festival* Overture. Reprinted by permission of the copyright owner, G. Schirmer, Inc.

Ex. 8–48b. Barber: *Piano Sonata,* IV. Reprinted by permission of the copyright owner, G. Schirmer, Inc.

Tonal patterns that do not adhere to the tonic-dominant or tonic-subdominant plan are usually based on a symmetrical order of one kind or another. Ex. 8–7 shows subject entrances arranged by rising semitones, while Ex. 8–49 shows entries that follow a series of fifths up and down. As a by-product of this latter arrangement, the texture grows with each entry from a thin midrange strand into a progressively thicker combination that encompasses the string orchestra range.

Ex. 8–49. Bartók: *Music for String Instruments, Percussion, and Celesta,* I. Copyright 1937 by Universal Edition; Renewed 1964. Copyright & Renewal assigned to Boosey & Hawkes, Inc., for U.S.A. and to Universal Edition for all other countries. Reprinted by permission.

This scheme disregards the traditional pairing by subject-answer–subject-answer that dominated most pre-twentieth-century fugue expositions. And yet, many recent fugues contain the paired order, although not always in the tonic-dominant scheme. In a three-voice fugue the last statement of such a pairing might return to the original note series, suggesting a return to the initial tonality.

Ex. 8–50. Hindemith: *Ludus Tonalis*, Fugue No. 4. © 1943 by Schott & Co., Ltd., London. Reprinted by permission.

It should be obvious that the composer's choice of tonal relations for subject entries must be determined by the pitch structure of his subject and the harmonic style within which his fugue will be couched. A relatively diatonic subject could well demand the tonally simpler and less disruptive *tonic-dominant* or *tonic-subdominant* scheme, whereas a more chromatic subject might justify a less simple order of entries that follows a nondiatonic relationship.

The Counter-subject; Invertible Counterpoint at Twelfth

In addition to a subject, most fugues draw upon another melodic pattern, called *countersubject*, for thematic materials.[4] As in the invention, this pattern usually appears in the exposition as a continuation of the subject along with the second entry.

Ex. 8–51. Schumann: *Fugue for Piano*, Op. 72.

---

[4] In some fugues several subjects are exposed and developed to an extent that justifies the title *double* or, as the case may be, *triple fugue*. It is beyond the scope of our work here to discuss these significant departures from the monothematic fugue design.

Ex. 8–52. Bach: *Well-tempered Clavier*, Book I, Fugue No. 6.

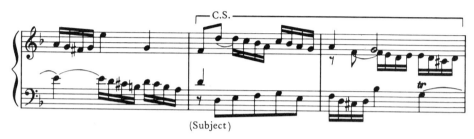

The countersubject isn't a full-blown melodic unit like the subject, nor does it occur in complete duplications later in the fugue. It is, rather, a characteristic pattern (or group of patterns) that provides accompanimental figures for later appearances of the subject. It also is used in some fugues as a source from which bridge passages are woven.

In some fugues the countersubject can be traced to a motive within the subject, thus unifying further the thematic basis of the whole fugue. The countersubject of Ex. 8–53 clearly originates from the second half of the fugue's subject.

Ex. 8–53. Bach: *Well-tempered Clavier*, Book I, Fugue No. 16.

A basic requirement of any countersubject is its adaptability to *inversion* (or *double counterpoint*) with the subject. Its continued association with the subject throughout the fugue requires that it form a satisfactory counterpoint above or below. We discussed this requirement of textural inversion in our study of the invention in Chapter 7, where inversion at the octave was cited. In addition to this relation of simple reversal of roles from top to bottom by octave transpositions, composers have occasionally brought about inversions at other intervallic relations. Inversion at the twelfth (fifth plus octave) and the tenth (third plus octave) occur most often.

As a simple illustration of invertible counterpoint at the twelfth, Ex. 8–54 shows two textures; the second is an inversion of the first at the twelfth.

Ex. 8–54. Inversion at twelfth.

Here the top voice of (a) has been transposed down one octave, while the bottom voice has been transposed up a fifth to create the reversal shown in (b). Notice that the following intervallic changes take place when inversion at the twelfth is used:

Ex. 8–55. Interval inversions at the twelfth.

Original Interval	1	2	3	4	5	6	7	8	9	10	11	12
	12	11	10	9	8	7	6	5	4	3	2	1

The same basic relation results regardless of which voice is transposed from its original note level by the interval of the fifth. The *upper* voice can be lowered a fifth when it moves to the lower part of the texture, or, as in Ex. 8–56, the *lower* can be raised a fifth when it becomes the top. Both procedures yield an inversion "at the twelfth," even though different pitches result.

Ex. 8–56. Interval inversions at the twelfth.

Both versions (y) and (z) are derived from the original (x) by inversion at the twelfth. In (y) the top voice of (x) has been shifted down one octave, the bottom voice up one fifth. Note that (z) contains the same intervals between the parts as (y) (5—3—5), but each contains different pitches—(y) is a perfect fourth below (z).

Transposition of one voice up a fifth or down a fifth (or compounds of these intervals) frequently necessitates pitch alterations to retain the desired tonality or to ensure workable harmonic relations between the two parts. Ex. 8–57 shows negligible pitch alterations of the first version when it is inverted at the twelfth.

Ex. 8–57. Bach: *Art of the Fugue*, Fugue No. 9.

(Parts are omitted which do not participate in the inversion)

The inverted texture may appear after an intervening section that separates it from its prototype, but it usually follows the statement of the original immediately, as in Ex. 8–58, where the original top voice has been dropped a twelfth (compound fifth) while the middle voice (highest of the *inverted texture*) has been raised an octave.

Ex. 8–58. Palestrina: *Mass, Dies Sanctificatus*, Agnus Dei, I.

The countersubject of the fugue from which the excerpts of Ex. 8–59 are taken is a clear example of invertible counterpoint. Bach uses it inverted at different interval relations during the course of the whole fugue.

Ex. **8–59.** Bach: *Well-tempered Clavier*, Book II, Fugue No. 16.

Inversion at 12th (inner voices of texture omitted)

Also see measures 28-31 of the same fugue

Invertible counterpoint achieves thematic unity. Since the same patterns are involved within the prototype and its inversion, no variety of thematic materials arises unless accompanying parts (which do not participate in the inversion) are altered or replaced. It is only the change of vertical relationships and intervals (harmonic relation) that provides any sense of variety.

Exercises

For more detailed assignments see *Materials and Structure of Music II, Workbook,* Chapter 8.

1. Analyze a number of fugue or fugato expositions found in the works of Palestrina, Buxtehude, Bach, Beethoven, Schumann, Shostakovitch, Hindemith, Bartók, Wm. Schuman. Pay particular attention to the following details:
    a. Structure of subject;
    b. Presence or absence of countersubject;
    c. Tonal relations of subject statements;
    d. Order of entries in terms of pitch range;
    e. Presence or absence of episode links between subject statements; nature of thematic material and contrapuntal devices used herein.
2. Follow the procedures of (1) above with a division of the whole fugue into major sections; then determine the following:
    a. Tonalities embraced by each section;
    b. Developmental techniques applied to subject;
    c. Uses of countersubject if present in the fugue;
    d. Appearances of subject in stretto (if present);

    e. Any uses of earlier material or earlier sections in textural inversions: at 8ve or at 12th or at 10th.

    f. Does final section or some "late section" serve as a clear reprise for the whole fugue, or does the work simply "end" without a return other than in terms of tonality?

3. Listen to a fugue several times, paying particular attention to the broad sections that are formed by tonality, textural, and thematic contrasts. Having heard the fugue several times, plot out in gross terms the basic form of the piece. (Make this in the form of a graphic design on a piece of paper.) Then listen again and in the process perfect your outline. By all means avoid seeing a score before or during this session. Then check the accuracy of your outline with the score.

4. From the literature, select a number of fugues for study. Pay particular attention to the following:

    a. Structure of the subject;

    b. Use of *tonal* or *real* answer and why;

    c. Order of voice entries in exposition and in subsequent expository sections;

    d. Tonality contrasts of subject entries in exposition.

5. With the same works selected for (1) above, study the following:

    a. Overall sectional divisions of the fugue; tonality plan;

    b. Developmental and contrapuntal processes applied in the various sections;

    c. Presence or absence of invertible counterpoint;

    d. Presence or absence of stretto; time gaps between voice entries in the stretti; total relations of voices.

6. Write a subject or select one from a fugue by one of the composers whose works have been discussed in the foregoing chapter. Add a contrapuntal accompaniment to this subject that is rhythmically complementary and that can be inverted with the subject at the octave. Write the original texture and then write the inverted version below. Follow the same procedure with a counterpoint that is invertible at the twelfth.

7. Write several subjects that seem appropriate for fugues. Write an exposition section for three voices using one of these subjects. (The exposition you write does not have to end with a logical sense of finality; it can merely break off after the third full statement of the subject.) Score the results for three instruments and perform.

8. Derive a brief fragment from the subject used for (4) above and write a two- or three-measure episode that is based on that fragment and that modulates from *tonic* to *relative major* or *minor*. Write another that modulates from tonic to a distant-related key.

9. Using one of the subjects written for (4), determine what kinds of development would work well and write fragmentary textures based on just these developmental processes.

10. Combine some of the above results into a fugue by adding a logical concluding section.

11. Find examples of inverted textures in the inventions and fugues of Bach. Copy the original measures on manuscript paper and place its inversion directly below so that the relations of the two can be studied clearly.

Chapter Nine

Sonata-Allegro Form

The form known as *sonata-allegro*[1] has dominated instrumental music since the mid-eighteenth century and is still a significant influence upon some composers today. Its roots can be traced to the binary form of the Baroque era, which has the overwhelming preference of seventeenth- and early eighteenth-century composers for shorter movements of instrumental compositions. The interesting process by which the simple

[1] At times referred to as just *sonata form* or *first-movement form*.

two-part Baroque binary evolved into the more complicated, three-part sonata-allegro will be briefly traced in the following paragraphs.

Pertinent Features of Baroque Binary Form [2]

The most obvious feature of the parent binary form is its division into two similar sections, the second of which is *thematically* identifiable with the first. The principal differences between the sections are tonal, not thematic. Instead of contrasting themes, the Baroque composer sought a highly unified musical web, the progress of the piece marked by smooth modulations between closely-related keys. Most binary movements from this period are characterized by a "sameness" of texture and theme throughout the movement.

The opening section of a typical binary form consists chiefly of a modulatory passage from the tonic key to a related tonal area, often the dominant or (when the tonic key is minor) to the relative major. The second section generally exhibits considerable tonal instability at the outset but reaches the tonic key at or near the end of the composition. The two sections then are parallel thematically, but each pursues a different tonal goal: the first *departs* from the tonic—the second *returns* to the tonic.

Each section is "open" tonally, since each begins and ends in a different key. The following diagram graphically illustrates this design:

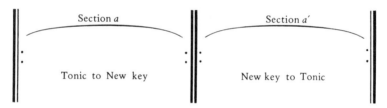

Early in the eighteenth century, isolated binary movements began to appear with formal procedures not found in the traditional two-part Baroque dance form. The simplicity of these innovations in no way indicated the impact they were to have upon musical structure in the next several hundred years. To the binary pattern the following two elements were added:

1. A restatement of the opening thematic material near the end of the movement, along with
2. the simultaneous arrival of the tonic key.

The coincidence of these two musical events (as in the pattern we call "rounded binary") produces a more profound effect than one might

[2] See *Materials and Structure of Music* I, Chapter 22, for an extended discussion of this formal design.

expect from such a simple device. First, the listener is immediately conscious of a third distinct section—a "return"—in the movement. The significance of this exact or partial duplication of the opening musical material can hardly be overstressed. Also, the arrival of the tonic key at the restatement produces an effect of completion and emphasizes it as a structural point for the listener.

It is not far from this simple expansion of the binary design to the sonata-allegro form, which we find in the symphony, quartet, and sonata movements of Haydn, Mozart, and their contemporaries.

The Classical Sonata-Allegro

The overwhelming preference of eighteenth-century composers for the sonata-allegro formal structure proves its psychological and musical effectiveness. This design became virtually the inevitable choice for first movements (hence the term "first-movement form" used by many English writers) and was popular for all of the movements in a multimovement work except when a type of dance movement—minuet or scherzo—was used (usually for a second or third movement). One of the most typical movement groupings is as follows:

Four-movement Symphony, Quartet, or Sonata			
First movement	Second movement	Third movement	Fourth movement
Rarely any but Sonata-allegro	Often S-A in a slower tempo; ternary or theme and variations are frequent alternatives	Minuet (or Scherzo) and Trio	Often S-A; rondo was the most common alternative

Sonata movements from the early eighteenth century to the present display uniformity in general outline—balanced, however, by a wealth of variety in detail. The result is a unique opportunity for the unfolding of musical ideas within an established framework.

If we examine any of the numerous eighteenth-century sonata-allegro movements, it is evident that the pattern outgrew many of its binary characteristics. In the mature compositions of Haydn and Mozart the dimensions of the sections clearly suggest a three-part division. If we compare this to its binary ancestor we see that the second section of the binary design is split into two sections. The start of the final section corresponds with the restatement of the opening theme and the return of the tonic key.

Another important change also took place: the thematic "sameness" of the older binary design was replaced by two new trends—thematic contrast and development. As the sonata-allegro form evolved, these features became more distinct.

Let us now view sonata-allegro form from a new point of view—as an established three-section form. Each of the three sections has a distinct function to fulfill, contributing to the overall plan. The terminology associated with the following diagram has become a standard part of the musical vocabulary:

	Exposition			Development	Recapitulation			Coda
Principal theme	Bridge	Subordinate theme	Closing theme	(sectional)	Principal theme	Bridge	Sub. th.	Cl. th.	(based on previous material)

Exposition

The *exposition* is a series of successive *statements* of the thematic materials, separated by transition or "bridge" passages (the two terms are synonymous). Most sonata movements feature themes that differ sharply from one another in contour, mood, or general melodic "personality." Although the exact number of themes is variable, the following pattern is the most common: the first or *principal* theme, followed by transitional material (sometimes with considerable thematic substance of its own), followed by a group of themes that often are separated by shorter bridge passages.

Some traditional names given to these themes include *subsidiary* or *subordinate* (used for the first theme in the second group of themes) and *closing* (the final theme of the exposition). This is often an unfortunate choice of terms, since the so-called subordinate theme may play a more prominent role than the first theme. Many writers prefer simply to designate the themes by number or alphabetic letter.

Ex. 9–1 illustrates a typical set of themes appropriate to this form. The contrasts in melodic contour, dynamics, and even articulation emphasize the individuality of each. Not all sonata movements display vividly contrasting melodic materials.

Ex. 9–1. Beethoven: *Piano Sonata in F Minor*, Op. 2, No. 1.

The function of the development section is likewise indicated by its name, since its primary objective is the "working out" (the development) of the musical ideas of the exposition, displaying them in dramatic new arrangement. Development is a basic part of the process of spinning out musical materials over a large form; in the development section this process is a primary feature.

Development sections are generally more active (in many ways) than expository sections, and the pace of musical events moves faster. Short, terse exclamations often replace the full sentences of the exposition. Even the occasional sections of relative repose are short-lived and are often followed by a vigorous return to the previous activity.

Perhaps the most widely-used developmental technique is fragmentation—the breaking up of thematic material into short, incisive motives so that they can be recombined in new and interesting ways, often in a contrapuntal texture. Motives thus derived lend themselves well to sequence, imitation, and other methods of extending melodic material.

Not all themes are appropriate for such a process. But Ex. 9–2, illustrates a theme perfectly suited to fragmentation, since it consists of extremely short, distinct motives. A short segment of the development of the same work demonstrates how these motives are combined.

Ex. 9–2. Haydn: *Symphony No. 104 (London),* IV.

Fragmentation is but one of a number of effective developmental procedures. The composer's strategy for the development section is greatly influenced by the character of his themes: long, finely-spun lyrical themes do not lend themselves to the type of development described above. In treating lyrical thematic material, composers have preferred to keep the theme more or less intact, elaborating the melodic line with variations and/or exploring different tonal regions.

And, in addition, fugato, textural change, dynamic contrast, change of register, and a number of tonal procedures discussed in earlier chapters (particularly those on motive development and fugue) are frequently encountered in development sections.

Composers have not followed any general pattern in choosing which themes to develop. In one composition, each of the themes of the exposition will be developed in turn; in another, the composer will concentrate attention on a single theme. A seemingly insignificant bridge theme will sometimes assume greater significance in the development until it overshadows the other themes.

Many other features are characteristic of the development: the evasion of cadence, changes in harmonic rhythm, new orchestral combinations, etc. All of these support the primary role of the development— to serve as a foil for the exposition and recapitulation, providing variety that helps to emphasize the unity established by the two outer sections of the formal plan.

Preparing for the recapitulation is the remaining task of the development. Since the type of preparation depends entirely on the individual composition, few generalizations are possible about this section. Its role is primarily tonal and, as such, will be discussed later in this chapter. Some elements, however, are helpful in creating the anticipation of a significant new musical event: the use of pedal point, a distinct change in harmonic rhythm, increased rhythmic activity, typical cadential approach procedures, etc. The development often ends with a strong cadence and a complete cessation of motion—sometimes even a fermata—before plunging into the recapitulation.

Recapitulation

The sonata-allegro design is completed by a restatement of the exposition that, in many respects, exactly balances the earlier section, although it is never a literal repeat. Thematically, the recapitulation is much like the exposition, generally displaying the same order of themes, similar transitional material, similar dimensions, and a similar conclusion.

Psychologically, the effect of the recapitulation is of relaxation after the intensity and unsettling effect of the development. The restatement of the thematic materials in their original forms aids in restoring the unity that is characteristic of this section.

Coda

A final section is often added to the recapitulation. Codas were relatively infrequent and of small dimension prior to Beethoven, but subsequently became to common and assumed larger proportions. With Beethoven the coda often turns out to be a second development section, balancing the first development in the overall design. The primary function of a coda, however, is to solidify the completeness of the movement and emphatically end it. Often we find material of a fanfare nature at the conclusion of a coda or, as in many of Beethoven's codas, repeated tonic chords, heavily orchestrated and at a high dynamic level, emphasizing the finality of the cadence chord.

The Tonal Design

The tonal organization of the classical sonata-allegro form helps to shape the work as much as does the thematic organization. It is in tonal relationships that the family resemblances between binary and sonata-allegro are most apparent. The eighteenth-century composer's preference for the dominant and relative major keys in the latter portion of the exposition indicates this relationship to the older form. Let us view the sonata-allegro pattern once again, this time considering key relationships and other tonal aspects of this form.

A fundamental characteristic of the exposition is its basic contrast of keys, between the key of the opening statement and the second group of themes. The principal theme generally remains in the tonic key. This is followed, however, by a transition, or bridge, that often grows out of the first theme. The tonal function of this passage is to effect a modulation from the tonic key to the key of the second group of themes. The principal theme group of a symphonic first movement appears in Ex. 9–3. The transition between principal and second theme groups demonstrates how thematic material from the first combines with a modulation to effect the transition.

Ex. 9–3. Mozart: *Symphony No. 38 (Prague)*, K. 504, I (piano reduction).

(Principal theme)

233

Several features typical of transition sections are evident in this example. In addition to the modulatory progression (producing temporary tonal instability) and use of motives from the principal theme, we find increased rhythmic drive, important changes of texture, dynamic contrasts, changes of harmonic rhythm, and many of the same procedures we observed in our discussion of development sections. Sequential imitation is particularly prominent.

As a rule, the key of the second theme group is maintained until the end of the exposition. Viewing the exposition as a whole, the following tonal pattern is established:

Principal theme group—Transition—Second theme group

stable tonality (tonic)—tonal instability—stable tonality (new key)
(modulatory)

This contrast between tonal stability and instability is as much a characteristic of sonata-allegro form as is the contrast in key.

Contrasting keys are further explored in the development section through the juxtaposition of several keys or tonal areas. In the music of the eighteenth century, most of these keys are closely-related, although the gradual trend was toward the inclusion of more distant keys. The following diagram presents in comparative form two typical development sections, and is clearly representative of the contrasting practices of the Classical (Haydn) and early Romantic (Schubert) composer.

Haydn: *Symphony No. 102 in B-flat Major*, I.

Keys:		c	E-flat	(unstable)	A-flat	c	d	(unstable)	c	C	c	(unstable)	dom. of B-flat
Duration in measures:	6	7		9	16	8	9	7	7	7	7	17	10

Schubert: *Symphony No. 4 in C Minor (Tragic)*, I.

Keys:	(unstable)	b-flat	G-flat	(unstable)
Duration in measures:	4	23	8	4

In his tonal plan, each of the above composers has included passages of unstable tonality: passages that are modulatory or that do not clearly suggest any single key. Schubert's plan features more distantly-related keys than those in the Haydn symphony. It is also noteworthy that Haydn employs a greater number of keys.

Preparation for and Beginning of the Recapitulation

The end of a development section must prepare for the return to the tonic key at the beginning of the recapitulation. This feeling of tonic expectancy can be produced by many means, and its advent may be either obvious or virtually imperceptible. Having avoided the tonic key during the development (so that the effect of its return will be fully realized), the composer's task is to make its return compelling.

An obvious device for producing this anticipation is the highly elaborated dominant or dominant seventh over a sustained pedal point. In subtler form, however, this section may consist of a sequential treatment of one of the thematic ideas that eventually arrives at the appropriate key without advance warning.

Ex. 9–4 illustrates a relatively simple preparation for the recapitulation. The previous section of development comes to a clear half-cadence in *g* minor (measure 3); in measure 4 the dominant of *B-flat* major is introduced and prolonged for the next seven measures. The resolution of this dominant signals the start of the recapitulation.

Ex. 9–4. Mozart: *Sonata in B-flat Major*, K. 333, I.

A much different procedure occurs in Ex. 9–5, where not the tonic key, D major, is implied, but rather its mediant, *f-sharp* minor. The final measures of this section preceding the recapitulation at measure 160 merely reiterate the dominant of *F-sharp*, ending with a long, sustained *C-sharp*. In a striking passage, this tone becomes the leading tone of D major and resolves accordingly, thus accomplishing a return to the tonic key.

Ex. 9–5. Beethoven: *Quartet in D Major*, Op. 18, No. 3, I.

In summary of Classical-period development sections, we quote the entire development of a Mozart sonata as Ex. 9–6. This excerpt contains the typical contrast of tonal stability/instability, exploration of closely-related keys, and a clear retransition to the tonic key—*A* major.

Ex. 9–6. Mozart: *Sonata for Violin and Piano*, K. 526, I.

The main and secondary tonal areas of the preceding development are graphically charted in the following basic framework. Note especially the dominant prolongation, beginning at O, that prepares the scene for recapitulation.

This contrast of tonal relationships is abandoned in the recapitulation, tonal strategy usually directed at reaffirming the tonic key. The key variety of the development gives way to key unity in this section. The recapitulation's beginning usually parallels closely the beginning of the exposition, since both feature the tonic key.

However, the transition section brings a new problem. Where the transition in the exposition modulated, the transition's function in the recapitulation is to avoid such a modulation so that the second theme group may sound in the tonic key. For this reason, it is precisely in this transition section that recapitulation differs the most from exposition.

Once the second theme group of the recapitulation is reached, the tonic key prevails: tonal unity has taken the place of tonal contrast. Although some slight tonal diversion often occurs near the beginning of the coda, this is of passing significance and serves merely to delay the inevitable drive toward the final cadence. In the concluding sections, anything out of the immediate orbit of the tonic key is a rarity.

Other Factors Influencing the Perception of Form

The sonata-allegro belongs to a small group of musical patterns featuring an "organic" process of growth and evolution that corresponds to the life process itself. Much of the effect of the form is produced by this gradually emerging, always changing "free-flow" of the musical elements.

It would be a mistake, however, to assume that smooth organic evolution is the only goal of sonata-allegro form. The perception of *distinct change*—either to a new section or a return to material (as in the recapitulation) suggesting an earlier section—is equally important in understanding musical form.

Composers have formulated many strategies for emphasizing the appearance of what seems to be new material: key change alone is one of the most effective means of delineating the start of a new section. But many other possibilities exist—contrast in theme, contrasting textures, change of register, dynamic change, contrast of timbre (orchestration)— all these function in an effective way to lead the listener toward the perception of a new formal event.

Ex. 9–7 illustrates this point. Using the motive that opens the composition, Brahms has employed several of the devices outlined in the previous paragraph to mark the start of successive sections within the development. In contrast to development sections which are cast in a fluid, continuous stream of musical activity, this development demarcates the beginning of each interior section by various tonal, dynamic, and textural means.

Ex. 9–7. Brahms: *Quartet in C Minor*, Op. 51, No. 1, opening motive.

(Section 1)

The Flexibility of the Pattern

It should be clearly understood that few sonata movements follow the *exact* thematic and tonal pattern described in the preceding pages. One can most accurately view sonata-allegro form as a *general* plan or a flexible procedure.

Many variants of this pattern exist. In one of these the development section is either omitted or is reduced to a mere transition between exposition and recapitulation. The term *sonatina* is often assigned to this type of piece, but readers should not confuse it with the type of keyboard piece written by Clementi, Kuhlau, and other eighteenth-century composers. Their "sonatinas" are miniature sonatas that generally contain all the standard sections. Thus the term *sonatina* can mean either a very brief sonata movement or one that lacks a development.

Ex. 9–8 scarcely justifies the name *development,* for not only is it extremely short but it contains few developmental techniques. More than half of its fourteen measures are an obvious transition to the recapitulation.

Ex. 9–8. Beethoven: *Sonata in G Major*, Op. 49, No. 2, I.

Other common deviations from the standard sonata-allegro are:

1. a *monothematic* exposition, one that uses basically the same thematic material for both main sections of the exposition—first in the tonic key and later in the contrasting key;

2. the omission of a *closing theme* in exposition;
3. the rearrangement of the order of themes in the recapitulation or the omission of one or more of these;
4. the use of key schemes that differ from conventional eighteenth-century practice;
5. the appearance of new themes in later sections—development, recapitulation, and/or coda; and
6. the incorporation of extensive development into bridge passages, thematic sections, codas, or elsewhere.

Ex. 9–9 illustrates the last of these and is a typical example of a short contrapuntal section used as an interlude between expository sections. This passage, a five-voice fugato based on the principal theme, separates the principal theme from the bridge (not reproduced here) in the exposition.

Ex. 9–9. Mozart: *Symphony in C Major (Jupiter)*, K. 551, IV.

Composers have chosen many different solutions to the main problem posed by the bridge between theme groups I and II in the recapitulation: how to retain most of the transition material of the exposition and yet avoid the change to the dominant key. One simple solution can be seen in the first movements of Schubert's *Trout Quintet* and *Symphony in B-flat*. His procedure is to begin the recapitulation in the *subdominant* key. This makes it possible to retain the same bridge material used in the exposition, modulating to the tonic for the final section (*exposition:*

tonic to dominant; *recapitulation:* subdominant to tonic). Thus the re-capitulation becomes a wholly transposed exposition.

Concerto movements in modified sonata-allegro form reveal a characteristic approach to the initial statement of thematic material in the exposition. The standard pattern in the Classical concerto is a double exposition in which the themes are first stated by the orchestra in the tonic key, then restated by soloist and orchestra, this time proceeding to the conventional dominant or relative major key in the second theme group. (This procedure is clearly illustrated in the first movement of Beethoven's *Piano Concerto No. 3,* Op. 37, a work that could serve as a model of formal clarity in the concerto idiom.)

The Function of the Introduction

Many sonata-allegro movements contain no introductory material, beginning directly with the exposition. However, a slow introduction frequently precedes the main body of the movement, forming an effective contrast not only of tempo but often of dynamics, thematic content, mood, and texture.

The introduction can serve several purposes. In many symphonies the slow introduction is not related thematically to the ensuing *allegro.* One concept of the introduction in these compositions seems to be a stately "frontispiece" to the main portion of the movement. In all cases the introduction does not participate in the sonata-allegro pattern itself; it generally remains outside of the three-part pattern of exposition-development-recapitulation.

The function of the introduction in Ex. 9–10 is clear: the fragmentary violin figures serve as a gradual winding up of motion. One scale degree after another is added until the movement is put "in gear" and moves on its way.

Ex. 9–10. Beethoven: *Symphony No. 1*, IV.

Introductory material can assume a tighter relationship with the remainder of the movement, however, when it shares thematic material. The common use of thematic material varies, of course, in degree; often the element in common is no more than a short motive that occurs both in the introduction and in the subsequent *allegro*. A more elaborate relationship is shown in Ex. 9–11. Here an entire passage from the introduction is transplanted into a new context. The material in the bracketed sections is similar melodically and harmonically.

Ex. 9–11. Brahms: *Symphony No. 1*, I (excerpts from introduction and *allegro*).

If we limited the use of the term "sonata-allegro" to movements conforming totally to the conventional eighteenth-century mold, we would be forced to conclude that the form is no longer a mode of organization for contemporary composers. It is clear that sonata-allegro is one of the least significant structural frameworks for *avant-garde* composers. If we argue, as many theorists do, that the essence of sonata-allegro form lies in the interplay of related keys or tonalities on a framework of time, then it is clear that we are describing the form as it existed for the Classic and Romantic composer.

However, as we have seen, most formal patterns take on specific style conventions of their chronological period; the essence of their form lies not in any specific characteristic but in a much broader concept that applies equally to all works organized in this fashion. Thus, for example, the conventions of key relationships that were typical of an early phase of sonata-allegro form were already beginning to undergo expansion and eventual obsolesence in the early nineteenth century.

Stripped of these "nonessentials," the sonata pattern emerges as a starkly simple design of *exposition-development-recapitulation*. And as such, it can be shown that some composers of the twentieth century have found it an effective framework for their musical ideas.

Two compositions will be cited in the following discussion: Paul Hindemith's *Piano Sonata No. 2*, the first movement, and the final movement of Béla Bartók's *Concerto for Orchestra*. Hindemith's movement corresponds so closely to traditional sonata design that its link with earlier examples will be readily apparent. The sequence of musical events is as follows:

Exposition:

1. Statement of a theme in a clear, stable tonality (*G* is the tonal center).
2. Transition, unstable tonally.
3. A second theme, stable and in the tonality of *F* (minor is implied).

Development:

4. A development by rhythmic ostinato, the transition material, and short scraps of the second theme; the tonality unstable throughout.

Recapitulation:

5. A restatement of the first theme in the original tonality, the ostinato continuing.
6. A short canonic passage replacing the original bridge passage (which was thoroughly explored in the development).
7. A restatement of the second theme—beginning in a new tonality but shortly returning to *G*.

Coda:

8. A short coda based upon the first theme, concluding in *G*.

The tonal organization of this movement warrants a closer look. It should first be observed that the relationship between tonalities is described in terms of the relationship between their *tonics*—a looser relationship than the interlocking web of related tones that we imply when we describe relationships between *keys*. Thus when we note that the first and second sections of Hindemith's exposition are in the tonalities of *G* and *F* respectively, we have still failed to relate their scales. However the basic point is clear: they establish the basic tonal contrast that is the hallmark of the sonata-allegro.

Secondly, tonal instability can now be realized through the *absence* of any tonality: passages that are (or seem to be) *atonal* can be used effectively to contrast with clearly tonal passages. In short, to contemporary composers, tonal/atonal can take on a meaning similar to stable/unstable for their predecessors.

Examining the tonal structure of the entire movement, we can diagram its tonal plan as follows:

EXPOSITION   *DEVELOPMENT*   *RECAPITULATION*

G—unstable –*f*minor —— unstable   (*F, B-flat, F-sharp, D, B, A*) —— G—unstable – *c*minor—G

These are obviously not the conventional tonal relationships of the eighteenth century or even of the late nineteenth century. The relationship between first and second themes (major 2nd) is perhaps the most apparent departure from tradition. Despite this, however, the return to and emphasis of the main tonality in the recapitulation, the alternation of points of tonal activity and repose, as well as the thematic organization, reveal this movement's close allegiance to the bedrock of sonata-allegro form.

This movement provides us with some clues to the kinds of deviations we might expect in other examples of twentieth-century sonata-allegro form. We should not expect to find tonality defined as in past centuries, nor should we expect to find the same near-related tonality schemes outlining main sections. We can expect to find, however, the relationships between thematic statements and their development, transition passages, alternation of tonal stability and instability, and the eventual return to the opening tonality that constitute the permanent features of this form.

A movement that displays a much freer approach is the final movement of Béla Bartók's *Concerto for Orchestra*. In his program notes for this work, Bartók admitted that he composed it with the sonata-allegro design in mind. In many ways, however, it differs from the outlines we have discussed thus far.

1. The recapitulation is much shorter than the exposition.
2. The second theme undergoes a significant transformation within the exposition and appears only in this latter form in the recapitulation.
3. Both the second and closing themes appear as *fugati* textures first in the exposition.
4. The closing material of the exposition is omitted in the recapitulation (although it figures prominently in the coda).

5. The movement begins and ends in *F*, yet *C-sharp/D-flat* appears to be the prevailing tonic of the exposition, while *F-sharp* is the tonic in the recapitulation.
6. The exposition contains much more contrast of tonality than would be present in classical examples of the form.
7. The development displays somewhat *less* contrast of tonal centers and tonal instability than one might expect.

Naturally, one should not assume that all composers of the present have discarded the exterior trappings of the sonata-allegro form they inherited. Composers who remained closer to the traditions of eighteenth- and nineteenth-century practice, such as Prokofiev, Shostakovitch, Sibelius, Vaughan Williams, and others, found in this form a source of formal strength and an appropriate vehicle for their thematic material. If there are any lessons to be learned from the past history of organization in music, one is that effective formal patterns do not die out but continue to coexist along with newer approaches. A subsequent chapter on twentieth-century formal procedures will explore the variety of experiments with formal structure in the music of this century.

Exercises

Additional materials and more detailed assignments are contained in *Materials and Structure of Music II, Workbook*, Chapter 9.

1. Analyze Ex. 9–2 for motive structure: identify the source of each motive used and the devices used to combine them (repetition, sequence, inversion, etc.).
2. Make a similar analysis of Ex. 9–3.
   a. Point out the source of each melodic idea in the transition.
   b. Analyze the modulation for type and exact location.
   c. Identify the various cadences occurring within this section.
   d. In what way is chromaticism a significant feature of this modulatory excerpt?
3. With recordings listen to the two movements outlined on page 254 and follow aurally the tonal plan of each development section. Does your aural experience substantiate the conclusions in the text?
4. Analyze the segments of Ex. 9–7 for key and identify each chromatic chord. Describe the texture at the beginning of each section in precise musical terms.
5. Name the various possible keys established in Ex. 9–6. Locate the areas of greatest tonal instability. Where does the retransition begin? Where does the recapitulation begin?
6. Listen to a recording of the first movement of Mozart's *Symphony in G Minor*, K. 550 and sketch out the main formal divisions. On repeated hearings determine the various developmental techniques used and as many of the key relationships as possible.

7. Listen to the following symphonic movements, noting in particular internal formal divisions and the means employed to mark the beginnings of main sections:
   a. Mozart: *Symphony in E-flat,* K. 543, I.
   b. Beethoven: *Symphony No. 2,* I.
   c. Brahms: *Symphony No. 3 in F,* I.
   d. Prokofiev: *Symphony No. 5 in B-flat,* I.
8. Contrast the introductions of the Mozart and Beethoven movements cited in 7a and 7b, noting key stability and changes of key, texture, and length of the sections.
9. Relate the thematic materials of Brahms' development section (7c) to the exposition.
10. Listen to the *Piano Concerto in A Major* (K. 488) by Mozart. Make a diagram of the main sections of the movement and compare to the structure of the *E-flat Symphony,* K. 543.
11. Listen to the opening movement of Bartók's *Third Piano Concerto* and determine the extent of its adherence to sonata-allegro design.

Chapter Ten

Enriched Harmonic Resources Ninth, Eleventh and Thirteenth Chords

We have seen how the family of seventh chords became established in musical practice. The richer textures of music composed during the late nineteenth century led to even more complex chords, chords incorporating intervals of the 9th, 11th, and 13th.

Ninth Chords   Example 10–1 shows ninths treated as decorative pitches. The accompanying reductions (on the third staff) represent the sonorities that are momentarily formed or implied where decorative ninths occur.

Ex. 10–1. Bach: Three-voice Invention in E-flat Major.

In contrast to ninths formed by decorative patterns, ninths occur as equal members of chords in the next example.

Ex. 10–2. Brahms: *Intermezzo,* Op. 116, No. 1.

The *f-sharp* in the previous example forms the major ninth of an arpeggiated chord built in thirds, whose root note is *e.* Since *b* is tonic, the chord is a subdominant ninth chord. A dominant ninth (lacking its 3rd) appears in Ex. 10–3.

Ex. 10–3. Wagner: *Tristan und Isolde,* Act I.

Ninth chords can be constructed on any scale degree by the same process used for triads and seventh chords. Note the kinds of ninth chords that can be derived from combining various major and minor scale tones.

Ex. 10–4. Diatonic ninth chords.

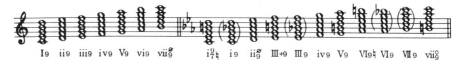

I_9 ii_9 iii_9 iv_9 V_9 vi_9 $vii^\varnothing_9$ $i^9_{7\natural}$ i_9 $ii^\varnothing_9$ $III+_9$ III_9 iv_9 V_9 $VI_{9\natural}$ VI_9 VII_9 $vii^\varnothing_9$

Compare the different qualities of ninth chords that can be built by using various scale forms. Some of the chords that can be derived from major and minor scales, such as iii_9 and $vii°_9$, seldom occur.

The Dominant Ninth Chords

A V_9 chord is a V_7 to which a major or minor third has been added. Thus V_9 is but a logical addition to the group of dominant functioning chords, as in Ex. 10–5.

Ex. 10–5. Brahms: *Intermezzo*, Op. 116.

V^{9-8}_{7-} V^9_7 V^{9-8}_{7-}
                          $6-5$
                          $4-3$

Typical resolutions of V_9—I (i) are illustrated in the next excerpt. Like the 7th, the 9th of the chord usually resolves by descending step.

Ex. 10–6. Typical resolutions of V_9.

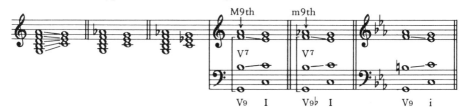

The 9th of the V_9 sometimes is mutated, composers freely using the major or minor 9th (or both) in the V_9—I relation. In minor keys such freedom does not prevail; we seldom find V_9 with a major ninth directly preceding a minor tonic triad.

Ex. 10–7. Minor ninth chord.

(Seldom found)

D: $V_9 - I$ $V^{\flat 9} - I$ d: $V_9 - I$ $V^{\natural 9} - i$

Deceptive resolutions of V_9 to vi are rare, perhaps because the ninth of the chord is identical with the root of vi, and the progression V_9—vi (or VI) would prohibit the normal 6—5 melodic movement of the ninth. When V_9 does move to vi or VI, as in Ex. 10–8, 6—5 melodic movement usually results in a reduction of harmonic tension *before* the change of chord to vi.

Ex. 10–8. Deceptive resolutions of V_9.

In the next example, V_9 is heard in measure 3 over a rearticulated dominant. The resolution in measure 4 of the ninth (*Ab*—*G*) creates a slackening of tension, although the dominant bass tone is maintained. Note that the 9th of this passage has the function of a suspension.

Ex. 10–9. Schubert: *Symphony No. 4 in C Minor (Tragic)*, I.

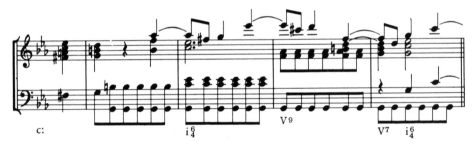

Approaches to V_9 are virtually identical to approaches to V or V_7. The same root relations prevail, and V_9 usually is found in relatively weak metric positions. Several common approaches to V_9 are illustrated in the group of excerpts in Ex. 10–10.

Ex. 10–10. Approaches to V_9.

Root position is the most frequent arrangement of ninth chords, the intervals formed above the bass note being 9, 7, 5, and 3 when five different pitch classes are present. The chord's 3rd, 7th, and 9th are usually present in four-part occurrences of the chord, its 5th frequently omitted, as in the V_7. Study the distribution of chord members in Ex. 10–11.

Ex. 10–11. Schumann: *Symphony No. 2, Adagio.*

Both first and second inversions of V_9 are found arpeggiated in Ex. 10–12. Note that the 5th is present in the first inversion, measure 2.

Ex. 10–12. Beethoven. *Piano Sonata in E-flat,* Op. 31, No. 3.

Although third and fourth inversions of ninth chords also occur, they are rare. The 9th most often lies in the top part of the chord, and only rarely is it placed in such a way as to form the interval of a 2nd with the chord root. The 9th is rarely found below the root, since such an arrangement would obscure the characteristic interval of the chord, the major or minor 9th. A variety of spacings of ninth chords in four and five parts is shown in the next example.

Ex. 10–13. Spacings of ninth chords.

The principles of spacing, doubling, and voice leading that generally apply to V_9 chords are the following:

1. The 9th, which usually occurs in the soprano or alto part, is always separated from the root by the interval of a 9th or more.
2. The 5th of the chord is most often omitted in four-voice textures.
3. Doubling does not normally occur in four-voice textures. In richer textures the root is usually doubled.
4. In inversions of the chord, the interval of a 9th is maintained between the root and the 9th.
5. The 9th of the chord resolves by descending step (6—5).
6. The tritone between the 3rd and 7th resolves according to the established principles.

Study the following examples of V_9 resolutions.

Ex. 10–14. Typical resolutions of V_9.

Like V_7, V_9 is susceptible to an enormous variety of resolutions, its use not limited to dominant-tonic relations, as the next example reveals.

Ex. 10–15. Other resolutions of V_9.

Nondominant Ninth Chords

The mmM ninth chord, comprised of a root, m3, p5, m7, and M9, occurs as ii_9 in major keys, as i_9 and iv_9 in minor.

Ex. 10–16. Different arrangements of ii_9 (mmM).

C: ii_9 ii_9 ii_9 ii_9

As attractive as these chords may be, they played only a nominal role in music until the twentieth century. Where they do occur in earlier music, the 9th (and often the 7th as well) are most often heard as appoggiaturas or suspensions. Unlike the V_9, nondominant ninth chords contain no tritone, and they normally appear within the phrase rather than as part of a cadence.

Ninth chords built on A (ii$_9$) and on D (V_9) form the harmonic basis for the passage shown in Ex. 10–17.

Ex. 10–17. Ravel: *Pavane.*

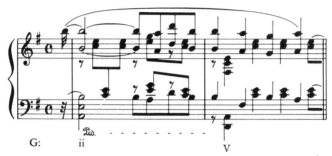

A more contrapuntal treatment of a mmM ninth chord (iv$_9$) is found in Ex. 10–18. Here the 9th and 7th are suspensions which form part of a sequence that begins in measure 2. Contrary motion dominates the outer voices leading to the cadence. Note here also that through a continuation of the sequence, the Neapolitan resolves to $^{\circ}_7$/VI, evading the expected V_7 until the last beat of measure 3.

Ex. 10–18. Mahler: *Songs of a Wayfarer,* No. 1.

Adding a minor 3rd above the 7th of a major-major seventh chord (MM$_7$) produces the MMM ninth chord. Again, the 5th is omitted from four-voice arrangements of the chord. The MMM ninth chord occurs as I$_9$ or as IV$_9$ in major keys, and as III$_9$ or VI$_9$ in minor.

Ex. 10–19. MMM Ninth Chords.

Leaps to and from ninths occur in the first two measures of Ex. 10–20. The same notes, *G* and *F*, which create iv₉ and III₉ chords, occur in the accompaniment as an appoggiatura and a suspension in that order.

Ex. 10–20. Schumann: *Symphony No. 2,* II.

The MMM ninth chord usually occurs as melodic embellishment of a simpler triad or seventh chord. A comparison of Ex. 10–21 and 10–22 will show the chord functioning in one case as a product of double suspensions, and in the other as a cadential tonic chord. The two treatments are music worlds apart.

Ex. 10–21. Bach: *Well-tempered Clavier,* Book I, Prelude in E♭.

Ex. 10–22. Ravel: *Le Tombeau de Couperin,* Minuet. Permission for reprint granted by Durand et Cie, Paris, copyright owners, and Elkan-Vogel Co., Inc., Philadelphia, agents.

In the following example, the 9th (*f-sharp*) of the chord in measure 2 has been "prepared" melodically in the previous measure.

Ex. 10–23. Wagner: *Tristan und Isolde,* Prelude to Act I.

Here the 9th occurs as a repetition of the preceding motive, and the V₉ resolves deceptively to VI. The whole passage seems to spring from the semitone motive of measure 1, since both the prevailing melodic intervals and root relations constitute developments of the same interval, the 2nd. Harmonic and melodic activity clearly stem from the same source.

Eleventh and Thirteenth Chords

Chords which contain as many as five or six different pitch classes are likely to possess an ambiguous root. It is possible to view such chords as (a) in different ways, since more than one of its tones may function as its basic pitch.

(a)

One possible interpretation of this chord would be as an eleventh chord based on *C* (its 9th omitted), as shown in (b).

(b)

A second way of viewing the same collection of pitch classes could be one in which *F* is interpreted as root, the result being an eleventh chord (whose 3rd is missing), as shown in (c).

(c)

Or we might even decide that this collection is in fact not a tertial chord, that it is indeed the product of stacked fourths, as (d) demonstrates. Our concern for the present is, of course, for *tertial* rather than *quartal* chords.

(d)

The possibilities for constructing different types of tertial eleventh chords so exceed their use in music that any comprehensive grouping of them would be unwarranted. Thirds of any size (but especially major and minor 3rds) may be added to any of the numerous kinds of ninth chords we have seen, thereby producing eleventh chords. Play the examples shown next and experiment with different spacings of each. All these chords contain perfect 11ths although others, such as augmented 11ths, are found in music of the late nineteenth and early twentieth centuries.

Ex. 10–24. Eleventh chords.

As with ninth chords, the 7th is present in four-voice (or more) arrangements of eleventh chords, while either the 3rd, 5th, or 9th may be absent. Eleventh chords usually occur in root position, the root being the most frequently doubled member. As a little experimentation will show, eleventh chords quickly lose their identity as tertian chords when the root is not at the bottom of the sonority.

The most common (and clearest) arrangement of this kind of chord occurs when its members are distributed as a series of stacked thirds, as in the next excerpt.

Ex. 10–25. Ravel: *Le Tombeau de Couperin*, Rigaudon.

C: ii$_9$ ii$_{11}$ V$_{13}$ I

This passage by Ravel contains a ii$_{11}$—V$_{13}$—I cadence in C major, and the effect of the cadence—supported as it is by roots related by perfect 5ths—is strong and direct. The supertonic eleventh chord on the second beat of measure 1 is a mmMp eleventh chord: minor 3rd, perfect 5th, minor 7th, major 9th, and perfect 11th. The V$_{13}$ chord contains both a perfect 11th and a major 13th above its root, and characteristically lacks the leading tone (the 3rd of the chord). Chords such as these and those in Ex. 10–26 are in some instances best regarded as combinations of two simpler chords that have been combined by stacking, one on the other, such as $\dfrac{\text{ii}}{\text{V}_7}$ or $\dfrac{\text{IV}}{\text{V}}$.

Ex. 10–26. Stravinsky: *Octet for Winds,* I. Copyright 1924 by Edition Russe de Musique; Renewed 1952. Copyright & Renewal assigned to Boosey & Hawkes, Inc. Revised Edition copyright 1952 by Boosey & Hawkes, Inc. Reprinted by permission.

We have seen that distinguishing between chord tones and non-chord tones is sometimes difficult. Eleventh chords frequently can be explained as much simpler chords that are embellished by prolonged or accented decorative pitches, such as 4–3 suspensions or appoggiaturas. The pitches on the second beat of measure 2 in the following excerpt momentarily form a V_{11} chord in f minor. Viewed another way, the 11th (F) of the chord is merely a rearticulated suspension, and the actual harmony is V_7.

Ex. 10–27. Wolf: *Spanish Songbook,* No. 26.

In measure 3 of the next example, *F* both creates an 11th of a V_{11} and acts as an appoggiatura of a V_7 chord. The entire passage prolongs dominant harmony; the function of the 11th of the chord is essentially melodic. As anticipated, the resolution of the 11th is by a descending step to *E* (4–3).

Pitches of essentially melodic function, but of sufficient duration to be heard as true chord members, may be indicated in analysis by placing parentheses around their numerical representatives, e.g., $V(\frac{11}{7})$. (See Ex. 10–28.)

In Ex. 10–29, the note *B* (11th above *F-sharp*) is heard for most of measure 3. Despite its treatment as a 4—3 suspension, *B* is established by its duration as a structural member of the harmony, and thus forming V_{11} in *E*. The pitch that resolves the 11th, *A-sharp*, is a passing tone. In contrast to the preceding illustrations, this chord (ii_{11}) represents an unusual use of the 11th since it is momentarily doubled and also left by a leap.

Ex. 10–29. Wagner: *Tristan und Isolde*, Prelude to Act I.

Augmented Eleventh Chords (+11)

The augmented eleventh chord is almost entirely a product of the early twentieth century, although it made a celebrated reappearance in jazz music of the period 1945 to 1955. Like the °7 and the Fr $^{+6}_{\ 3}$ the +11 contains two tritones. Its sound is similar to that of the French augmented sixth chord, but its harmonic function is quite different, as illustrated in the next example.

Ex. 10–30. Comparison of Fr $^{+6}_{4\ 3}$ and V_{+11}.

The first chord, the Fr +6, precedes the dominant and is based on a root that is a semitone above that chord's root, the fifth degree of the scale. The second chord, by contrast, is a *dominant chord*, and thus it is structurally more important. A notational difference between the two chords also exists, in that the Fr +6 contains an augmented 6th above the bass, in contrast to the minor 7th contained in the +11th chord.

Ex. 10–31. Fundamental positions of the two chords.

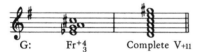

The complete +11th chord consists of a major 3rd (usually present), a perfect 5th, a minor 7th, a major 9th, and an augmented 11th. The 5th and the 9th of the chord are frequently omitted.

Augmented 11th chords can be built on any scale degree. Their most common function, however, is that of V. They frequently are built on the lowered second degree (Neapolitan) of a scale, there functioning as embellishments of tonic. This function can be expressed as $^{\flat}II_{+11}$. Study Ex. 10–32 and note the tonal functions of the several augmented eleventh chords.

Ex. 10–32. Augmented eleventh chords embellishing diatonic chords.

Observe in the next excerpt how +11th chords on *A* and *D* resolve as delayed appoggiaturas. This passage is tonally unstable, characteristic of the fact that these chords frequently occur in transitional passages, heralding a change of key or a new formal section (or both). The

tonal instability of such passages serves to heighten the expectancy of
a more definite tonality, while affording an opportunity to exploit harmonic color.

Ex. 10–33. Brahms: *Symphony No. 3*, II.

Mutations of the members of the +11th chord are common, usually
as a raised (and thus major) 7th, a raised (and thus augmented) 5th,
and as a raised or lowered 9th. In Ex. 10–34 two +11th chords built
on the subdominant appear between articulations of the tonic triad.

Ex. 10–34. Ravel: *Le Tombeau de Couperin*, Forlane. Permission for reprint
granted by Durand et Cie, Paris, copyright owners, and Elkan-Vogel Co., Inc.,
Philadelphia, agents.

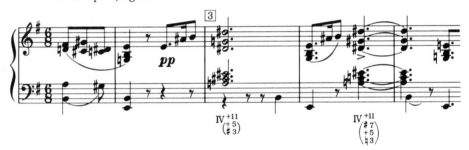

The chord in measure 3 of this excerpt contains a M3, +5, m7, and +11,
while its successor contains a m3, +5, M7, and +11. In both cases the
+11th member has been doubled.

 An idea of the variety of sonority obtainable through alterations
of +11th chords can be gained by playing over the chords shown in
Ex. 10–35. All these contain the +11 interval.

Ex. 10–35. Alterations of the +11 chord.

Like seventh, ninth, and eleventh chords, thirteenth chords function in most cases as dominants, although they too may be built on any scale degree. The V_{13} chords of G and C are shown resolving to their respective tonics in the next example.

Ex. 10–36. Schumann: *Phantasiestücke*, Op. 12, Fabel.

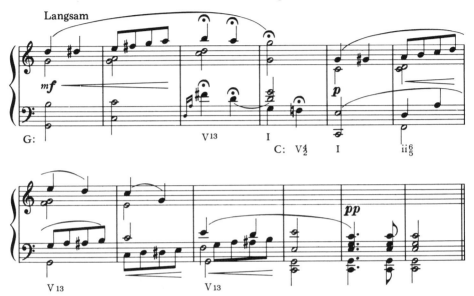

Chord members often omitted from V_{13} are its 5th and 9th. All the principles of resolution of the V_7 apply to resolution of V_{13}—I. The 13th itself has two common resolutions, one by descending step to the 5th of the V_7 chord, the other by a descending leap of a 3rd to the tonic note.

Ex. 10–37. Resolutions of dominant thirteenth chords.

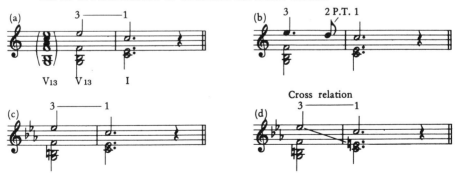

A typical V_{13} cadence is shown in Ex. 10–38, the 13th resolved by a descending leap to tonic.

Ex. 10–38. Gounod: *Faust*, Act I.

C: V7   V13

The V_{13} chord members are usually arranged so that they clearly project the characteristic sound of that chord. When the 5th is present it is spaced at least a ninth below the 13th, which is true of the C in the thirteenth chord of the next example.

Ex. 10–39. Kodaly: Cello Sonata, Op. 4, III. Copyright by Universal Editions. Reprinted with their permission.

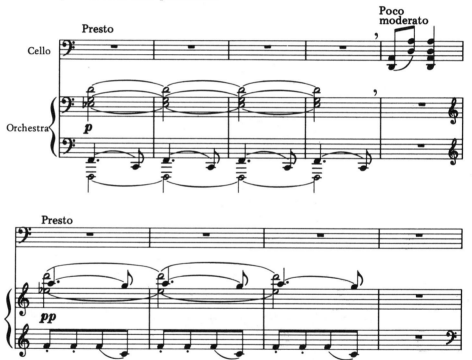

The expectation of resolution created by the V_{13} chord is a product of two factors: (1) the tritone formed between the chord's 3rd and 7th (as in any V_7 chord), and (2) the two interlocking 7ths formed between the root and 7th and the 7th and 13th, see below.

Note especially the 3–1 melodic patterns in the next excerpt, as well as the interlocking 7ths (*A—G* and *G—F*) in measure 1. (The tritone occurs between *G* and *C-sharp*.) The chord is V_{13} in *D* minor. The *F* is a pitch of essentially melodic function, a function confirmed by the fact that the *F* is not doubled in the piano accompaniment.

Ex. 10–40. Schubert: *Standchen*.

Ex. 10–41 provides examples of a variety of ninth, eleventh, and thirteenth chords.

Ex. 10–41. Schumann: *Davidsbundler*, No. 1.

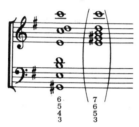

The chord on the second beat of measure 14 in this excerpt is a V_{13} in *A* minor. It is shown in the following example as a block chord in fundamental position.

The chord's 3rd is in the bass, and thus the chord is a V^{13}_3. Inversions of thirteenth chords, like those of ninth and eleventh chords, are infrequent. Granting the possibility that such chords are invertible, theoretically speaking, we shall consider them as root position sonorities, inversions being quite rare occurrences.

Dominant thirteenth chords furnish numerous possibilities for mutation, some of which are shown next.

Ex. 10–42. Dominant and secondary dominant thirteenths.

Although virtually every chord member (except the root) can be mutated, the major 3rd and minor 7th, which form the tritone of the chord, must be retained if the V_{13} is to function as a dominant sonority.

Ex. 10–43. Alterations of V_{13} in *F* major.

Study Ex. 10–44 to observe how the composer has merged interesting counterpoint and a full complement of seventh, ninth, eleventh, and thirteenth chords, noting the various melodic patterns that unify the excerpt.

Ex. 10–44. Rachmaninoff: *Piano Prelude in E-flat.*

Nondominant Thirteenth Chords

On occasion, several composers of the late nineteenth century—notably Scriabin and Debussy, as well as the American Charles Ives—used harmonic color as an end in itself, making chords and their varied qualities the basic organizing principle. For example, in the following excerpt rich chords (ninths and thirteenths) succeed each other to produce a stream of sounds that are related more by chord quality and voice leading than by functions within a key.

Ex. 10–45. Ravel: *Le Gibet.* Permission for reprint granted by Durand et Cie., Paris, copyright owners, and Elkan-Vogel Co., Inc., Philadelphia, agents.

Thirteenth chords of nondominant function, called *added sixth chords*, play a basic role in both art music and jazz. Stravinsky's *Symphony in Three Movements* closes with the chord shown in the next example, a tonic thirteenth (or perhaps a tonic ninth chord with added sixth).

Ex. 10–46. Stravinsky: *Symphony in Three Movements*, III. Copyright 1946 by Schott & Co., Ltd., London. Reprinted by permission.

D♭:   I₉(add 6)

Incomplete eleventh and thirteenth chords on *B-flat* and *G* occur on the third and fourth beats of measure 1 in the next excerpt. Both chords produce a heightening of tension in the unfolding contrapuntal phrase.

Ex. 10–47. Hindemith: *Ludus Tonalis*, Interludium. Copyright 1943 by Schott & Co., Ltd., London. Reprinted by permission.

Having become acquainted with some of the more complex chords introduced toward the close of the past century, in the next chapter we shall consider other developments of that same era that also were to influence, even more significantly, the course of music to follow.

Exercises

Additional materials are contained in *Materials and Structure of Music II, Workbook,* Chapter 10.

1. Build ninth chords on the various scale degrees of *F* major and *f* minor, indicating the quality of each resulting chord.
2. Build and resolve dominant ninth chords in several keys, major and minor.
3. Compose short examples for various combinations of four voices or instruments which contain typical illustrations of V₉ resolving to I.
4. Compose a vocalise which illustrates melodically outlined seventh and ninth chords on different scale degrees.
5. Listen to a recording of the first principal section of Ravel's *Pavane to a Dead Princess* and identify the ninth chords that occur.
6. Play major triads on the piano and superpose ninths and sevenths above each triad vocally.
7. Make harmonic reductions of the chordal sections of Bach's *E-flat* Prelude, Book I, *Well-tempered Clavier*, noting particularly the use of ninths as decorative pitches.

Chapter Eleven

Enriched Tonal Resources Variable Tonal Relations and Harmonic Ambiguity

In this chapter we shall discuss the expansion of harmonic resources (and the general weakening of tonality) that occurred in the music of the late nineteenth century. The reduced dependence of this music upon the major-minor key system forged an important link in the chain of development of Western music.

Tonic focus in melody and harmony is very much related to the strong metric placement of certain pitches and chords, especially pitches and chords that can stand in the relationship of I to V. With the enriched harmonic pallette of the nineteenth century came new practices in which the role and nature of tonality were considerably changed. For example, the tonic note, *A*, is almost hidden as a prominent melodic or harmonic pitch within the first nineteen measures of the Chopin *Mazurka* illustrated in the first example.

Ex. 11–1. Chopin: *Mazurka*, Op. 17, No. 4.

A is prominent in the bass at measure 13, but our anticipation of a tonic (*a* minor) triad here is thwarted by the appoggiatura (*b*) and a progression of V_7 to iv   rather than V_7—i. Strong confirmation of tonic is withheld until the terminal cadence at measure 20. Here, the interaction between harmony and melody has achieved two important effects: (1) tonality has remained obscured for eighteen measures by avoiding assertions of the tonic chord, and (2) the tonality has been clarified (after eighteen measures) through an assertion of the tonic triad (preceded by its dominant) in a strong metric position.

Tonality is asserted through interplay of prominent tonic and dominant pitches in Ex. 11–2. However, Brahms has accompanied the tonic note with chords other than tonic, or with inversions of the tonic triad. Not a single tonic chord in root position occurs after the first beat of measure 1; nor can we find a dominant-tonic progression after measure 2. The entire passage, however, operates within the broad tonal outlines of tonic-dominant. (Note the first and last chords of the excerpt.)

Ex. 11–2. Brahms: *Symphony No. 1*, II.

Brahms has extended the tonality-establishing pattern of tonic- dominant by using it as a framework for a long span of music, rather than as a simple harmonic progression. Every occurrence of the dominant chord is deemphasized by avoiding root position or strong beat placement.

Clear and emphatic assertions of tonic, dramatically reinforced by powerful rhythmic-dynamic force, occur in the opening of Beethoven's *Third Symphony*.

Ex. 11–3. Beethoven: *Symphony No. 3*, I.

After such a beginning it is improbable that any pitch other than *e-flat* will be perceived as tonic. Compare the Beethoven example with the Wagner excerpt of Ex. 11–4, and note the remarkably different expressions of tonic (*E-flat*) in the two works.

Ex. 11–4. Wagner: *Tristan und Isolde*, Act I.

One difference between the two is that *e-flat* is never heard in a strong metric position accompanied by tonic harmony in Ex. 11–4. Wagner consistently evades our "tonic expectations" by accompanying strong *melodic* assertions of tonic with *nontonic chords*; rhythm, melody, and harmony never really converge to confirm E-flat. This is particularly evident in measures 5, 10, and 15. At measure 15 the voice reaches a climactic strong beat on e^2-*flat*; our expectation of the tonic triad is very strong, especially in view of the previous dominant emphasis. Tonic harmony, however, is withheld in favor of $°_7$/V.

The point to remember from the preceding illustration is that a tonic may be implied melodically *even though the supporting chords fail to confirm it.*

Summing up the rhythmic considerations cited thus far we should note that:

1. Tonic and dominant chords in prominent positions, particularly terminal cadences, are important to the perception of tonality, even though they may be separated in time by considerable musical development.
2. The prominence of the tonic chord is lessened when it occurs in weak metric positions, especially when it is in an inversion.
3. Structural melodic pitches may affirm tonic, even though the tonic chord is avoided in the accompanying chords.
4. Tonality is most clearly established by the coordinate activity of melody and rhythmically-stressed tonic chords.

Deceptive Harmonic Action

The deceptive cadence provides a significant way for harmonic action to expand a phrase. By avoiding the tonic chord, a deceptive resolution broadens the tonal scope of a phrase or section by postponing the harmonic confirmation of tonic. For V—vi to be deceptive requires that tonic be previously established. In the progression of Ex. 11–5, E-flat rather than G might easily be perceived as tonic, for there has been no previous clear indication of tonic.

Ex. 11–5. Deceptive progression.

By way of contrast, *G* evolves as tonic in measures 1 and 2 of Ex. 11–6, and it is therefore easily understood as an evaded chord root at the close of the example. The result is a deceptive cadence.

Ex. 11–6. Deceptive cadence.

Reviewing various resolutions of a V_7 in *G,* we can see that the resolutions shown in Ex. 11–7 are typified by *step* root relations and voice-leading.

Ex. 11–7. Various resolutions of V_7 in *g* minor.

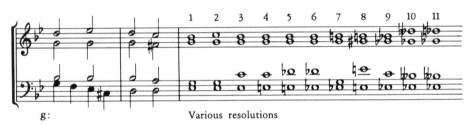

Three step resolutions appear in Ex. 11–8, each characterized by step motion in the bass.

Ex. 11–8. Franck: Prelude, Aria, and Finale.

In measure 5 of Ex. 11–9a, Wagner avoids the finality of a tonic resolution of $V_{9-(8)}$—I through a deceptive resolution to an *f-flat* major $\overline{A^b \text{ (pedal)}}$ triad.

Ex. 11–9a. Wagner: *Tristan und Isolde.*

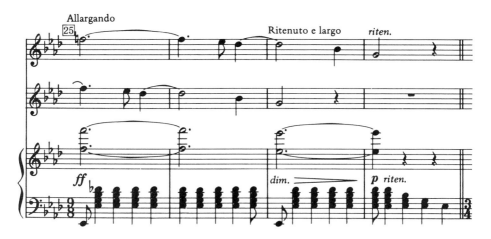

The *f-flat* chord at measure 5, then, acts as the launching point for sixteen measures of music which shift tonality continuously before *A-flat* is reaffirmed in measure 21. The same *f-flat* chord, so effectively used to evade tonic, is employed again at measure 20 as the Neapolitan of the dominant (N/V). It is from this chord that Wagner moves to a reassertion of tonic. The entire excerpt might be reduced harmonically to the progression: I—V₇—♭VI—I—V₇ in *A-flat*. Since it is these chords which underline the tonality, the passage can be viewed tonally as an expansion of them. This will be more apparent from a study of the harmonic reduction in Ex. 11–9b.

Ex. 11–9b. Reduction of Ex. 11–9a.

The structural importance of a deceptive resolution as a critical point in the form of the example above cannot be overstressed. We can summarize by pointing out that tonality has been virtually suspended for some fourteen measures (5–19) on the heels of a remarkably simple harmonic event.

Harmonic Sequences

Harmonic sequence is produced by the repetition of a chord pattern at different pitch levels. Harmonic sequence is perhaps most easily understood as a sequence of root relations, as seen in the following two examples.

Ex. 11–10a. Harmonic sequence.

Ex. 11–10b. Resulting root pattern.

Sequence has often been used to elaborate an essentially diatonic key scheme, acting as a vehicle for rich and varied chord patterns, frequently weakening or obscuring tonality altogether.

Any chord pattern may be the basis for a sequence, although root relations by fifths are most often found in music before the close of the nineteenth century. Triads, seventh chords, and more complex nontertian chords may be found in sequence, as well as patterns involving an alteration between stable and unstable sonorities.

Harmonic sequences, like melodic, constitute one of the most common developmental techniques in music. Three statements of a sequence "at the third" (repetitions of an initial pattern at successive levels of a third below) comprise the opening of Ex. 11–11. The root pattern (lower stave) is changed at measure 4 with the reassertion of tonic. The *b-flat, g,* and *e-flat* chords (I, vi, and IV), form the harmonic centers of each unit of the sequence.

Ex. 11–11. Beethoven: *Piano Sonata*, Op. 106, Scherzo.

Sequential repetition commonly involves pitch relations that exceed those of the prevailing key, as can be seen in the preceding Beethoven excerpt. The *f-sharp*, introduced as the leading tone of a V/vi, creates a momentary diversion from the main tonal level of *B-flat*.

A considerably more unstable tonal digression occurs in the next example.

Ex. 11–12. Schubert: *Sonata for Piano*, Op. 53, Scherzo (Trio).

In this innovative passage, the composer has juxtaposed four-measure phrases in a sequence of third relations moving from *C* to *E-flat* to *G-flat* and returning via *b* minor and V of *C* to *C*. Passages such as this clearly reveal some of the means by which nineteenth-century composers, such as Schubert, enriched the harmonic spectrum of tonal music.

Compare the previous sequence with the one by Chopin that follows; the sequential units (marked on the music) consist entirely of root relations by semitone. This passage's roving progression almost completely wipes out any feeling of key. The tonic, *A-flat*, is reinstituted at the close of the excerpt. (Note that the final sequence unit is shortened by one chord.)

Enriched Tonal
Resources

Roots: f♭   E♭   E♭♭   D♭   E♭♭   D♭   C

   B   C   C♭   B♭

The first two measures of Ex. 11–14a form a *real* sequence, that is,
a sequence produced by the exact duplication of a harmonic-melodic
pattern on a different pitch level. An analysis of roots shows how the
music unfolds in a drive to the cadence on *A* at measure 5.

Ex. 11–14a. Hindemith: *Sonata for Flute and Piano,* I. Copyright 1937 by
B. Schott's Soehne, Mainz. Reprinted by permission.

Fl.

Piano

Ex. 11–14b. Root analysis of Ex. 11–14a.

As in the previous illustrations of Beethoven, Mozart, and Wagner, Hindemith has balanced the instability of a sequence with a dominant-tonic cadence that asserts a sense of tonality. Sequences often are altered rhythmically or intervallically to avoid literal repetition, especially in works of the twentieth century.

Expanded Key Relations

Two related processes that contributed to the enrichment and variability of tonality in nineteenth-century music are: (1) flexible key relations, which include all possibilities of key succession, and (2) the minimizing of the role of a main key, by beginning and ending movements or large sections in different keys (open tonality), and by employing continuously changing keys or avoiding prolonged emphasis on any one key.

Ex. 11–15, an introductory adagio to the finale of a piano sonata, illustrates (1) above. The main key of the movement is *F*. However, the opening four measures clearly center pitch focus on *E* (the leading tone of *F*). Heard as part of the opening phrase, the beginning *F* major chord is treated as a +6 approach (note the "added" *d-sharp*) to an *E* major triad. And *E* (mutated to *e* minor) is confirmed by its dominant, *B*, in measure 4. This opening is clearly a departure from more traditional tonal schemes.

Ex. 11–15. Beethoven: *Piano Sonata, Op. 53, Adagio.*

289

A somewhat different process can be seen in Ex. 11–16. Like Ex. 11–15, the excerpt is part of an introduction to a finale.

Ex. 11–16. Beethoven: *Piano Sonata*, Op. 81a.

Andante espressivo
In gehender Bewegung, doch mit Ausdruck

The main key is *c* minor, affirmed cadentially in measure 8. Similar to Ex. 11–15, the opening chord's tonal orientation is vague. The second phrase (beginning in measure 5), which is entirely in *c* minor, forms a sequence with the first. Following this brief establishment of C, eleven measures occur which prolong *g* minor, briefly touching *c* minor again in measure 20. The structural "meaning" of the tonic key in this movement has been so minimized that it has become just another of several related keys.

Relationships by Seconds and Thirds

Musicians often cite the late works of Beethoven as precedents for many of the tonal and formal curiosities found in later music.

The unusual tonal successions found in Ex. 11–17 occur in the introduction of a Beethoven sonata movement, which is built out of three characteristic Baroque forms, *recitative, arioso,* and *fugue.* It seems paradoxical to find a merging of harmonic relationships that *forecast* the dissolution of the major-minor key system in a composition based on forms from an *earlier* historical period. An analysis of some of the significant key relations of the work is shown below. The principal key is *A-flat*. (A more detailed study of the music is strongly recommended.)

Beethoven: *Piano Sonata*, Op. 110.
Principal Key Relations

1st Section (quasi recitative)   *2nd Section* (arioso dolente)
    b-flat, E (a-flat implied)   a-flat
3rd Section (fugue)   *4th Section* (arioso dolente)
    A-flat, c, D-flat, A-flat   g (closes in G major)
                            5th Section (fugue)
                                G, g, trans-A-flat

Ex. 11–17. Beethoven: *Piano Sonata*, Op. 110, Introduction.

Several observations can be made about the movement: (1) The eventual tonic, A-flat, is avoided at the outset, which begins in *b-flat* minor. (Beethoven assigned the signature of five, not four, flats at the opening of the piece.) (2) The dominant *key* of E-flat is almost completely absent throughout the movement, and tonic-dominant key relations are consistently skirted in favor of more distant ones. (3) The keys of *A-flat* major and *a-flat minor* are mixed with keys a second removed, such as *g* minor, *G* major, and *b-flat* minor. Although both the subdominant and mediant keys are confirmed in the movement, the characteristic key relationship is that of a minor second, *A-flat—g*.

The overall effect of the Introduction (Ex. 11–17) is that of tonal elusiveness, because no key is stressed for an extended time. Furthermore, chords which have the longest durations are unstable (Mm7th chords), while chords that create tonic feeling are of only one beat's duration or less. The duration of the tonic chord (X at measure 4) is equal to the briefest chord in the example. Again we find that tonal instability often corresponds to the duration and placement of tonality-establishing chords.

The next excerpt contains an extended shift from *f-sharp* minor to *f* minor.

Ex. 11–18. Schubert: *Schwanengesang.*

(V7

This shift down a minor 2nd is begun by chromatic inflections in measure 1 (*c-natural* and *f-natural*) and accomplished in measures 4–5 through an unusual chromatic third relation, *a* minor to *f* minor. Tonal instability prevails through measures 6 (last beat) and 7, when there is a brief return to *G-flat* (*F-sharp* enharmonic), which forms a Neapolitan relation with *f*. All voices resolve the conflict between *f* and *f-sharp* with the parallel descent to *f* in measure 8 and the subsequent V—i close.

Chords containing tritones, related by root movement of seconds and thirds, reveal all twelve tones of the chromatic scale in Ex. 11–18. Tonic is *a*. The chord succession through measure 3 consists of Mm7th chords on *b-flat*, *b*, and *a* and °7ths on *b-flat*. It would be hard to imagine a clearer illustration of how every chromatic pitch may appear in a passage oriented to *one* tonic.

Chords Containing Tritones

You are familiar with many of the chord types that contain one or more tritones:

I. *One Tritone*
 ° triad
 Mm 7th chord
 ° 7th chord

II. *Two Tritones*
 ° 7th chord
 Mmm 9th chord
 Fr $^{+6}_{\;\;3}$ chord (and other +6ths)
 +11th chord
 V $_{+11}^{13}$

Ex. 11–19. Chords containing tritones.

Many of these chords involve chromatic alteration. Chords containing tritones create harmonic tension and are frequently aligned with chromatic pitch relations, both harmonic and melodic. It is through a study of the juxtaposition of these chords that we can easily trace the enrichment of tonality and the increased harmonic color of much music of the nineteenth and twentieth centuries.

In Ex. 11–20, all but two of the twenty chords contain tritones (see measures 3 and 11), and the entire excerpt lacks strong key confirmation. Sequence, motive repetition, and contrasts of register are important in the organization of this orchestral texture, but sustained harmonic tension is the most obvious cause of its continuity.

Ex. 11–20. Wagner: *Tristan und Isolde.*

In contrast to the smoothly connected tritone chords in Ex. 11–20, the chords in Ex. 11–21 show very little contrapuntal relationship and involve a use of the tritone that is virtually "keyless" and essentially coloristic. Here the tritone's ambiguity is exploited both vertically and horizontally, as can be seen from the root relationship of *A-flat* in measure 3 and *D* in measure 4. Tonality is achieved—to the degree it is— through accented melodic repetitions of the tone *c*.

Ex. 11–21. Moussorgsky: *Boris Godunov,* Coronation Scene.

Andantino alla marcia

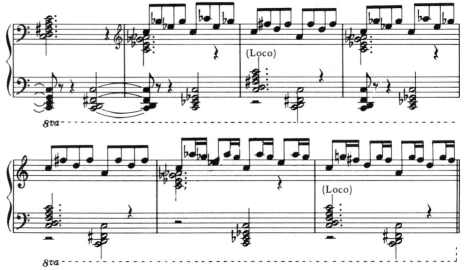

Melodic tritones often confirm the instability of chords containing tritones. For example, the cadential tritone leaps in melodies of the Classical period usually are supported by the V_7 chord, and they resolve in conjunction with the arrival of the tonic chord.

The tritones in the melodic fragments of Ex. 11–22 reveal a more structural use of that melodic interval; none "resolves" to a more reposeful tone.

Ex. 11–22a. Debussy: *Afternoon of a Faun.*

Ex. 11–22b. Strauss: *Thus Spake Zarathustra.*

Ex. 11–22c. Sibelius: *Third Symphony,* I.

Ex. 11–22d. Schoenberg: *Moses and Aaron,* Act I, Scene 2. Reprinted by permission of Mrs. Gertrud Schoenberg, copyright owner.

Moses

We are often so diverted by the rich palette of chords composers such as Wagner and Strauss have assailed us with that we overlook the importance of melodic relations in their music. Although contrapuntal forms such as the fugue and passacaglia occur rarely in music composed during the late nineteenth-century, contrapuntal procedures are nonetheless important to the organization of that music.

The passage in Ex. 11–23a unfolds with movement from the dominant of *b-flat* minor to *b* (-*natural*) minor. Syncopated chords, broken by the triplet motive in the right hand, are accompanied by octave repetitions of chords in the left hand that form an ascending chromatic line from *F* in measure 1 to *f* in measure 7. Although the effect is essentially chordal, the two textural levels can be seen as a simple two-voice frame.

Ex. 11–23a. Brahms: *Rhapsody*, Op. 79, No. 1.

Ex. 11–23b. Two-voice reduction of Ex. 11–23a.

Several contrapuntal factors contribute to the organization of the passage. The dissonances in the second part of measure 1 (in the bass) and in the first part of measure 2 are passing tones. Further contrapuntal variety is created through a mixture of similar, parallel, oblique, and contrary motion, contrary motion highlighting the tonal and contoural climax in measures 7 and 8. A rhythmic intensification is reached

297

in measure 8 with the introduction of stretto. Rhythmic independence between the two textural levels (as seen in the right- and left-hand parts) is consistently maintained through displacements of the right-hand chords in contrast with the on-the-beat sonorities of the left-hand part.

Two chromatic lines that frame successions of unstable chords often move in contrary motion. The possibilities for "filling in" two outer parts, related by contrary motion, are numerous. In Ex. 11–24 two lines, both moving consistently by step in contrary motion, have been filled in with a complement of chords, most of which contain tritones.

Ex. 11–24. Contrapuntally organized chord succession.

A similar linear harmonic design is the basis of measures 4–8 of Ex. 11–25.

Ex. 11–25. Wagner: *Tristan und Isolde*, II.

By themselves, the chords in measures 4–8 of the Wagner excerpt would be virtually keyless. In other words, measures 4–8 are ambiguous tonally, and they prolong harmonic tension, which has no real release in the passage. The excerpt ends with a progressive cadence that suggests *d* minor.

Linear chords, undergirded by an essentially diatonic chord pattern in *A-flat* major, result in the tonal instability of Ex. 11–26. Play the reduction and the complete excerpt and compare the two.

Enriched Tonal
Resources

Ex. 11–26b. Harmonic reduction of Ex. 11–26a.

The role of the underlying harmony (as exemplified in the reduction) is to provide a solid foundation for the web of counterpoint and decorative chords that constitute the foreground of the passage.

In measures 2–4 of the same example, continuous eighth-notes unfold in the upper orchestral accompaniment. All of this activity, shown in Ex. 11–27, can be regarded as melodic elaboration of the *A-flat* tonic triad, the basic (melodic) pitches shown in the example.

Ex. 11–27a. Wagner: *Tristan und Isolde,* II.

However, when this same voice is heard in relation to the three (upper) moving parts, we are aware of a tension and rhythm, established by the resulting linear chords.

Ex. 11–27b. Ibid., upper voices.

The result is a progression of chord roots above an *A-flat* bass pedal, as shown below.

Ex. 11–27c. Ibid., root pattern of linear chords.

By isolating different levels of activity, as discussed above, we can better understand a complex musical foreground made up of counterpoint and chords, supported by a stable substructure.

Two opposite trends, one involving extended chromaticism, the other the use of modes other than major and minor, contributed to the ultimate dissolution of the major-minor system in the period from about 1880 to 1918. We should note, however, that just as chromaticism dominates the music of particular composers (such as Wagner and Franck), modality is a matter of a specific composer's style or is even characteristic of individual works, rather than a widespread trend. As we shall see, it is not until the twentieth century that the full weight of either of these two contradictory trends, the former of which has greater impact, is felt.

Modality

Few late nineteenth-century works are organized entirely on a modal basis. On the contrary, the use of modality was limited mainly to occasional themes and cadence patterns. These are mere allusions to modes involving materials that imply rather than rigidly adhere to a single mode. Compositions organized entirely within the scope of a single mode are practically nonexistent, with the exception of some ancient chant melodies and folk songs. We shall probe further the incorporation of modal scales into basically nonmodal music in Chapter 12, where Impressionism is the subject of discussion.

The introduction of the late nineteenth-century song shown in Ex. 11–28 might be interpreted as Aeolian on *E*, closing with a Picardy Third.

Ex. 11–28. Wolf: *Mörike—Lied*, No. 23.

The same pattern is repeated throughout the song on different tonal levels. It is shown in Ex. 11–29 as a Phrygian reference.

Ex. 11–29. Ibid.

Even in these basically diatonic modal references, some chromaticism is evident as mutations of the mediant degree, such as the $g^\#$ in measure 2 of Ex. 11–29.

An allusion to the Phrygian mode is found in the unaccompanied first statement of the principal theme of the final of Brahms' *Third Symphony* cited below. The movement as a whole is clearly in f minor, even though the theme itself apparently unfolds on c (the dominant of f).

Ex. 11–30. Brahms: *Symphony No. 3*, IV (first theme).

This same movement incorporates frequent Phrygian suggestions, particularly with Phrygian cadences on the dominant. Ex. 11–31 contains one of many Phrygian cadences from the movement.

Ex. 11–31. Ibid.

The inscription "In der Lydischen Tonart" ("In the Lydian Mode") is part of the title of the third movement of a string quartet by Beethoven. The closing of this movement is on an F major triad, yet not a single $B^\flat$ appears throughout the closing section of the movement. As shown in the next example, the passage is tonally ambiguous. The first part hangs between the tonics of C and F (C major and F Lydian).

Ex. 11–32. Beethoven: *String Quartet*, Op. 132, III (close).

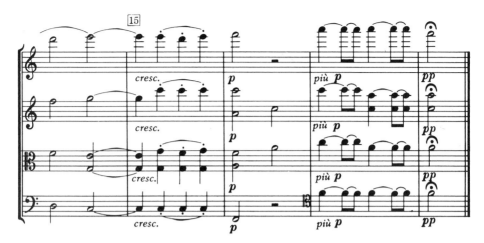

Beethoven's Lydian inflections result from melodic and harmonic centering on F while using a scale consisting of *f g a b c d e*. Beethoven has, in effect, created an ambiguous tonality, which unfolds by a series of shifts between an apparent tonic C and its subdominant, *f*. It is precisely this ambiguity that is heightened by the cadence on *f*.

As pointed out earlier, entire movements or sections that adhere to a single diatonic scale without some use of chromatic inflection, mutation, or modulation are rare.

Ex. 11–33. Mussorgsky: *Boris Godunov*, III.

The opening passage suggests Lydian mode on C (*C D E F♯ G A B*), characterized by the repeated use of *F♯* melodically and harmonically, as in measures 4–7. Dominant-tonic root relationships are negligible, occurring only in measures 1 and 12. The composer has used a chord pattern that embodies the most characteristic element of the Lydian mode, the tritone formed between the 1 and 4 scale degrees.

305

Tonal Regions As we have seen in previous examples, passages frequently involve sudden departures from the principal key, or a secondary dominant creates momentary emphasis on a degree other than tonic without bringing about an actual modulation. In contrast to brief areas supported by secondary dominants, tonal regions are short passages, usually contained within a phrase or short section, which clearly change tonic but lack the confirmation identified with a modulation. Many of the brief shifts of tonic discussed earlier as transitory modulations can be described as tonal regions. In other words, a tonal region is a short passage that weakens the polarity of a previous tonic, creates the expectation that a new tonic will be confirmed, yet fails to fulfill that expectation. As we shall see, tonal regions vary in length, this variability dependent to a great extent upon both tempo and harmonic rhythm.

The use of the term *region* implies that the tonic of the region is related to the main key, much as a secondary dominant is related to its "tonic." But a secondary dominant is a single chord, usually with a predictable relationship to the chord that it precedes, while a tonal region embraces a group of chords *of any function* that constitute more than a simple embellishing relationship to a chord of resolution. For example, the region of V (in a given key) is a short passage that centers tonally on the dominant degree of the main key. Any scale degree or nonscale degree can act as "tonic" of a tonal region.

A series of brief regions succeed each other in Ex. 11–34, whose principal key is *B-flat* major: *D-flat, d, c,* and *g*. Each region contains two different chords, usually tonic and dominant. Passages of this kind are susceptible to more than one analysis or interpretation. Looking at the passage as a whole, we may well regard the polarity of *B-flat* as strong enough to perceive the "tonic" of each region as a member of the *B-flat* tonality, embellished by a secondary dominant, or, as in measures 9–10, by a German augmented sixth chord. On the other hand, it is also possible to hear each two-measure unit, beginning with measure 7, in a different region of *B-flat* (as shown in the example). Either analysis should be based on the listener's *aural* experience of the passage, considering both possibilities.

Ex. 11–34. Schubert: *Sei mir gegrüsst.*

In making an analysis, the point at which a tonal region begins is shown by: (1) indicating the "tonic" of the region; (2) showing the relation of "tonic" of the region to the principal key by a bracketed roman numeral; (3) indicating the function of those chords that occur in the region by roman numerals; and (4) indicating the return to the initial key.

In Ex. 11–35, a *c* minor triad, heard for four measures, is treated as a N/V in *e* minor. The remote relation of this chord to the prevailing key weakens the "pull" of *E*, and *c* minor is heard as a point of focus for four measure, thus creating a tonal region of its own. As examples of this kind suggest, the "tonic" chords of regions are often not members of the diatonic family of chords of the principal key.

Ex. 11–35. Schubert: *Schwanengesang,* No. 5.

Tonal regions sometimes involve cadential confirmation of a new key. The subsequent phrase, however, reaffirms the principal key or begins yet a new region. Since the subsequent key does not reaffirm the key, no modulation occurs.

In Ex. 11–36 the principal key, *C* major, is established in measures 1–6. The next four measures involve the region of *A* (both *a* minor and *A* major), with a rhythmically weak cadence in measure 12. The next phrase, however, returns directly to *C* major and thus does not confirm a modulation to *A*.

Ex. 11–36. Brahms: Op. 119, No. 3.

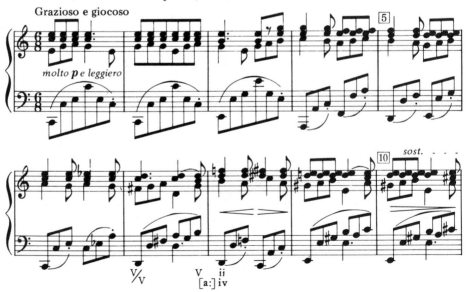

In the previous example the shift to *a* minor is accomplished through a pivot[1] chord that is common to both *C* major and *a* minor. The *d* minor triad, first beat of measure 8, functions as the pivot chord. The return to *C*, however, involves the common tone *E*, which is sustained through a change of harmony from vi $\frac{6}{5}$ in *A* to I in *C*. The change of key back to *C* is more abrupt than the previous shift to *A*, since no real pivot chord is heard.

A striking shift to the Neapolitan region is illustrated in the next example.

Ex. 11–37. Beethoven: *Piano Sonata,* Op. 106, III.

Some compositions consist of successions of regions, with little use of prolonged tonalities. Regions are most easily detected when they occur as brief departures from a clearly established key that is immediately reasserted on the heels of the region. The next excerpt illustrates two successive regions of unequal length between assertions of the main key of *A-flat* major.

---

[1] Pivot chords occurring between regions, or between regions and principal keys, are indicated the same as in modulations.

Ex. 11–38. Wolf: *Spanish Songbook II*, No. 2.

Exercises

Additional materials are contained in *Materials and Structure of Music II, Workbook*, Chapter 11.

1. Use examples from development sections of eighteenth- and nineteenth-century compositions for analysis and recognition of tonal regions.
2. Plan a short composition for piano around a series of regions, interpolated between class assertions of a principal major or minor key.

3. Use examples from the works of the Russian nationalistic composers of the close of the nineteenth century for continued study of modality and modal reference.

4. Compose a vocalise which illustrates modality in the form of thematic construction, cadences, and mutation. Then add a suitable piano accompaniment.

5. Listen to the Prelude to Act I of *Tristan und Isolde,* by Wagner. Follow the music with a score, then answer the following questions:

   a. Describe the overall form of the movement in terms of large sections.

   b. What repetitive-developmental techniques constitute the melodic organization of the main voice(s)?

   c. Cite several contrapuntal techniques in the example.

   d. What are some of the characteristic chords that occur?

   e. What expression would best describe cadence types in the movement?

   f. Make a harmonic reduction of a short section of the movement.

   g. Cite several ways in which this movement represents an expansion of the tonal materials found in the music of Haydn and Mozart.

   h. In what way(s) are major and minor keys evident in this composition?

Chapter Twelve

Impressionism:
Bridge to
the Twentieth Century

During the 200 years before the twentieth century, Western art music generally conformed to established patterns of melody, rhythm, texture, timbre, harmony, and form. Variations of personal styles certainly existed, yet they were transcended by a norm of common practice. In fact, many historians refer to the period of 1700 to 1900 as the *common practice period*.

Some music composed toward the end of the nineteenth century reveals a wide divergence of musical practices. Composers altered the course of music in a period of unprecedented change, both in terms of rate and extent. While many composers of that era still embraced musical styles of the past, others evolved a bridge to the future. One collection of composers, whose music plowed the ground for the music of the twentieth century, were called "Impressionists." While the body of impressionistic music is comparatively small, it exemplifies important changes that took place between 1880 and 1920. We shall consider some of the most important aspects of its materials and structure before moving on, in subsequent chapters, to more in-depth study of the resources of twentieth century composers.

The term *impressionistic music* is loosely applied to the music of a small group of composers of the late nineteenth and early twentieth centuries. Most notable were the Frenchmen Claude Debussy and Maurice Ravel, with the Englishman Frederick Delius and the American Charles Griffes providing a more international arena for this new approach. Musical impressionism was influenced by a trend in French painting exemplified by the works of artists such as Degas, Monet, and Renoir. Theirs was a gentle art, rich in color, indistinct in outline, hazy in detail, suggestive rather than literal in its representation of nature.

Composers of impressionistic music sought to create similar general effects through the use of musical materials. In broad terms, compact motives unfolded through subtle variations, and fragmentary allusions replaced the extended themes and the thematic development of earlier music. Counterpoint, exact sequences, and imitation were generally abandoned for such organizational procedures as modified repetition, extended pedal point, ostinato, and compelling new sounds from the instruments of the orchestra. Sectional forms, transparent in texture and sometimes vague in outline, replaced the larger developmental forms perfected in the eighteenth century by Haydn, Mozart, and Beethoven. Tonality, once a powerful organizing force, became veiled and at times obscure through the use of exotic scales, evaded or blurred cadences, and chromatic elements that weakened the key systems of earlier music. Kaleidoscopic sound effects were achieved through numerous rapid and abrupt changes of tonality, timbre, texture, dynamics, and register, as well as changes of melodic, rhythmic, and harmonic patterns. Composers were pursuing their new goal of creating "sound for sound's sake."

Expanded Pitch Resources

Prior to the late nineteenth century, melodies and harmonies had been confined for the most part to resources derived from seven-note scales, especially the major and minor scales. Although some late Romantic composers, such as Wagner and Skryabin, created passages of extreme chromaticism, and a number of composers made occasional use of pentatonic and whole-tone scales, music was essentially bound to the major/minor key system passed on from the eighteenth century. The Impressionists, in their quest for dramatic color, made new pitch resources a more dominant ingredient in their works. Some of these "new" pitch resources were fresh only because they had not been used extensively in music of the preceding 200 years.

While they explored these new pitch resources, Impressionist composers did not wholly forsake major and minor scales as common fare, but they no longer served as the exclusive reservoir from which all musical relationships flowed.

Whole-tone Scale

Given the twelve pitch classes of the chromatic scale, only two different whole-tone scales are possible: *C D E F♯ G♯ A♯* and *D♭ E♭ F G A B*. Any other whole-tone scale is necessarily a respelling or alteration of one of these forms. Since this scale consists of all equal steps, its sound is tonally ambiguous, no pitch class dominating as a potential tonic. The closing measures of Ex. 12–1 show a complete whole-tone scale in the approach to a cadence on the major third *C—E*. (Some members of this scale are spelled enharmonically.)

Ex. 12–1. Debussy: *Prelude No. 2*, Book I. Permission for reprint granted by Durand et Cie., Paris, copyright owners, and Elkan-Vogel Co., Inc., Philadelphia, agents.

Pentatonic Scales

Another scale associated with Impressionism is the pentatonic scale. This five-note pattern may appear in a great variety of interval arrangements; our examples are limited to the so-called *tonal pentatonic* form, a five-note grouping that contains no half-steps. In this version, any one of the five notes may act as tonic, depending on the way its pitches are organized in relation one to another. In the following excerpt *D♯* is the tonic note.

Ex. 12–2. Debussy: *Nocturnes,* "Nuages" (piano reduction).

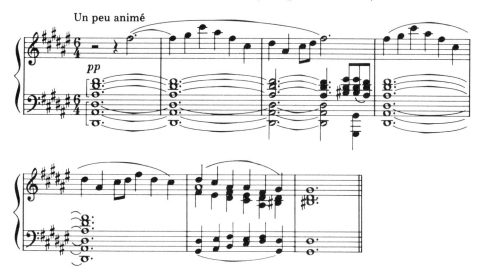

Modes

Although examples of extended modality do not occur often in this music, they provide some of the aura of the ancient past that marks frequent passages in the Impressionist's output. In the next example the basic scale (considering *C* tonic) is *C D E F G A B♭,* or Mixolydian based on *C.*

Ex. 12–3. Debussy: *Prelude No. 10,* Book I (theme). Permission for reprint granted by Durand et Cie., Paris, copyright owners, and Elkan-Vogel Co., Inc., Philadelphia, agents.

The pitch basis of the next melody is the Phrygian mode on *G,* the passage ending with a progressive cadence on the dominant note.

Ex. 12–4. Debussy: *String Quartet*, Op. 10, No. 1, I.

Chromatic Scales

Passages that utilize all twelve pitch classes in close succession occur with some frequency in impressionistic music. (Instances of the chromatic scale as an actual melodic pattern are rare.) The next excerpt crowds all twelve notes into a single rising passage. Note how the three different collections of five notes each—A^b B^b C D^b E^b, E F♯ G♯ A B, and C D E^b F G—more than exhaust the twelve different pitch classes.

Ex. 12–5. Debussy: *Prelude No. 11*, Book 1. Permission for reprint granted by Durand et Cie., Paris, copyright owners, and Elkan-Vogel Co., Inc., Philadelphia, agents.

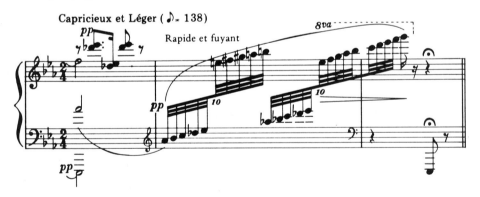

Melody and Form

Since they expanded the musical vocabulary, the Impressionists were faced anew with the problem of maintaining tonal coherence. At times their solution was immediate repetition (usually *varied* repetition). They also dwelt on particular motives, intervals or timbres to unify their materials. Some of their melodies are the by-product of harmonic progression, instrumental figuration, or repeated melodic-rhythmic units. In some instances, phrase lengths are unclear because stereotyped cadence formulae are avoided. Strong meter is often discarded in favor of *tempo rubato* and through elaborate beat subdivisions and ornamentation.

Repetitions of melodic and harmonic patterns are at times varied through change of interval, rhythmic alteration, or merely by change of register. A short melodic portion may be introduced, then followed by its varied repetition. The successive variants often proceed to higher and higher melodic peaks. The bracketed figures of the next example illustrate how slightly modified repetitions of a short motive can lead to a climactic point, producing a rising step progression from F to the final B♭.

Ex. 12–6. A. Skryabin: *Album Leaf*, Op. 45, No. 1. Used by permission of Leeds Music Corporation, New York, N.Y. All Rights Reserved.

A composer can mold an extended line from such simple ideas by means of literal and varied repetitions. The first two measures of the next example are first repeated literally, then repeated in varied ways twice. Note how the top line of measures 7–8 forms a melodic sequence with measures 5–6.

Ex. 12–7. Ravel: *Piano Sonatine, III.*

In many impressionistic works, short motives unify a large section through various techniques of motivic transformation. There is nothing new about this, yet the degree to which it is employed represents a departure from the practice of the past. Debussy's *Prelude No. 5*, Book I (*Les Collines d'Anacapri*) exemplifies the extended use of this technique. The following analysis provides a skeletal idea of the motives used in this composition, the essential materials of which appear in the following examples.

Section:	Introduction		A		B		C	
Materials:	Motives 1 & 2	Theme A	Motive 2	Theme B	Theme B Motive 1	Theme C1	C2 C2	
Measures:	(1-13)	(14-21)	(21-31)	(32-39)	(40-48)	(49-52)	(53-62)	

Section:	Transition	A	B	Close	
Materials:	Motive 1	Theme A	Theme A Motive 1	Theme B Motive 1	Motives 1 & 2	Motive 1
Measures:	(63-67)	(68-74)	(75-80)	(81-84)	(84-89)	(90-96)

This composition's form is a repetitive scheme in which two short motives function as unifying factors throughout, except within the brief *C* section in the middle. The *Prelude* opens with a statement of two motives (Ex. 12–8), both of which forecast the pentatonic character of the ensuing themes.

Ex. 12–8. Debussy: *Prelude No. 5*, Book I. Permission for reprint granted by Durand et Cie., Paris, copyright owners, and Elkan-Vogel Co., Inc., Philadelphia, agents.

Theme *A* arrives later (measures 14–21), followed by a return of *motive 2* (bass of measure 21) that is attended by the rhythmic accompaniment of *theme A*.

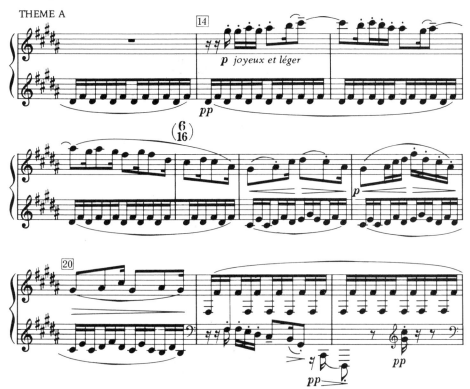

THEME A

This process continues to measure 32, where *theme B* appears.

Ex. 12–10. Ibid.

A few measures later *theme B* is repeated at a higher level (measures 40–43), *motive 1* skillfully woven into its accompanying fabric.

Ex. 12–11. Ibid.

The *Prelude's* middle section, C, encompasses fourteen measures (49–62). Its melodic elements are dominated by the pitch F♯, thus providing a brief tonal contrast. Its last four measures are a textural variant of its first four measures.

Ex. 12–12. Ibid.

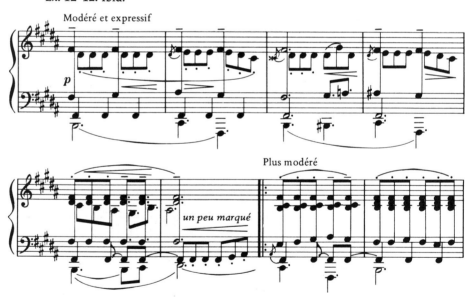

This section is closed by a transition to *theme A* that is built from *motive 1.*

Ex. 12–13. Ibid.

Impressionism

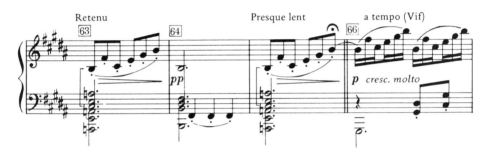

Motive 1 subsequently becomes part of an ostinato pattern that accompanies the restatement of *theme A*.

Ex. 12–14. Ibid.

Motive 2 returns in measures 80–81 with the rhythm of *motive 1* as an accompanying line. They are repeated (measures 86–93) with *motive 1*, but now couched in a new texture. It persists in this new form as an ostinato, the basis of the closing section of the *Prelude*.

Ex. 12–15. Ibid.

This Debussy *Prelude* reveals a form molded from literal and varied repetitions of two motives. Although the process is not peculiarly impressionistic, it served as a prime unifying procedure in many works by impressionistic composers. (For an example of this technique on a grander scale, study Debussy's *String Quartet,* Op. 10.)

Pedal Point and Ostinato

Pedals and ostinato figures are abundant in impressionistic music. For example, in the middle of the second movement of Debussy's *Fetes,* a D^b—A^b bass pedal persists for fifty-five of the work's fifty-seven measures. As is generally true, the pedal establishes a tonal reference, the composer ranging far afield in the rest of the music's texture, yet producing a cohesive and impressive tonal result.

Ex. 12–16. Debussy: *Prelude No. 3,* Book II. Permission for reprint granted by Durand et Cie., Paris, copyright owners, and Elkan-Vogel Co., Inc., Philadelphia, agents.

Movt. de Habanera

Ex. 12–17 illustrates a passage in which a rearticulated pedal (*A*) provides the only clue to what might be the tonic, once the tonic triad has sounded within the first two measures.

Ex. 12–17. Debussy: *Prelude No. 4*, Book I. Permission for reprint granted by Durand et Cie., Paris, copyright owners, and Elkan-Vogel Co., Inc., Philadelphia, agents.

Harmony

Although much of the harmonic vocabulary of Impressionism consists of diatonic triads and seventh chords, greater use is made of ninth, eleventh, and thirteenth chords. The more complex intervals are treated freely without regard for conventional melodic preparation and resolution. These harmonies occur for the most part in two ways: (1) in progressions in which there is a balance of parallel, contrary, and oblique motion between lines, and (2) in progressions in which all lines move in parallel motion (planing).

Traditional harmonic influences are apparent in the next example; the key of $D^{\flat}$ is established and diatonic harmonies are present. But close inspection reveals emphasis on root relationships of seconds and thirds, and chords that are not diatonic comprise a major part of the passage.

Ex. 12–18. Debussy: *Clair de Lune.*

Certain features of this and subsequent examples are characteristic of the harmonic practice of the Impressionists, particularly that of Debussy.

1. There is an increased use of seventh and ninth chords.
2. Dominant-tonic relations do not predominate.
3. Chords are frequently mutated to obtain a change of color.

Note that a triad does not appear within the next excerpt.

Ex. 12–19. Debussy: *Nocturnes*, "Sirènes" (adapted).

Use of richer chords (eleventh and thirteenth chords) is better illustrated in the section of this chapter devoted to parallelism. For the moment, however, consider an excerpt in which thirteenth chords appear in measure two. Observe that they are MmM chords to which major thirteenths have been added along with major ninths.

Ex. 12–20. Debussy: *Nocturnes*, "Fêtes" (adapted).

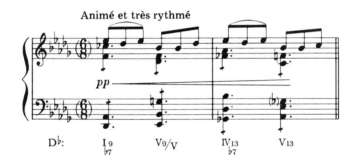

Added Tones

In some instances the chords of Impressionism seem to defy analysis as exclusively tertial patterns. One often must resort to a description based on the notion of adding tones to an otherwise triadic structure. This kind of sonority occurs in the form of an "added sixth" to the tonic chord in the next excerpt. Notice that this chord is the same as that discussed in Chapter 4, page 000.

Ex. 12–21. Debussy: *Nocturnes*, "Fêtes."

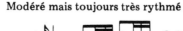

Through the addition of tones to simpler tertian structures, the harmonic vocabulary is greatly expanded, thus enlarging the spectrum of musical resources while maintaining a tie to the past. It is but a short step from this practice to chords containing a number of consecutive scale degrees sounding simultaneously, sonorities called *tone clusters*.

Ex. 12–22. Debussy: *Prelude No. 3*, Book II. Permission for reprint granted by Durand et Cie., Paris, copyright owners, and Elkan-Vogel Co., Inc., Philadelphia, agents.

Similar chords are frequently found in the music of such later composers as Béla Bartók and Henry Cowell, to name but two.

Whole-Tone Chords

You may recall that the mediant triad in minor can occur as an augmented chord. This triad, and similar constructs, appear infrequently prior to the Impressionistic period. The Impressionists made greater use of augmented sounds, and it appears reasonable that whole-tone chords have their basis in the augmented triad.

The sonorities in Ex. 12–23 retain tertian characteristics which lend themselves to conventional analysis. For example, the first chord, a French $^{+6}_{\ \ 4}_{\ \ 3}$, alternates with an augmented eleventh chord. All six degrees of the whole-tone scale appear in these two chords and the whole-tone effect is intensified by the tritone root relation.

Ex. 12–23. Debussy: *Pelleas and Melisande*, Act I, Scene 1.

While some of the chords in Ex. 12–24 can be rearranged to spell tertial structures, others cannot, with any plausibility. A more reasonable description of this passage—and of others similar to it—notes that its source is a single whole-tone scale, *B♭ C D E F♯ G♯.*

Ex. 12–24. Debussy: *Prelude No. 2,* Book I. Permission for reprint granted by Durand et Cie., Paris, copyright owners, and Elkan-Vogel Co., Inc., Philadelphia, agents.

Quartal Harmony

There is limited use of quartal harmonies (chords built of superposed fourths) in impressionistic music. Such harmonies are illustrated in Ex. 12–25. Except for the third chord in measures 1 and 2, all the chords in the first two measures are made up of three superposed perfect fourths with their octave doublings.

Ex. 12–25. Debussy: *Prelude No. 10,* Book I. Permission for reprint granted by Durand et Cie., Paris, copyright owners, and Elkan-Vogel Co., Inc., Philadelphia, agents.

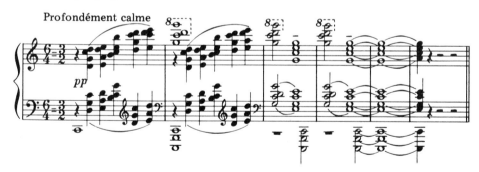

Planing

One of the most distinctive features of Impressionism is harmonic parallelism, or *planing,* which consists of constant similar motion between the parts of a texture. In its simplest form planing consists of melodic reinforcement (doubling) at a particular interval relationship, and in more complex arrangements melodic lines may be thickened by a series of parallel chords.

Ex. 12–26. Debussy: *Prelude No. 10*, Book II. Permission for reprint granted by Durand et Cie., Paris, copyright owners, and Elkan-Vogel Co., Inc., Philadelphia, agents.

The goal of counterpoint is individuality of parts; extensive parallelism does not produce counterpoint. In fact, parallel movement is generally avoided until the beginning of the twentieth century. Debussy and his followers utilized this procedure to the extent that it became a feature of their music. It expanded the coloristic potential of harmonic progression, diminishing the functional role of individual chords within a series. Textures of planing occur in short incidental, transitional, and modulatory passages, as well as in more extended sections. While some passages may be confined to diatonic triads, others consist of ninth chords in a highly chromatic setting. In any event, the use of planing imparts a characteristic flavor which, although not uniquely impressionistic, is a notable feature of the style.

Before discussing this technique in detail, we might consider a few examples of planing from the works of composers before the time of the Impressionists.

Ex. 12–27a. Musica enchiriadis, Ninth Century A.D. Composite Organum at the Fifth.

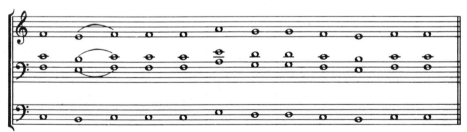

Ex. 12–27b. Glück: *Alceste*, Aria, "Divinités du Styx."

In Ex. 12–27c, $°_7$ chords are planed chromatically in a way that foreshadows later practices.

Ex. 12–27c. Liszt: *Les Préludes.*

Parallelism in impressionistic music is manifested in both simple and complex ways. In regard to the first, a melody may be reinforced by the simple addition of a doubling line at a particular interval distance, as in the following example.

Ex. 12–28. Ravel: *L'Enfant et Les Sortilèges.* Permission for reprint granted by Durand et Cie., Paris, copyright owners, and Elkan-Vogel Co., Inc., Philadelphia, agents.

More frequently, melodic figures are accompanied by a series of chords that move in parallel motion. In one instance the planed material may constitute the total texture, while in another it may be the accompaniment only. In Ex. 12–29 the melodic line is accompanied by parallel diatonic triads in G^b major.

Ex. 12–29. Debussy: *Prelude No. 6*, Book I. Permission for reprint granted by Durand et Cie., Paris, copyright owners, and Elkan-Vogel Co., Inc., Philadelphia, agents.

In passages of ambiguous tonality, seventh chords frequently are used in planed texture. The theme of Ex. 12–30 is enriched by a series of planed Mm7 chords. This is a particularly dramatic moment in this composition because of the sound produced by the multiple divisions of violins and violas.

Ex. 12–30. Ravel: *Daphnis and Chloe Suite No. 2.* Permission for reprint granted by Durand et Cie., Paris, copyright owners, and Elkan-Vogel Co., Inc., Philadelphia, agents.

Tonality

The growing adoption of a standard system of tuning (equal temperament) that made any key relation practical for performance, and the gradual abandonment of the major/minor scale systems brought greater freedom to composers in their choices of chords and chord progressions. They explored more remote key relations, and stereotyped cadential patterns were either discarded for new patterns or were modified; the strong leading tone to tonic relationship was often avoided, and the concept of tonality, as it had prevailed for two centuries, was broadened dramatically. No longer were composers content to work within limited key schemes upheld by clear cadences, unequivocal chord progressions, and key relationships of only fifths and fourths.

Changes of tonal center in impressionistic music frequently occur with an abruptness that would have occurred in a Mozart or Beethoven composition only in a developmental section. Sudden shifts from one tonic to another replace the conventional modulation process. Once a tonality is established, it may be abandoned, or at least weakened, by the sudden injection of a new element, perhaps preparing the way for a new thematic idea at a different tonal level, or serving only to interrupt momentarily the established tonality.

In the next example a wealth of different chord types occur in close succession within a highly chromatic scheme. After only four measures —themselves tonally indefinite—the opening material has shifted up by a semitone.

Ex. 12–31. Debussy: *Prelude No. 4*, Book I. Permission for reprint granted by Durand et Cie., Paris, copyright owners, and Elkan-Vogel Co., Inc., Philadelphia, agents.

Key feeling tends to be vague or absent in much of this music for a number of reasons, but two conditions are particularly evident: (1) root relationships of seconds, thirds, and tritone; and (2) the presence of tritones in the chords themselves. Ex. 12–32 provides a typical instance, planing of ninth chords (measure 1) joining the curious root relationship of E—A$^\sharp$ to produce an engaging mixture of ambiguity *and* decisive tonic (the A$^\sharp$ major triads in measure 1, beat 3, and measure 2, beats 2 and 4).

Ex. 12–32. Ravel: *Jeux d' Eau*. (C) 1941 by Editions Max Eschig, Paris. Reprinted by permission.

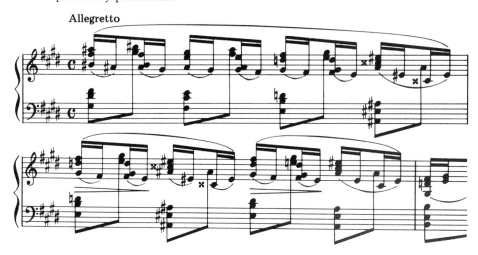

Relatively weak cadences contribute to a reduction of tonal decisiveness, even when traditional patterns such as V—I and IV—I are present. Prolonged nonharmonic tones, enriched chords, chromatic alterations, and other factors sometimes disguise a basic cadence. The added sixth (to the E major tonic) and the prolonged appoggiatura (melodic G♯) in the following excerpt combine with a I—V pedal figure to create a colorful final cadence that is merely a refurbished V—I progression.

Ex. 12–33. Delius: *Sea Drift.* Copyright 1951 by Hawkes & Son Ltd. Reprinted by permission of Boosey & Hawkes Inc.

A less decisive final cadence is illustrated next. The texture thins abruptly, finally leaving the single D♭ as a cadential pitch.

Ex. 12–34. Debussy: *Prelude No. 4,* Book II. Permission for reprint granted by Durand et Cie., Paris, copyright owners, and Elkan-Vogel Co., Inc., Philadelphia, agents.

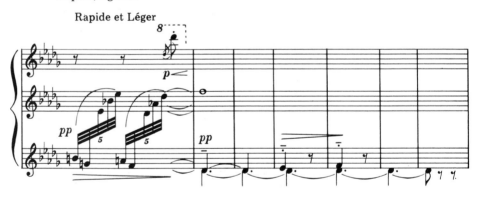

On occasion a texture projects a sense of tonality only because of a pedal point. The passages illustrated in Ex. 12–16 and Ex. 12–17 are informative because they show how a tonic can be established through action of a pedal rather than through progressions of key-defining chords. Look back to Ex. 12–17 (Debussy, *Prelude No. 4*) to note how the pitch A is a persistent reference point over which wholly foreign melodic and chordal patterns are woven.

In closing our discussion of tonality here, let us consider just one more excerpt. Ex. 12–35 is chosen because of the several typical features it contains. Note the planed major triads with roots a third apart (measures 1–2), the planed augmented triads (measures 3–4), and the ending which, although suggesting an authentic cadence, contains a modified dominant chord. The tonality is unsettled by the planed major triads, suspended by the augmented chords, then decisively confirmed at the final cadence. All this takes place within the key of $B\flat$ major, yet the filler is far removed from the harmonic content used by composers of the previous century.

Ex. 12–35. Debussy: *Prelude No. 1*, Book I. Permission for reprint granted by Durand et Cie., Paris, copyright owners, and Elkan-Vogel Co., Inc., Philadelphia, agents.

Orchestration

No discussion of the path-breaking role played by the Impressionist composers is complete without recognition of their marvelous expansion of orchestral sounds. In the hands of Debussy and Ravel the orchestra's wealth of untapped effects became the very essence of the musical substance. The size of the orchestra was expanded, new instrumental timbres were emphasized, and different mixes of instruments were highlighted. We can call attention to seven significant departures from the past:

1. frequent division of string parts (*divisi*) into many parts rather than the traditional division into the five sections of 1st vlns, 2nd vlns, violas, cellos, basses;
2. expanded attention to solo woodwinds as principal thematic instruments (flute, oboe, English horn, clarinet);
3. extensive use of mutes (*sourdines*) in string and brass families;
4. emphasis on new instruments such as alto flute, harp, saxophone, various exotic percussion such as tam-tam and antique cymbals;
5. exploration of extreme instrumental timbres, such as the low register of the flute;
6. emphasis on unmixed orchestral choir sounds, such as string section, woodwinds, as opposed to mixed voicings of earlier orchestral styles;
7. an enlarged palette of timbres achieved through the use of unusual (for then) techniques such as strings bowing over the fingerboard (*sur la touche*).

While the strings of the classical orchestra played the principal thematic role, their position in the Impressionists' orchestration was slightly reduced by greater attention to solo woodwinds, the woodwind choir, and the brass choir. Nonetheless, the hazy, shimmering sound of the orchestra was achieved mainly through the use in the string section of mutes, special bowings, and frequent tremolo patterns.

Exercises

For more detailed assignments see *Materials and Structure of Music II, Workbook,* Chapter 12.

1. Create two phrases of music, based on the following harmonic scheme, that are separated by a series of planed chords, this midsection providing a transition between the two keys.
   a. Phrase 1, *c* minor: i, III, IV$_6$, V$_9$, iv Fr $^{+6}_{\substack{4\\3}}$, III$_9$, iv$_7$, ii$^{4}_{3}$, i.
   b. Phrase 2, *A*♭ major: I, vi$_7$, iii, IV$^{4}_{2}$, ii$_7$, iii$^{6}_{5}$, V$_{13}$, I$^{5}_{3}$ (tonic with added sixth).
2. Arrange passages created for No. 1 for string quartet.
3. Construct examples in which planed chords are used to accompany the melody of   Ex. 12.3. Experiment with the following:
   a. M and m triads
   b. Mm $^{4}_{2}$ chords
   c. quartal chords
4. For additional attention to planing, see Debussy, *La Soiree dans Granada* (measures 29–32); *Nocturnes,* Fêtes (23–34); *Prelude No. 5,* Book II (last 14 measures).

5. Make a piano setting using only one whole-tone scale (or enharmonic equivalents). Use as your model Ex. 12–22 and experiment with tertian and nontertian chords, choosing those that you feel are most effective. Test your product at the piano.

6. Analyze (formal and materials) the following Debussy works:
   a. *Prelude No. 8*, Book I
   b. *Prelude No. 10*, Book I

7. Describe the harmony of the following passages by Debussy:
   a. *Nocturnes*, Fêtes, measures 9–22.
   b. *Nocturnes*, Sirênes, measures 38–41
   c. *Prelude No. 6*, Book II, final 30 measures

8. Find examples in the music composed for your performance instrument (including voice) of ninth, eleventh, and thirteenth chords, chords with added tones, and quartal and whole-tone chords.

9. Use the following ostinato pattern to compose eight measures of music for the piano. Maintain the ostinato throughout with no alterations. Use at least four of the following: $^0_6{}_5$, mm₇, V⁴₂ V, Fr $^{+6}_3$, mm⁴₂, N₆.

Debussy: *Prelude No. 6*, Book I.

10. Make a setting for flute, oboe, clarinet, and bassoon of the theme in Ex. 12–4. Introduce minimum chromaticism, avoiding overpowering the basic scale of the melody. Compare your setting with Debussy's.

11. Analyze the form of Ravel's *Jeux d'Eau,* indicating the basic formal scheme, measure numbers of main events, tonal centers, transitory materials, etc. Then summarize this work's impressionistic features. Start your work by listening to it several times, only then turning to the score.

Chapter Thirteen

Melody
in Twentieth-Century
Music

Twentieth-century music reflects new attitudes about sound resources and new approaches to the organization of musical materials. Some of the changes in attitude appear to be radical departures from previous times, particularly when dimensions other than pitch and rhythm become primary musical ingredients. It is not unusual to hear compositions in which loudness, timbre, texture, and different types of articulation shape the musical form. Recent music also makes greater use of the sound potentials of traditional instruments, for example, extremes of range, and percussive sounds produced by tapping the body of instruments. The electronic means of sound production available today did not exist prior to 1945.

Along with the multiplicity of sounds now available, there are changes in the organization of materials. In this chapter we shall examine some of these that distinguish twentieth-century melodies from those of earlier times. We also shall point out organizational patterns that are clearly derived from earlier musical styles.

Rhythm

The rhythm of many melodies of this century represents a distinct departure from earlier music. Generally speaking, rhythm is less closely aligned with meter. Even though meter signatures are usually retained, notation frequently indicates only the accents that shape a phrase or section.

Ex. 13–1 illustrates rhythms that fail to confirm the meter signature. In this melody a beam designates grouping; the result is a change from predominant duple patterns to a grouping by three (as $\frac{3}{8}$) in measures 7–8. This shift is immediately apparent, as is the relation of the triple grouping to the closing of the phrase.

Ex. 13–1. Bartók: *Mikrokosmos*, Vol. VI, No. 146. Copyright 1940 by Hawkes & Son (London) Ltd. Renewed 1967. Reprinted by permission of Boosey & Hawkes, Inc.

Ties may be used with conventional meters to create asymmetrical patterns. In Ex. 13–2 agogic accents are produced by ties. Because the first note is tied, a four-unit rhythmic group results, whereas the next rhythmic group contains three units. The stressed a^1-*flat* in measure 3 resembles a downbeat, as do both the e^2-*flat* in measure 5 and the *b-flat* in measure 7. Such aperiodic stresses lead to asymmetric rhythmic structures, traditionally not associated with compound meters.

Ex. 13–2. Carter: *Piano Sonata,* II. Copyright 1948, by Music Press, Inc.

Furthermore, meter signatures sometimes seem completely divorced from the rhythmic accents of passages within a composition. When this is the case, the indicated meter is merely a *notational* framework that has been retained, even though it may have little to do with the organization of the actual durations, as in Ex. 13–3.

Ex. 13–3. Schoenberg: Op. 10, IV. Reprinted with permission of Universal Edition (London and Vienna).

In some recent music patterns consistently vary in length. In Ex. 13–4 the bar lines designate accents. The ♪ is constant throughout; therefore, the duration of each rhythmic unit and the time that elapses between each dynamic accent is variable except for the last four measures.

Ex. 13–4. Boris Blacher: *Epitaph,* Op. 41. © 1952 by Bote & Bock, Berlin. Reprinted by permission.

This melody's ♩♪ motive marks a series of rhythmic groups. Each of these groups elides with the next. The entire melody consists of eight groups, each of which has a different rhythmic content. Since there is no clearly defined cadence until the end of the excerpt, the motive marks off each group by serving as its beginning. To produce the cadence, periodic accents (in measures 22–25) and repetition of the motive (measures 24–25) are brought into play.

Each of the rhythmic groupings in composer Blacher's melody might have been designated by a different meter signature, $\frac{2}{4}$, $\frac{3}{8}$, $\frac{2}{4}$, $\frac{3}{8}$, $\frac{5}{8}$, etc. Changes like this can be seen in Ex. 13–5. Even with the use of changing meters, however, the composer also uses beaming to indicate rhythmic grouping. The rhythm of both phrases is asymmetrical, as is the formal unit that results from the combination of the two phrases.

Ex. 13–5. Stravinsky: Octet, I. Copyright 1924 by Edition Russe de Musique; Renewed 1952. Copyright & Renewal assigned to Boosey & Hawkes, Inc. Revised Edition copyright 1952 by Boosey & Hawkes, Inc. Reprinted by permission.

Some successions of different meters have the effect of lengthening or shortening the metric pattern that has been established. The first two measures of Ex. 13–6 lead us to expect a continuation of the $\frac{3}{8}$ meter; suddenly, however, the abbreviated third measure destroys this regularity.

Ex. 13–6. Bartók: *Concerto for Orchestra*, I. Copyright 1946 by Hawkes & Son (London) Ltd. Reprinted by permission of Boosey & Hawkes, Inc.

339

Composite meters [1] also are common in recent music. Since they contain recurring accents, they are similar to simple and compound meters. Ex. 13–7 has two meters; one is composite ($\frac{5}{8}$), the other is simple. Note how the $\frac{5}{8}$ measures vary between a $3 + 2$ and a $2 + 3$ grouping.

Ex. 13–7. Ravel: *Quartet in F Major*, IV.

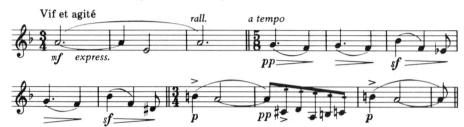

In Ex. 13–8 the composite meter is grouped in two ways, $4 + 3$ and $3 + 4$. In measures 1–2 and 3–4 the grouping is alternated so that the phrase structure is $4 + 3 + 3 + 4$, producing a type of rhythmic symmetry. Measures 5 and 6 contain the same arrangement, indicating that $4 + 3$ followed by $3 + 4$ can be regarded as symmetrical.

Ex. 13–8. Henri Dutilleux: Sonatine for Flute and Piano. By permission of Alphonse Leduc & Co., 175 rue Saint-Honoré, Paris, Owners and Publishers. Copyright 1946. Reprinted by permission.

Unequal divisions of a common meter are another possibility. For example, although $\frac{9}{8}$ meter is usually divided $3 + 3 + 3$; it can be divided $4 + 2 + 3$. Even though both divisions contain nine eighth notes to the measure, the latter is no longer a compound meter; it is composite.

Ex. 13–9. Bartók: *Mikrokosmos*, Vol. VI, No. 148. Copyright 1940 by Hawkes & Son (London) Ltd. Renewed 1967. Reprinted by permission of Boosey & Hawkes, Inc.

---

[1] Meters with other than two, three, and four beats; e.g., groupings of 5, 7, or 11. Their interior arrangement reveals uneven groupings such as $2 + 3$, $3 + 2$, or $4 + 3$, etc.

And observe a few more examples of meters which, although traditionally simple or compound, can be made composite by simple changes of
groupings.

Rhythmic complexities multiply when there is a constant changing
of basic durations, as in Ex. 13–10. Although the composer designates common meter signatures, only in measures 3 and 5 are the beat
patterns those ordinarily associated with these simple meters. Measures
1 and 3 illustrate a type of proportional notation. Measure 1 contains
seven ♪ rather than the customary six of a $\frac{3}{8}$ meter. Measure 3 with
its meter signature of $4/2^3$ illustrates a subtle proportional scheme; the
meter signature designates that the measure is to be performed as if
four triplets are occupying the time allotted to three triplets.

Ex. 13–10. Boulez: *Le marteau sans maître*, III.

Proportional rhythms may be notated in various ways; one way is
shown in Ex. 13–11. The notes above the staff designate the duration
of events (an event may contain only one element or several); thus, the
first event has the duration of a quarter note and the second event equals
a double whole note plus an eighth ◗ ♪ . The angles of beams connecting the elements of an event indicate relative velocity, as ⌐⌐⌐ =
very fast; ⌐⌐⌐ = accelerando; and ⌐⌐⌐ = ritardando. In compositions of this type *chance* is an important musical factor.

Ex. 13–11. Stockhausen: *Klavierstück X.*

dicke Noten betont (pp, p oder mf)

     Proportional rhythms may be notated by designating the duration of a passage in clock time. In Ex. 13–12 the passage is to last from 40 to 45 seconds. None of the note values (stemless note-heads with horizontal line and "eighth notes") has an "absolute" length. The duration of each note is approximated by the length of the horizontal line used, e.g., +▬ as compared to +▬▬▬ .

Ex. 13–12. Ligeti: *Aventures*. Copyright © 1964 by Henry Litolff's Verlag. Reprint permission granted by C. F. Peters Corporation, 373 Park Avenue South, New York, N.Y. 10016.

Senza tempo, 40—45˜

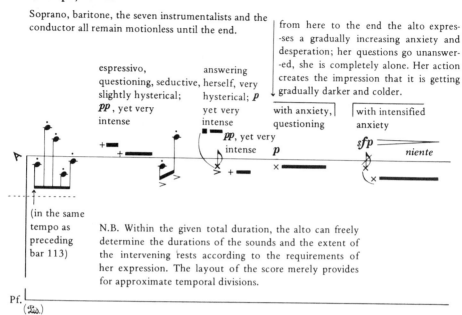

Soprano, baritone, the seven instrumentalists and the conductor all remain motionless until the end.

from here to the end the alto expres- -ses a gradually increasing anxiety and desperation; her questions go unanswer- -ed, she is completely alone. Her action creates the impression that it is getting gradually darker and colder.

espressivo, questioning, seductive, slightly hysterical; *pp*, yet very intense

answering herself, very hysterical; *p* yet very intense

with anxiety, questioning

with intensified anxiety

pp, yet very intense *p*

sfp

niente

(in the same tempo as preceding bar 113)

N.B. Within the given total duration, the alto can freely determine the durations of the sounds and the extent of the intervening rests according to the requirements of her expression. The layout of the score merely provides for approximate temporal divisions.

Pf.
(Ped.)

Pitch Organization

While diatonic pitch collections still form the basis of many melodies, other ways of organizing pitches, including even sounds of indefinite pitch, have been developed. While in some compositions the pitch resources drawn upon are greater than in the past, in others the pitch materials are fewer. In this section we shall discuss various types of organization representative of twentieth-century melody.

The natural minor scale basis of the melody of Ex. 13–13 does not distinguish it from many other melodies, yet the way these notes are used is distinctive. For example, the successive skips by fourths in measures 2 and 3 form a nontertian chordal outline rather than the major and minor triads that we associate with natural minor.

Ex. 13–13. Vaughan Williams: *Symphony No. 5 in D Major*, III. © 1946 by Oxford University Press, London. Reprinted by permission.

Sometimes melodic structure is even more closely akin to pre-twentieth-century diatonic melodies than the Vaughan Williams excerpt. The scale basis of Ex. 13–14 is *G* Mixolydian. One chromatic tone, *f¹-sharp*, is used to embellish tonic in the final cadence. The subtonic appears only twice, and in each case as an embellishing tone. Limited range and simple tonality frame add to the illusion of something ancient.

Ex. 13–14. Henry Cowell: *Persian Set*, III. Copyright © 1957 by C. F. Peters Corporation, 373 Park Avenue South, New York, N.Y. 10016. Reprinted with permission of the copyright owner.

In part, the use of modal pitch resources in the present century is a reaction to the expectations associated with major and minor melodies. This is especially true of modes that do not contain the leading tone.

In Ex. 13–15 segments of more than one scale are implied. The opening measures (1–6) suggest a pentatonic scale basis because only five notes appear. In measure 7, however, other tones are introduced that counteract this implication.

Ex. 13–15. Bartók: *String Quartet No. 3*, Prima Parte. Copyright 1929 by Universal Edition; Renewed 1956. Copyright and Renewal assigned to Boosey & Hawkes, Inc., for the U.S.A. and to Universal Edition for all other countries of the world. Reprinted by permission.

By scanning the notes of this example, you can find a twelve-note scale. However, an examination of the melody's tonality frame (Ex. 13–16) reveals that the chromatic notes do not have a consistent secondary or embellishing function as is found in melodies of earlier periods. In melodies like Ex. 13–15 tonic is an important organizational factor, but the tonal significance of tones other than tonic is not as easily determined, often not consistent within the melody.

Ex. 13–15a. Tonality frame of Ex. 13–15.

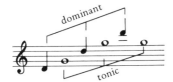

In Ex. 13–16 the outlined augmented triads create tonal instability, as well as presenting all twelve pitch classes. Consequently, any note could be used to create a tonic effect, provided that emphasis be given it by some means, such as harmonization or rhythmic duration.

Ex. 13–16. Liszt: *Faust* Symphony.

Similar pitch patterns prevail in Ex. 13–17. Here each four-measure phrase is clearly punctuated by an octave skip and a silent beat. Each cadence tone is a potential tonic. The patterns within the phrases do not point conclusively to a single note. Unity is created by the repeated intervallic relationships (augmented triads, recurrent octaves) and the durational accents produced by a beat's rest after each cadence tone.

Ex. 13–17. Bartók: Suite, Op. 14, II. Copyright 1918 by Universal Edition; Renewed 1945. Copyright & Renewal assigned to Boosey & Hawkes, Inc., for the U.S.A. an'd to Universal Edition for all other countries of the world. Reprinted by permission.

Tonic (perhaps *C*) receives little emphasis in Ex. 13–18. Tonal unity results mainly from the repetition of simple chordal and rhythmic patterns rather than from continued affirmation of a tonic.

Ex. 13–18. Hindemith: *Philharmonic* Concerto. © 1932 by B. Schott's Soehne, Mainz. Renewed 1960. Reprinted by permission.

Ex. 13–19 illustrates tonality expanded through chromaticism. Here duration gives importance to some pitches, but ultimately, f^1 is most important because of its location at the end of the excerpt, because f^2 appeared as cadence pitch earlier (measure 4), and because it completes the overall descending pitch motion.

Ex. 13–19. Bartók: *Sonata for Two Pianos and Percussion*, II. Copyright 1942 by Hawkes & Son (London) Ltd. Renewed 1969. Reprinted by permission of Boosey & Hawkes, Inc.

Confirmation of a tonic and its consequent role as a unifying factor is a prominent feature of many compositions of this century. As we have seen, the tonic effect is produced mainly by rhythm contour and recurrence, which in reality link it to earlier practices.

Atonal and
Serial Melody

Tonality is not always a factor in music. Other means of organizing pitched sounds dominate much music composed since the turn of the century.

A basic premise for any atonal melody is that no single pitch or interval is more important tonally than any other. Such a premise presupposes that key feeling is to be avoided. It is apparent, then, that other means for organizing the available pitches are used.

The melodic line shown in Ex. 13–20 has a simple motivic structure, but its pitch materials do not create a tonic. The recurrence of a set of three notes provides unity. This group of notes is a pitch set, and although the set may contribute to unity, it does not replace the function of a tonic.

Ex. 13–20. Webern: Movements for String Quartet, Op. 5, I.

In Ex. 13–20 a pitch set occurs at three different levels: measure

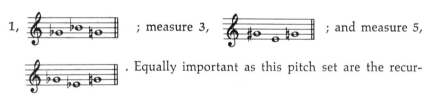

. Equally important as this pitch set are the recurrent rhythms and the step progression from a^3 to f^3 in measures 4–6.

Repetition of note groups also is a prominent factor in the next excerpt, but this repetition does not lead to the creation of a tonic or a hierarchy of pitch relations. The overall pitch line moves in a gradual way from f^1 to f^2-*sharp*, followed by three statements of a motive having f^2-*sharp* as its beginning pitch. If any prominence is gained by one pitch, it is *E*, because of its continuing role as lowest note, and then, toward the end, highest note.

Ex. 13–21. Lutoslawski: *Paroles Tisseés*. Reprinted by permission of J & W Chester Limited. © Copyright, 1967, Edition Wilhelm Hansen, London, E.C.I. Copyright for socialist countries by PWM—Edition, Krakow, Poland.

In serial compositions the elements of a set are ordered precompositionally. These elements may be pitches, durations, types of attack, degrees of loudness, etc. Very often only one dimension is serialized. If a composer elects to serialize pitch, he arranges the pitches in any succession that does not reuse any note.

A tone row or set may contain some or all of the twelve notes of the chromatic scale. The melody of Ex. 13–22 is based on the twelve-tone arrangement shown above it. This row establishes the order in which pitch classes are presented. In many works the total melodic and harmonic pitch relationships are predetermined by the tone row. A row is an abstract set of relationships to which rhythm and registers are applied, thereby producing melodic patterns. The set is *abstract*, for it represents only note names or pitch classes [2] without consideration for octave register or, as we shall see, enharmonic spelling.

Ex. 13–22. Schoenberg: *String Quartet*, Op. 37, I. Reprinted by permission of the copyright owner, G. Schirmer, Inc.

[2] Pitch class designates all pitches having the same name; thus, C, c^1, c^2, c^3, etc. all belong to the pitch class (P.C. or p.c.) C.

Segments of a tone row are frequently singled out for emphasis, much as motives or figures are given prominence in earlier music. In atonal music, these short segments, often drawn from a tone row, are commonly called *pitch sets*. Pitch sets are described in terms of their interval content based on a given starting pitch class (0). The various pitches constituting the set are numbered (*integer notation*) from 0 to 11, and a particular pitch's integer is determined by the number of semitones separating it from the starting pitch class, 0. For example, the following set, consisting of F♯, D and F, begins Ex. 13–21. Arranged in its most compact form (within an octave) the set is shown as:

* Normal order.

Since the number of semitones separating *D* from *F* equals 3, and the number separating *D* from *F♯* equals 4, this set is designated as 0 3 4. Such sets often appear with the ordering of their pitches changed, but they still are described in terms of their original (most compact) ordering, called *normal order*.

Another twelve-note series is given in Ex. 13–23, together with a melody derived from it. As in the Schoenberg melody, the predetermined row specifies only note succession. The coherence of the pattern that results is produced from the limited variety of durations, the symmetrical contour, and the constant motion by wide leaps.

Ex. 13–23. Webern: *Symphony*, Op. 21, II. © by Universal Edition; Reprinted with their permission.

In spinning out a serial work the tone row can be repeated, divided into segments, inverted, reversed, or both reversed and inverted. Of course, it also can be transposed to a different set of pitch classes.

Ex. 13–24 shows the *inversion* (*I*), the *retrograde* (*R*), and the *retrograde inversion* (*RI*) of the series of Ex. 13–23. Together with transpositions of each, these arrangements, or other derived arrangements of the twelve notes, can form the basis of a *serial composition*, all successions and combinations of pitches directly derived from the original matrix, the "O" (= *original*) or P (= *prime*) [3] form of the row.

Ex. 13–24. *I*, *R*, and *RI* forms of Ex. 13–23.

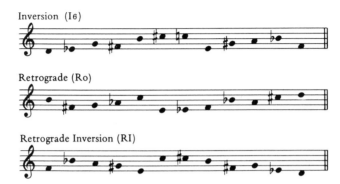

The second phrase of Ex. 13–25 is based on a transposed *inversion* of the pitch series found in the first phrase. This brings into play a pitch pattern that would not be possible if transposition were not used. Note the preservation of the interval successions of the original row.

Ex. 13–25. Dallapiccola: *Cinque Canti,* "Aspettiamo la stella mattutina." © 1957 by Edizioni Suvini Zerboni, Milan.

Other Organizational Factors

Many contemporary melodic contours are remarkable because of their wide range. A wide range gives added prominence to high and low points, accentuating contour patterns that are, generally speaking, variations of common shapes. The extended arch of Ex. 13–26 distinguishes

[3]The *prime* (untransposed) form of the row is often designated with zero (0); thus I₀ is the inverted form of the row beginning on the prime note. I₁ would be I transposed up one half-step.

this line from similarly contoured melodies by separating widely the high and low points.

Ex. 13–26. Carter: *Piano Sonata*, I. Used with the permission of the copyright owner, Mercury Music Corporation.

In sharp contrast is the contour formed by a limited number of tones moving in a tightly restricted range. The pitch activity in such melodies often consists of motion by seconds, as in Ex. 13–27. Here the outer pitch limit of a perfect fifth is filled in with combinations of only three intervals, the minor second, major third, and minor third. The resulting contour is a series of miniature arches, each of which is a variant of the one preceding it.

Ex. 13–27. Bartók: *Music for Strings, Percussion and Celeste*, I. Copyright 1937 by Universal Edition; Renewed 1964. Copyright & Renewal assigned to Boosey & Hawkes, Inc., for U.S.A. and to Universal Edition for all other countries of the world. Reprinted by permission.

Some melodic contours are distinctive because the high and low points are punctuated by disjunct pitch activity producing a "jagged" design. High and low pitch relationships between phrases may form an extended arch; in a single phrase or in parts of a phrase, "jaggedness" may be the primary contour factor.

Ex. 13–28. Schoenberg: *Serenade*, Op. 24, IV. © Copyright 1924 & 1952 by Wilhelm Hansen, Copenhagen. By permission of the Publishers.

Chordal outlining also occurs in many twentieth-century melodies. Various chord types are outlined in Ex. 13–29, the prolonged ascending melody suggesting seventh and ninth chords as well as a minor and a diminished triad. Beginning in measure 11 the characteristic intervals, sixths and sevenths, are used sequentially. In measures 14–26 the outlining of quartal chords is important.

Ex. 13–29. Barber: *Concerto for Violin*, I. Reprinted by permission of the copyright owner, G. Schirmer, Inc.

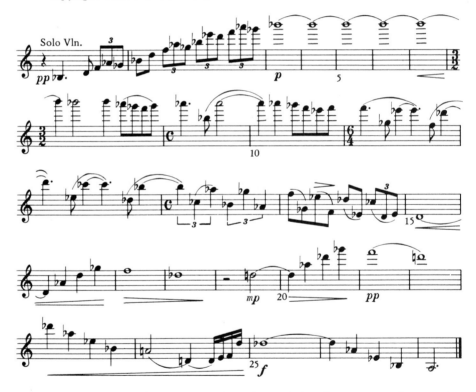

The second phrase of the next melody illustrates outlining of a quintal chord. Throughout this example the fifth and its inversion (the fourth) provide the characteristic intervallic content.

Ex. 13–30. Hindemith: *Second Sonata for Piano,* III. © 1936 by B. Schott's Soehne, Mainz. Renewed 1963. Used by permission.

The tonal materials of contemporary melody are more diverse than those of previous periods, yet general principles of pitch organization—contour, durational emphasis, metric position, relation to tonic, etc.—still form the basis of coherent structure. Because of the changing role of tonality, however, structural unity often results from factors other than pitch resources.

Exercises

For more detailed assignments see *Materials and Structure of Music II, Workbook,* Chapter 13.

1. Write several melodies using a modal scale basis, but in which nontertian chord outlining plays a predominant role.
2. Create several motives that will become the primary unifying factor of one or more melodies that you write. Organize your melodies so that little or no implication of major or minor keys is present.
3. Devise a tone row and use it as the basis for an instrumental melody.
4. Analyze several contemporary melodies assigned by your teacher. Follow the analytic procedures that he outlines. Select the melodic lines from such works as:

> Bartók: *Concerto for Orchestra; Second String Quartet*
> Boulez: *Structures*
> Copland: *Piano Variations*
> Dallapiccola: *Notebook for Anna Libera*
> Hindemith: *String Quartet* No. 2
> Kagel: *Sonant*
> Ligeti: *Aventures*
> Penderecki: *Anaklasis*
> Webern: *Cantata No. 2,* Op. 31.

5. Write a melody in which new tonics appear in close succession, but that ends and begins with the same tonic. Use an uneven grouping of a compound meter such as $\frac{9}{8}$ as the metric basis.

6. Make a plan for an extended melody for oboe (approximately thirty measures long). Sketch in cadences, tonal centers, unifying rhythmic patterns, unifying pitch patterns, etc.

Chapter Fourteen

Harmony in Twentieth-Century Music

Harmony in contemporary music includes sonorities used in music of the past as well as some that are strikingly new. The most apparent link with the past in some music is the incorporation of triads and seventh chords. Other tertian chords, such as ninths, elevenths, and thirteenths, also form part of the harmonic fabric of some twentieth-century music.

We first shall discuss chords composed of stacked thirds, turning later to chords that depart radically from the harmonic conventions of the past.

Tertian Chords

Major and minor triads provide the harmonic material for Ex. 14–1. These triads appear in simple sequential relations, their root pattern one of ascending second separated by a descending 4th.

Ex. 14–1. Prokofiev: *Piano Sonata No. 2*, Op. 14, I. © Copyright MCMLVII by Leeds Music Corporation, New York, N.Y. Used by permission. All rights reserved.

Major and minor triads are not always associated with functional relationships. In Ex. 14–2 major and minor triads that share the same root are alternated. The juxtaposition takes place in different registers, so that the minor triads are always higher than the major. The result is a parallelism of inverted triads separated in register. (In measures 57 and 58 the triadic spelling is enharmonic. The pattern continues, even though notation suggests a change.)

Ex. 14–2. Bartók: *Contrasts*, III, "Sebes." Copyright 1942 by Hawkes & Son (London) Ltd. Renewed 1969. Reprinted by permission of Boosey & Hawkes, Inc.

356

Both of the preceding examples illustrate two possible uses of simple triads. In music of the twentieth century, extended passages containing only major and minor triads often occur in contrast to surrounding sections dominated by more varied sonorities. In still other instances, major and minor triads may appear in their traditional roles as points of departure and arrival.

The *e-flat* minor triad in Ex. 14–3 is succeeded by chords having *b-flat* for their lowest note. Each of the structures on the first beats of measures 1–3 is of a different type.

Ex. 14–3. Hindemith: *Sonata for Organ*, No. 1, II. © 1937 by B. Schott's Soehne, Mainz. Reprinted by permission.

Tertian chords often provide the main harmonic material of a section. Parallel sevenths are used exclusively over the double pedal in Ex. 14–4. As such, the stream of seventh chords continues the coloristic use of chords begun by Debussy.

Ex. 14–4. Paul Creston: *Symphony No. 2,* I. Reprinted by permission of the copyright owner, G. Schirmer, Inc.

Both chords in measures 1 and 2 of Ex. 14–5 contain major sevenths as their delimiting intervals. The first chord contains intervals other than thirds; it contains the tritone *d-flat—g* that moves to *c—g* in the augmented major seventh chord that follows. Note that this "resolution" chord is more stable than the preceding chord. Each of the chords in this excerpt is connected by the common tone *g*.

Ex. 14–5. Barber: *Piano Sonata,* I. Reprinted by permission of the copyright owner, G. Schirmer, Inc.

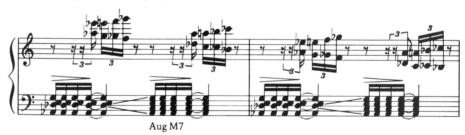

Mm$_7$ chords are the simplest chords in Ex. 14–6. The first two sonorities are composite chords of both tertian and nontertian elements. Harmonic motion is created by the succession of different sonority types. Because of its greater complexity and spacing, the first chord produces a textural accent, its repetition at regular intervals creating $\frac{5}{4}$ meter, in spite of the notation in $\frac{4}{4}$.

Ex. 14–6. Honegger: *Symphony No. 1*, I. © 1942 by Editions Salabert, Paris, by permission of Franco Colombo, Inc., New York.

Basically tertian chords are frequently enriched by the inclusion of "added tones." The chords shown in the next example can be interpreted as seventh chords, yet a pitch that forms a 7th is consistently placed below the root of each chord. As a result, a second interpretation is possible: the passage consists of major and minor triads with "added tones," all of which form seconds with another chord member.

Ex. 14–7. Stravinsky: *Firebird Suite*, Finale.

Nontertian Chords

Chords based on stacked perfect 4ths (such as *C—F—B♭*) occur in much music written just before mid-century. Chords consisting of mixtures of perfect and augmented 4ths (such as *C—F—B*) also are called *quartal*. Although the latter is a mixture of two different types of fourths, we shall use the term *quartal* to refer to any chord in which the *perfect* fourth is the characteristic interval.

Quartal chords containing only perfect 4ths are illustrated next. The dyad (*G—D*) at the beginning of this passage fits with quartal chords because its intervals are octave, 5th and 4th.

Ex. 14–8. Hindemith: *Nobilissima Visione*, III. Used by permission of the copyright owner, B. Schott's Soehne, Mainz.

Quartal chords are the principal harmonic material in Ex. 14–9.

Ex. 14–9. Copland: *Piano Fantasy.* Copyright 1957 by Aaron Copland. Reprinted by permission of Aaron Copland, Copyright Owner, and Boosey & Hawkes, Inc., Sole Licensees.

Each of the four- or five-note chords in Ex. 14–10 contains a fourth, yet some of the chords also contain a third. Chords such as those on the first beat of measures 1 and 3 might be considered seventh chords, but they probably are not heard as third inversion seventh chords. Clearly the section is based on combinations of fourths.

Ex. 14–10. Berg: *Wozzeck.* © by Universal Editions. Used by permission.

Chords of superposed fifths (*quintal chords*) occur in some scores. In Ex. 14–11 a quintal chord is used cadentially. Since the last chord contains the doubled *a*'s, it takes on the character of a quartal chord, with which it has much in common because of the fourth-fifth inversion relationship. Note that in a spread position the chord can be shown to consist of the series *A–E–B–F♯.*

Ex. 14–11. Bartók: *Sonata for Piano*, III. Copyright 1927 by Universal Edition; Renewed 1954. Copyright & Renewal assigned to Boosey & Hawkes, Inc., for U.S.A. and to Universal Edition for all other countries of the world. Reprinted by permission.

Seconds and sevenths constitute the basic harmonic building blocks in many contemporary compositions. Sometimes these secundal chords are used to accompany simple melodic lines. The texture shown in Ex. 14–12 continues for about twelve measures, creating a static harmonic rhythm in which the dynamic accents tussle with the notated meter of $\frac{2}{4}$.

Ex. 14–12. Villa-Lobos: *String Quartet No. 3*, IV. © 1929 by B. Schott's Soehne, Mainz. Reprinted by permission.

Three adjacent seconds sound together in Ex. 14–13. This type of chord is called a *tone cluster*. Normal use of this term indicates that a combination of three or more adjacent seconds forms a tone cluster.

Ex. 14–13. Bartók: *Sonata for Piano*, III. Copyright 1927 by Universal Edition; Renewed 1954. Copyright & Renewal assigned to Boosey & Hawkes, Inc., for U.S.A. and to Universal Edition for all other countries of the world. Reprinted by permission.

In comparison to Ex. 14–12, the secundal chords here are unstable. In the former excerpt, e^1 and d^1 of the accompaniment are a perfect fifth above a and g, while the most stable interval in Ex. 14–14 is the major third (except in measures 2–4 with the fifth between the melody and one of the accompanying voices).

A tone cluster is used as a pedal to set into relief the simple melodic line in Ex. 14–14. In contrast to Ex. 14–13, the chord in the left-hand part produces a resonance that becomes background to the simpler relations formed in voice and right hand.

Ex. 14–14. Ives: "Majority." From *Nineteen Songs,* copyright 1935, Merion Music, Inc. Used by permission.

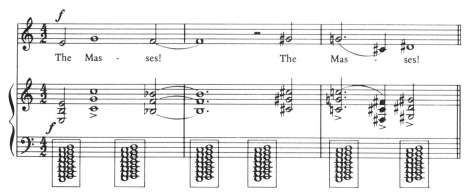

Stacked Chords

Some contemporary compositions contain sonorities created by stacking simpler chords together. The result is commonly called *bichords* or *polychords*. This means that two or more simple units are combined to form one complex chord.

Spacing is an important factor in the effectiveness of bichords. If the individual members of the chordal units involved are rearranged so that the component structures are masked, the bichord identity is lost. Both chords in Ex. 14–15 contain the same notes, yet the first consists of stacked chords (*G-sharp* major over *A* major), while the second implies a harmonic piling of several different intervals.

Ex. 14–15. Chords of identical notes but different structures.

The bichords in Ex. 14–16 are created by combining either major or minor triads, or both. Variety is maintained by varying the mixtures. Here the two lowest notes always form a fifth, which contributes to the unity of the excerpt, as does the planing in contrary motion.

Ex. 14–16. Honegger: *Symphony No. 5,* © 1951 by Editions Salabert, Paris,
by permission of Franco Colombo, Inc., New York.

Bichords also form the harmonies of Ex. 14–17. In contrast to the
Honegger excerpt, the stable fifth does not appear as the lowest interval,
and the two strata of voices do not move in contrary motion. Notice
that each of the bichords forms a second inversion MM9th chord in
measures 1 and 2.

Ex. 14–17. Wm. Schuman: *A Free Song.* Reprinted by permission of the copyright owner, G. Schirmer, Inc.

The accompaniment in Ex. 14–18 consists of arpeggiated bichords.
Even though the roots of the combined chords are consistently a half-
step apart, the arpeggiated patterns form sixths throughout the passage, suggesting two simultaneous tonalities, or *bitonality.*

Ex. 14–18. Stravinsky: *Rake's Progress.* Copyright 1949, 1950, 1951 by
Boosey & Hawkes, Inc. Reprinted by permission.

Bichords often appear at climactic points. In Ex. 14–19 the phrase begins and ends with a *D* major triad. As the climax is reached, bichords are introduced, supporting the peak of the melodic arch. The first chord in measure 2 suggests a combination of two chords, a *C-sharp* mm₇ over a *C-sharp* major triad. The chord on the third beat in measure 2 begins as the combination of a *d-sharp* °₇ chord over an *F* Mm₇.

Ex. 14–19. Hindemith: *Second Sonata for Piano,* III. © 1936 by B. Schott's Soehne, Mainz. Reprinted by permission.

Combining thirds that do not share the same root creates another type of bichord similar to those already illustrated. The first chord of measure 1 (accompaniment) in Ex. 14–20 could be spelled *a-c-sharp-e-g-sharp*. However, the spacing separates the two thirds and gives the effect of harmony produced by joining two different harmonic units of the same type (major thirds).

Ex. 14–20. Bartók: *Sonata for Violin* No. 2, I. Copyright 1923 by Universal Edition; Renewed 1950. Copyright & Renewal assigned to Boosey & Hawkes, Inc., for U.S.A. and to Universal Edition for all other countries of the world. Reprinted by permission.

Frequently, great independence exists between the parts of a texture, as in Ex. 14–21. In such cases, the mere sounding of parts together produces the chordal effects, rather than some systematic chordal ordering.

Ex. 14–21. Carter: *Sonata for Flute, Oboe, Cello, and Harpsichord*, II. Used by permission of Associated Music Publishers, Inc., New York.

Other Chord Types

Most of the chords discussed earlier in this chapter consist of combinations that *could* be reduced to a tertian basis. For example, all of the chords in Ex. 14–22 could be reduced to the tertian structure shown at the end. Because of such factors as spacing, however, some of the chords bear little resemblance to this hypothetical reduction. It seems unproductive to relate them as such.

Ex. 14–22. Chords containing identical tones but of different structures.

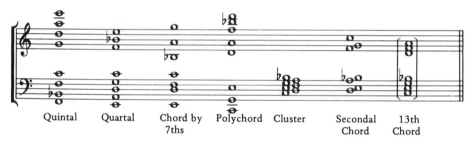

| Quintal | Quartal | Chord by 7ths | Polychord | Cluster | Secondal Chord | 13th Chord |

The chords in Ex. 14–22 have intervallic components that distinguish each as a particular chord type. Since one interval type dominates each chord, we can identify it by this singular characteristic; i.e., *secundal* chords (built of seconds), *quartal* chords (built of fourths).

The chords discussed in the following paragraphs do not always contain such common factors, although a certain interval type may be more prominent because it appears more than once, or because of spacing.

Various means for describing sonority types have evolved gradually. In general, spacing and register are discounted for the purposes of classification; two means for describing sonority types and for determining harmonic similarities are (1) calculating the total interval content and (2) showing the pitch content in relation to a prime.

To calculate the interval content of any chord, each interval is accounted for as belonging to one of six interval classes (I.C. or i.c.).[1]

Ex. 14–23. Interval content analysis.

I.C.   6   1   3   2   5   3   4   4   1   5

Total interval content: I.C. 1 = 2 occurrences
2 = 1 occurrence
3 = 2 occurrences
4 = 2 occurrences
5 = 2 occurrences
6 = 1 occurrence

A second procedure is to determine the pitch content of a collection of notes in relation to a prime, which is shown in terms of half-steps above it.[2] Any of the notes of a group can be selected to represent the prime, provided the arrangement expresses the pitch content arranged in the smallest possible span.

Ex. 14–24. Pitch content analysis.

0   1   2   5   8

As Ex. 14–24 demonstrates, the five-note collection in its reduced form spans a minor sixth.

In Ex. 14–25 chords containing various combinations of major and minor thirds, perfect fourths, augmented fourths (diminished fifths), and sixths occur over a stable lower part. The interval content analysis shows that each of the chords has certain intervals in common; each of the chords contains the same number of first and second class intervals, whereas the number of class three intervals alternates between two and three. Most notable is the absence of a class six interval in the last chord. Such an analysis assists in describing similarities and dissimilarities of chords in a composition, as well as providing one means for establishing relations between chords based on similar interval content.

---

[1] The six interval classes are: 1 = m2, M7
2 = M2, m7
3 = m3, M6
4 = M3, m6
5 = P4, P5
6 = tritone

[2] This method of classification has much to recommend it. For example, a single number identifies an interval; thus 4 = major third; 7 = perfect fifth.

Ex. **14–25.** Webern: *Five Pieces for String Quartet*, Op. 5, No. 5. © by Universal Editions. Used by permission.

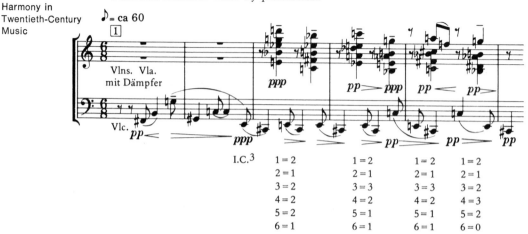

By contrast, notice the different content of the harmony in Ex. 14–26, whose chords are less complex.

Ex. **14–26.** Schoenberg: Song No. 12, from *Das Buch der hängenden Gärten.* Reprinted by permission of Belmont Music Publishers, Los Angeles 90049.

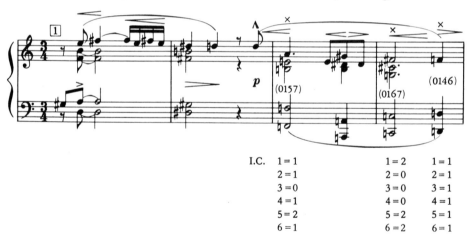

In Ex. 14–27 the cadence chord contains twelve different notes. These notes are arranged so that seconds are concentrated in the middle register, sixths, fifths, fourths, and thirds in the outer registers.

---

[3] This analysis applies only to the notes in the treble clef of the excerpt.

Ex. 14–27. Helm: Concerto for Five Solo Instruments, Percussion and Strings, II. © 1954 by Schott & Co., Ltd., London. Used by permission.

Since twelve different notes can form a single chord, it is possible to arrange them to form twelve-note quintal chords, twelve-note quartal chords, or in any other symmetrical arrangement of twelve separate notes. However, the tones would have to be spaced over a wide range to make evident the two types just mentioned.

Harmonic Succession

Harmonic predictability for all twentieth-century music defies formulation. In other words, norms cannot be clearly identified for all contemporary music as though it were all cut from the same cloth. We are limited to generalized descriptions of chord types and generalized observations about chord succession.

Some general principles of harmonic succession are apparent. For example, common-tone relations, connection by contrary motion or similar motion, and familiar root or bass progressions still are basic to much music. Harmonic succession also may be predicated on serialized organization or any other system, as is discussed later in this chapter. If simple major and minor triads form the principal harmonic material, composers often connect chords in ways that obscure or expand tonality. Thus certain relationships (such as root movement by a tritone) occur more frequently than in earlier music.

Root movement of a tritone and of a second are illustrated in Ex. 14–28. Here major and minor triads form the principal harmonic material. The root movement by major seconds connects the parallel harmonic construction and leads to a section containing tritone root relationships.

Major and minor triads are again the basic harmonies in Ex. 14–29. Although longer relative duration gives emphasis to the *G-flat* chord in measure 2 and the *A-flat* chord in measure 5, the prevailing activity does not enable us to predict the appearance of these chords as harmonic goals. Even so, the succession of chords is smooth, a result of the contrary motion between the parts. Note that the most frequent root relation is by thirds.

In measures 5 and 6 of the excerpt shown in Ex. 14–30, the basic quintal chords are smoothly connected by the contrary motion of the voice pairs. A similar procedure occurs in measures 3–4 and 8–9. Note that in measure 4 quartal chords are joined by this same procedure. The linear chords that fill in the span between the two *A*-major chords in measures 1–2 are all joined together by the common tone *A*.

Ex. 14–30. Hindemith: *Piano Sonata No. 1*, I. Used by permission of the copyright owner, B. Schott's Soehne, Mainz.

In Ex. 14–31, three-note clusters (measures 1–4) accompany a simple, diatonic melody. Here harmonic succession is the result of parallel step motion except for the progression to the chord in measure 5.

Ex. 14–31. Cowell: *String Quartet No. 5*, II. Copyright 1962 by C. F. Peters Corporation, 37 Park Avenue South, New York, N.Y. 10016. Reprinted with permission of the publisher.

Common-tone relationships help to unify Ex. 14–32. Each of the chords in measures 7–10 has at least one tone in common with its successor. The presence of this melodic link produces smooth succession between different chord types.

Serialized Harmony

Harmonic materials can be derived systematically from serialized note combinations. The chords that result from this procedure may be of diverse or similar types. For instance, if twelve notes are arranged as in the series shown in Ex. 14–29, the chords noted in Ex. 14–33 are potential harmonic structures through a simple partitioning of the row into four parts of three notes.

Ex. 14–33. Partitioning of a row into chords.

The resulting chords are the product of the combination of three successive notes, and the sonorities created are dependent upon the relative positions assigned them. Consequently, the members of individual chords are determined by the order in which they appear in the tone row.

A passage consisting of serially derived chords is shown in Ex. 14–34. Chords containing successive groups of three notes occur at the outset and proceed in that manner until all twelve notes of the row have occurred. In measure 2, a six-note chord is produced by combining the first six notes of the row, followed by a chord (measure 3) that contains the last six notes.[4] The seventh through twelfth notes of the row are rearranged in measure 4, creating a new chord.

Ex. 14–34. George Rochberg: *Bagatelle No. 5* © by Theodore Presser Company. Reprinted by permission.

[4] This division of a twelve-note row into two units of six is commonly referred to as *hexachordal*, i.e., a hexa (or six-part) set division.

As can be seen, notes 0 1 2 and 9 10 11 combine to form the same chord type, while 3 4 5 create an augmented triad, and 6 7 8 create still a different type.

A composer who uses serial technique frequently chooses certain note combinations to the exclusion of others because they contribute to continuity. Each of the three bracketed notes in Ex. 14–35 represents a potential chord. Some of the segments contain identical notes, and some segments contain identical interval relations.

Ex. 14–35. Schoenberg: *String Quartet No. 4*, Op. 37, tone row. Reprinted by permission of the copyright owner, G. Schirmer, Inc.

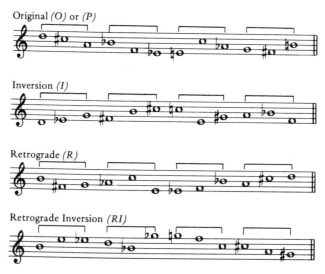

In Ex. 14–36 the first five measures of the melody are based on the *P* form of the row cited in Ex. 14–36, as are most of the accompanying chords. Considering only the chords in measure 1, each is the result of combinations of the segments 3 4 5, 6 7 8, and 9 10 11. The chord appearing on the fourth beat of measure 2 is derived from the set 8 9 10 of the *RI* form.

Ex. 14–36. Schoenberg: *String Quartet No. 4*, Op. 37, I. Reprinted by permission of the copyright owner, G. Schirmer, Inc.

Chords derived from tone rows, then, are based on the original and its derivative forms. If a tone row is ordered so that it can yield chords of a similar sonority, then that type conceivably might be heard as an important organizational factor. But such harmonic successions are only a by-product of the note organization of the original row (or its segments); they certainly are not related to a key system in the conventional sense.

Although the procedures and examples cited in our discussion are typical of serial techniques, they are based specifically on rows of twelve tones. It should be clear that rows of less than twelve tones could also serve as the basis for the same techniques.

**Melodic and
Harmonic
Interaction**

It remains now to examine some of the ways melody and harmony interact in serial music. Since composers are less dependent upon traditional tonal organization and draw upon a much larger body of musical resources, a far richer set of possibilities exists for the serial composer. In this discussion we shall explore some of these by examining several representative examples.

Initially, melodic and harmonic elements may seem to be independent in Ex. 14–37. That this is not the case becomes clear through studying some of the principal lines in that passage.

Ex. 14–37. Berg: *Schlafend trägt man*, Op. 2, No. 2.

Although the voice and piano in measures 1–4 may appear to be independent, several related figures are presented in each. The opening figure in the voice part consists of the interval relations 0, 4, and 3. This pattern is duplicated, transposed and reordered in the piano (designated as "X" in the example).

The half-step pattern (0 1 2) designated "Y" in measures 3–4 also appears, transposed by a tritone, in the piano's top line. This vertical joining by a tritone between voice and piano is consistent with the harmonic substance, for each chord of measures 1–4 contains two tritones. Still another aspect of interaction relates to the three-note melodic figure designated as "Z." This whole-step pattern is an important vertical factor since each of the chords of measures 1–4 is relatable to a symmetrical whole-tone segment. The first chord serves as a model for the other chords in the phrase in this respect:

Vertical and linear relations in serial compositions are directly determined by the manner in which a composer derives harmonic structures. The excerpt shown (Ex. 14–38) illustrates a serialized melody and accompaniment in which both dimensions are based on four-note segments of the row.

Ex. 14–38. Webern: *Variations for Orchestra*, Op. 30.

The four-note chords in measures 1–10 are derived from R_0; the melodic line is derived from both P_0 (measures 1–3 and measures 7–10) and P_1 (measures 4–6). It is evident that in measures 1–3 and 7–10 there are no pitch class duplications in the melody and accompaniment; the interval content, however, of both the melody and accompaniment in these measures is the same. In measures 4–6 there is intentional pitch class duplication in that *B* and *D* occur in the same register in both melody and accompaniment. Considering only chords, it is evident that the four notes are spaced to produce expansion (measures 1–9) and contraction (measure 10).

Ex. 14–39. Messiaen: *Couleurs de la Cité Céleste.* By permission of Alphonse Leduc & Cie., 175 rue Saint-Honoré, Paris Ier, Owners and Publishers. Copyright 1966.

Sometimes melody and harmony are not as distinctly separated texturally; Ex. 14–39 illustrates one such instance. The lines designated with a ★ contain the principal melodic material, but in each instance these starred lines are coupled to produce a "color line"; for example, the three clarinets, *petite* trumpet, and French horns are coupled to produce a melodic stratum, with the piano and *cencerros* forming another. Counterpointed against these two melodies are trumpets and trombones, xylophone, xylorima, and marimba. Although there is rich harmony in this excerpt, it is the color combinations that draw our attention. Such emphasis on color is a logical extension of coloristic uses of harmony by Impressionistic composers such as Debussy. The total effect is similar to that of color threads weaving through a multicolored fabric.

A quite different concept of horizontal-vertical interaction in musical texture is illustrated by Ex. 14–40. Both the vertical and the horizontal are made of the same stuff, with the horizontal starts and stops punctuating moments of the total event rather than separating parts of a texture into melody and harmony. Harmonic progression in a conventional sense is absent. It is changes in vertical density, together with the horizontal starts and stops that provide a sense of motion toward a musical goal.

Ex. 14–40. Penderecki: *Anaklasis.*

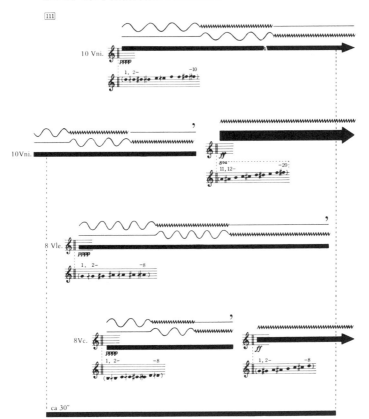

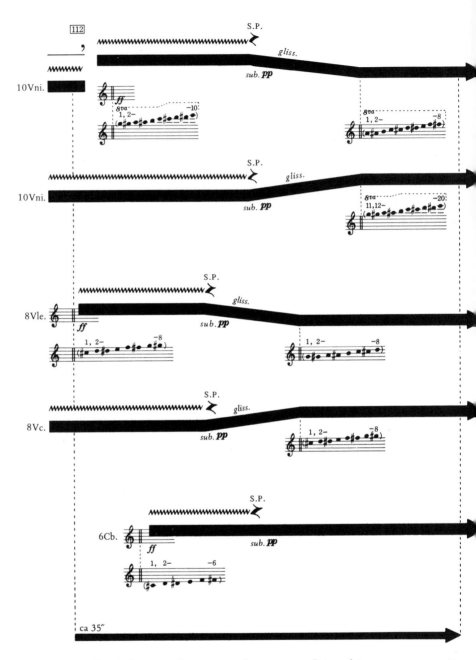

Each of the preceding examples uses traditional instruments as its sound sources. In our day, electronically produced sounds (pitched and nonpitched) are used as the basis for compositions. Ex. 14–41 is a graphic representation (a score) providing instructions for recreating an electronic composition on tape.

Ex. 14–41. Stockhausen: *Electronic Study No. II.*

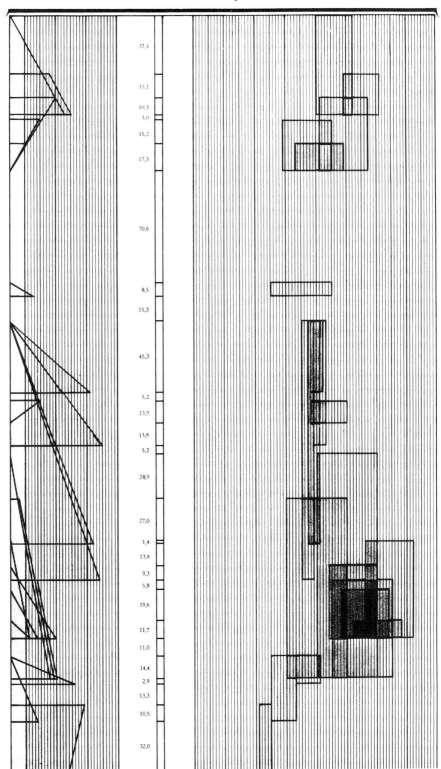

The duration of each pitch in this score is designated in terms of centimeters of tape (76.2 centimeters = 1 second); pitches and pitch mixtures are obtained from a frequency scale of 81 steps selected from a frequency range of 100 to 17,200 cycles per second. The loudness of any event is selected from an intensity scale of 31 steps ranging from 0 to 30 decibels.

As the graphic score vividly illustrates, the harmonic component is one of varying degrees of lesser or greater vertical density; similarly, the linear component is produced by proximity of attack or frequency of attacks.

Exercises

For more detailed assignments see *Materials and Structure of Music II, Workbook*, Chapter 14.

1. Write a composition for flute and piano (approximately 16 measures) in which the harmonic material of the accompaniment consists only of successive and superposed major and minor triads. The scale basis of the flute part might be pentatonic.
2. Make a harmonic plan for a three-part composition in which sonorities are the foremost factor in delineating the form; for example, Section I might contain only tertial chords; Section II might contain quartal, quintal, or superposed chords; Section III might be similar to Section I or different.
3. Devise a row of twelve different tones; then use this row and its derivative forms as the basis of a short composition for clarinet, violin, and piano.
4. Analyze each of the examples in this chapter to determine the factors that govern harmonic succession. In addition, analyze and listen to works by Shostakovitch, Bartók, Stravinsky, and Hindemith for more study relating to harmonic succession.
5. Find examples from literature that contain quartal, quintal, and secundal chords.
6. Listen to and analyze in detail the sonorities of composition such as those found in Volume VI of Bartók's *Mikrokosmos*. Identify chord types and describe the principles of harmonic succession found in each of the examples studied.
7. Make a sketch of an experimental composition in which some sections are based on serial techniques and in which other sections are not. Include in your sketch ways in which the materials of each section might be commonly related because of similar sonority types, or by some other means.

8. Listen to and analyze horizontal-vertical relations in works such as those listed below.

Berio: *Rounds* (both piano and harpsichord versions)
Boulez: *Le marteau sans mâitre*
Dallapiccola: *Quaderno Musicale di Annalibera*
Davidovsky: *Study No. 2*
Erb: *In no strange land*
Gaburo: *Antiphony IV*
Kagel: *Sonant*
Ligeti: *Atmospheres*
Partch: *And on the Seventh Day Petals Fell in Petaluma*
Penderecki: *Stabat Mater*
Stockhausen: *Klavierstücke* I–IV
Varèse: *Déserts*

Chapter Fifteen

Tonality and Atonality in Twentieth-Century Music

Many factors that contributed to the broadening of the tonal spectrum paved the way for relationships in contemporary music. In this chapter we shall examine some of these common relational patterns.

Tonal Relations

Tonality demands a focal pitch and relationships of pitches to that focal point as well. Although disguised or transformed, these relationships frequently occur in music of the twentieth century.

Ex. 15–1 illustrates one type of modification of traditional relational patterns. *F* is the tonic—it is the first melodic and harmonic root,
the last pitch heard, and it is the first note of the phrase beginning in
measure 7. However, it is the final occurrence of *f* that confirms its significance. Other factors corroborate it as a focal point: (1) the radical
change of texture and sonority in measure 16; and (2) the bass movement from *C* to *f* in measures 15–16. It is insignificant that every note
of the chromatic scale occurs within the passage; interval and rhythm
relationships still can conspire to project a sense of pitch focus.

Ex. 15–1. Bartók: *Concerto for Orchestra*, 1. Copyright 1946 by Hawkes &
Son (London) Ltd. Reprinted by permission of Boosey & Hawkes, Inc.

Yet another example of broadened tonal sense is illustrated in Ex.
15–2. Here the final cadence confirms *E-flat* as a stable point of arrival.
With the exception of the opening measures, *E-flat* is not a *predictable*
convergence point for the passage. The tonal relationships of this excerpt
are not wholly different from those of the past. For example, notice the
emphasis on the *e-flat—b-flat* fifth early in the accompaniment, the
triadic harmony, and the modified plagal cadence at the end. What is
different is the absence of *E-flat* as a structural pitch within the interior
of the passage, measures 5–10.

Ex. 15–2. Vincent Persichetti: *Fourth Piano Sonata*, II. Permission for reprint granted by Elkan-Vogel Co., Inc., Philadelphia, copyright owner.

Modification of conventional harmonic patterns is only one of many techniques that establish a tonal center in some contemporary music. Sometimes durational emphasis is the primary factor in creating a tonic. In Ex. 15–3 tonic is immediately established by the pedal. By the end of the excerpt a motion to *C* occurs, a result of the individual lines converging on that pitch, as well as the duration and terminating position assigned to it.

Ex. 15–3. Hindemith: *Mathis der Maler*, 1. © 1934 by B. Schott's Soehne, Mainz. Renewed 1961.

Tonal stability often is achieved by an ostinato, as in Ex. 15–4. The persistent bass pattern establishes *F* as tonic, even though the melodic activity does not. Tonic, then, is the product mainly of repetition and, in the bass line, melodic contour.

Ex. 15–4. Hindemith: *Second Sonata for Piano*, 1 © 1936 by B. Schott's Soehne, Mainz. Renewed 1963.

Recurrence of a notable harmonic pattern also has a stabilizing effect, even if the constituent chords are complex. In Ex. 15–5 the recurrent chord with *E* as lowest note has a tonic function; it is consistently preceded by a *D-sharp* major chord, forming a leading-tone relation. The tonal digressions beginning at the end of measure 5 are transpositions of this opening figure. The return of the opening progression in measure 8 reaffirms *E* as the tonal center.

Ex. 15–5. Copland: *Music for the Theatre*, Prologue. Copyright 1932 by Cos Cob Press, Inc.; renewed 1960 by Aaron Copland. Reprinted by permission of Aaron Copland, copyright owner, and Boosey & Hawkes, Inc., sole licensees.

Bitonality and Polytonality

The presentation of two or more tonalities together is a considerable expansion of tonal relationships. Although we can hear two different pitches simultaneously, we probably can perceive only one tonic at a time. In bitonal passages, then, we have the option of focusing on one or the other tonic successively. Composers often make this easier for us by using simple melodic patterns that are separated by register and texture.

Two keys, *C* and *G-flat*, occur together in Ex. 15–6, illustrating *bitonality.* Both the right- and left-hand parts have their own textural identity because the upper part contains the melodic material, the lower the accompaniment. Their identities are created by their respective outlined major triads. Registral and rhythmic separation also play roles here.

Ex. 15–6. Milhaud: *Saudades do Brazil,* "Ipanema." © 1925 by Editions Max Eschig, Paris. Renewed 1953.

Sometimes the parts of a bitonal passage are entwined within the same pitch register. Separation of the parts in this case is generally established by making one or the other part prominent as melody, the other as accompaniment. This type of separation can be seen in Ex. 15–7.

Ex. 15–7. Honegger: *Symphony for Strings,* III. © 1942 by Editions Salabert, Paris, by permission of Franco Colombo, Inc., New York.

Hearing a tonal center becomes even more difficult when as many as three potential tonics exist. In such *polytonal* sections textural spread is more essential than in bitonal passages. Ex. 15–8 contains three possible tonics, *B-flat, E,* and *C-sharp.* Notice the textural separation, the *B-flat* pedal on the bottom, in the left hand, the middle layer of the left hand part that emphasizes *E,* and the top layer that focuses on *C-sharp.* The individuality of the upper two strands is further intensified by contrary motion.

Ex. 15–8. Bartók: *Sonata for Piano,* I. Copyright 1927 by Universal Editions. Renewed 1954. Copyright & Renewal assigned to Boosey & Hawkes, Inc., for U.S.A. and to Universal Editions for all other countries of the world. Reprinted by permission.

A similar polytonal effect may occur when one or more of the parts is not in an obvious key, as in Ex. 15–9. Here separation is established by the contour and articulation of the lowest part in opposition to the conjunct motion of the coupled upper parts. Although the upper parts do not clearly establish any tonality, they produce in combination with the lower part a bitonal texture. Note, however, that the upper and lower parts converge at cadential points to a simple *B* major triad (enharmonically).

Ex. 15–9. Stravinsky: *Symphony of Wind Instruments.* Copyright 1926 by Edition Russe de Musique. Copyright assigned to Boosey & Hawkes, Inc. Revised Version copyright 1952 by Boosey & Hawkes, Inc. Reprinted by permission.

Atonality

In contrast to tonality, *atonality* is the absence of a tonal center. Atonality often is associated only with serially organized music. This is not wholly justified because a serial composition might well be tonal, and a nonserial work can be atonal. In passages such as Ex. 15–10 the descriptive term *atonality* is appropriate. The pitch content is derived from a twelve-note row.

Ex. 15–10. Webern: *Symphony,* Op. 21, II. Copyright by Universal Editions. Reprinted by permission.

Tonality may be minimized or avoided simply by ensuring that no one tone or interval stands out as a focal point. Such a process can be seen in Ex. 15–11, where *B*, *G-sharp*, and *G* (minor 3rd—minor 2nd) form an important three-note contour motive. This motive provides the primary material for the pitch structure of the movement. These same intervals also occur together as a harmonic component in measures 4, 6, and 8.

Ex. 15–11. Schoenberg: *Piano Piece,* Op. 11, No. 1. Reprinted by permission of Belmont Music Publishers, Los Angeles 90049.

Schoenberg's contour motive functions as a melodic binder rather than as a true focal point; other tones have equal significance. The relationships, then, are more "tone to tone" than "tones to a tonic."

Another characteristic of many atonal compositions is the persistent appearance of successive complex chords that never resolve. A high degree of harmonic tension is maintained, and thus the need for resolution to a central point is eliminated. In Ex. 15–12 complex sonorities prevail. There are decided changes in rhythm, loudness, and texture that produce a sense of tension and release, but these do not lead to pitch emphasis.

Ex. 15–12. Ernst Krenek: *Toccata*. Used with the permission of the copyright owner, Mercury Music Corporation.

Pandiatonicism The basic pitch material of *pandiatonic* music is the diatonic scale, usually the major scale. Pandiatonicism is not a return to the functional tonal relations of pre-twentieth-century music. On the contrary, it incorporates a very free use of the diatonic pitches, resulting in harmonic successions that follow no apparent calculated order.

Ex. 15–13 illustrates a pandiatonic passage. Although it is in C major, the bare harmonies here are not those of clear tonic and dominant interplay that we associate with music of the eighteenth century.

Ex. 15–13. Richard Donovan: *Adventure.* Copyright 1957, Merion Music, Inc. Used by permission.

In the next excerpt a harmonic ostinato in the upper staff establishes the tonality. Three other lines, two of which are in canon, form a pandiatonic texture that includes only the notes of *G-flat* major. Note again the random way in which chords are formed by the coinciding melodic tones.

Ex. 15–14. Copland: *Appalachian Spring.* Copyright 1945 by Aaron Copland, renewed 1972. Reprinted by permission of Aaron Copland, copyright owner, and Boosey & Hawkes, Inc., sole licensees.

Like many atonal compositions, most pandiatonic passages are contrapuntal, as in Ex. 15–15. Here the participating parts for the two pianos are differentiated by melodic contour, register placement, and rhythmic separation (beginning in measure 2).

Ex. 15–15. Stravinsky: *Sonata for Two Pianos*, I. © 1945 by Associated Music Publishers, Inc., New York. Reprinted by permission.

Tonality Schemes

Since tonality remains an important facet in a great amount of music composed during this century, tonality changes also are a vital factor. In contrast to earlier music, much twentieth-century music incorporates tonal relations that are vague. Even in works that contain a straight-forward sense of tonality, temporary tonal centers, such as tonal regions, frequently appear in close succession. If such successions are followed by the return of an initial tonality, then that factor assumes a more prominent role in musical organization.

The passage shown in Ex. 15–16 is at times referred to as *tonally free*, because the changing tonal centers are in distant relationships and are so brief. This example begins in *C*, cadences on *G-sharp* in measure 4, returns to *C* in measure 6, and then moves to *C-sharp* in measure 10.

Ex. 15–16. Hindemith: *Mathis der Maler*, II. © 1934 by B. Schott's Soehne, Mainz. Renewed 1961. Reprinted by permission.

Two principal tonal centers, *D* in the beginning and *E* at the end, occur in Ex. 15–17. In contrast to Ex. 15–16, the common-chord relation smooths out the tonal digression.

Ex. 15–17. Copland: *Third Symphony*, I. Copyright 1947 by Aaron Copland. Reprinted by permission of Aaron Copland, copyright owner, and Boosey & Hawkes, Inc., sole licensees.

The traditional device of shifting abruptly to a new tonal center occurs in many passages composed by the Russians Shostakovitch and Prokofiev. Such shifts often involve a common-tone relation between keys. Ex. 15–18 begins in *F*, followed by a shift to *A-flat* in measure 7. The pitch *C* provides the common-tone relationship, both as beginning and ending melodic note.

Ex. 15–18. Shostakovitch: *Symphony No. 5*, Op. 47, I. © Copyright MCMXLV by Leeds Music Corporation, New York, N.Y. Used by Permission. All Rights Reserved.

The next excerpt contains two successive tonal centers, E and G. In this example the new tonic is reached by a modulatory sequence, beginning in measure 5, that descends by major seconds.

Ex. 15–19. Bartók: *Mikrokosmos*, Vol. VI, No. 150. Copyright 1940 by Hawkes & Son (London) Ltd. Renewed 1967. Reprinted by permission of Boosey & Hawkes, Inc.

Tonality changes have had a direct bearing on musical form since our key systems were developed in the late sixteenth century. In general, changes occur more frequently in contemporary music than in most compositions of the eighteenth and nineteenth centuries. All types of tonal relationships occur. Many may first appear to be uncommon or complex; in context, however, they occur as new solutions to old problems. In much contemporary music, however, tonality has no relevance to musical organization because it is not even present.

Exercises

For more detailed assignments see *Materials and Structure of Music II, Workbook*, Chapter 15.

1. Using Ex. 15–1 as your guide for meter and tonal relationships only, write a sixteen-measure piano piece in *G*.
2. Write a brief composition for four different instruments in which bitonality provides the tonal basis.
3. Analyze portions of a composition such as Berg's *Piano Sonata* to determine what unifying factors occur in place of tonal centers.
4. Compose two phrases for oboe and piano. Within these two phrases include at least three common-tone shifts to new tonal regions.
5. Plan a short composition for string quartet in which quartal chords are the most "consonant" sonorities and no tonic is established.
6. Make an aural and visual analysis of the tonality scheme of a work such as the first movement of Paul Hindemith's symphony *Mathis der Maler.*
7. Listen to and analyze bitonal passages in de Falla's *Harpsichord Concerto,* Milhaud's *String Quartet No. 5,* and similar works.
8. Make an aural and visual analysis of atonal works of Schoenberg and Webern, e.g., Webern: *Movements for String Quartet,* Op. 5 or *Pieces for Orchestra,* Op. 6; Schoenberg, *Piano Pieces,* Op. 11 or sections from *Pierrot Lunaire.* Determine what musical factors provide coherence in the absence of tonality.

Chapter Sixteen

Formal Processes in Twentieth-Century Music

Since far-reaching innovations of melody, harmony, rhythm, texture, and timbre have taken place in twentieth-century music, we also might expect sweeping changes in formal processes. This is not the case with much of the music composed within the past twenty-five years, as repetition, contrast, and variation continue to function in most music as the determinants of musical form.

Forms have been adapted by composers to serve their individual styles, but they remain essentially the same as their earlier prototypes, particularly in works of early twentieth-century composers such as Hindemith, Barber, Mahler, and Bartók.

A second group of composers, consisting of such a diverse collection as Arthur Honegger, Charles Ives, and Igor Stravinsky, used novel means to organize compositions that still adhere nominally to the broad outlines of earlier forms.

A third group of composers has, in effect, renounced organizing principles such as melodic repetition and tonality in favor of procedures derived from serialism. Composers such as Arnold Schoenberg, Anton Webern, Alban Berg, and composers influenced by them have employed serial techniques in one way or another, and the forms of their works are in many instances radical departures from traditional formal designs.

Still another group of composers has elevated chance processes, both in composition and in performance, to heights never before attempted. Such compositions are "of the moment," each performance presenting a slightly different version of the same basic composition. Composers such as John Cage, Earl Brown, Pierre Boulez, Karlheinz Stockhausen, and Donald Erb have incorporated chance operations in some of their works.

Formal Punctuation

Even in recent music, cadences punctuate phrases, large sections, and the ends of compositions. In some contemporary works melodic, harmonic, and harmonic forces do not operate together to create strong cadences of the kind one expects to find in the music of Mozart and Beethoven. Consequently, formal units are marked off less conspicuously by contrasts of texture, rhythm, sonority types, tempo, or tone-colors.

Nonetheless, much music of this century, especially music of the first half, still relies on the harmonic/melodic cadence as a formal delineator. In Ex. 16–1 the close of the introduction of a piano concerto is marked by a V—I cadence in C major (colored by a kind of unresolved double suspension in the middle voices). The subsequent section is different, with its change of tempo and figurative pattern in sixteenth notes.

Ex. 16–1. Prokofiev: *Concerto for Piano No. 3*, I. Copyright by Edition Gutheil. Copyright assigned to Boosey & Hawkes, Inc., 1947. Reprinted by permission.

The beginning of the development section of a sonata-allegro movement is illustrated in measure 5 of our next excerpt. The composer's instructions (*molto rit.*), accompanied by two successive *fermati*, clearly separate the two sections. The cadential effect of such a passage is achieved by both a change of pace and a relative absence of activity. The change of texture (from four voices to one) confirms the division.[1]

Ex. 16–2. Schoenberg: Quartet No. 4. Reprinted by permission of the copyright owner, G. Schirmer, Inc.

Several general observations about cadences in twentieth-century music will explain the role they may play in delineating form. For example, a cadence may occur as a short pause in only one of several voices. Or harmonic tension may be reduced suddenly, thereby implying arrival at a structural point. It should be understood that rhythmic and harmonic factors may be independent, the one not confirming the other at cadential points. Or the harmonic relationships traditionally associated with cadences may be completely avoided.

The cadence in the second full measure of the next example gives C no more duration than the eighth notes that dominate the preceding measure. Furthermore, it is overlapped by the contrasting pattern in the first violin. The pitch C is nonetheless a cadential pitch. It creates a completion of the preceding harmonic-melodic action, reasserts the tonic of the movement, and heralds a restatement of the first theme.

---

[1] The beginning of this section also corresponds with the introduction of a transposed statement of the 12-note row that is used in this piece.

Ex. 16–3. Bartók: *Quartet No. 4,* I. Reprinted by permission of Belmont Music Publishers, Los Angeles 90049.

The sounds that close some compositions appear to be final only in the sense that they are the last thing heard. This makes it possible to close a work with a complex sonority that in no way represents *harmonic resolution* of preceding activity.

The chord that appears at the end of Ex. 16–4 closes a movement. It bears no resemblance to traditional "final" chords. In the context of the movement, however, both the descending half-step in the bass and the symmetric chord produce a logical close. They both are events that are significant throughout the movement; the descending half-step is the final interval of the basic theme and the symmetric chord occurs repeatedly. By bringing these aspects together, the close is a type of final musical synthesis.

Ex. 16–4. Schoenberg: *Piano Piece,* Op. 11, No. 1. Reprinted by permission of Belmont Music Publishers, Los Angeles 90049.

The formal delineation in Ex. 16–5 is accomplished through an interaction of several factors, the most prominent of which are clearly articularly cadences to tonic, *B-flat* (measures 5, 7, and 12). Tonic is supported by its dominant in the flute part of measures 2, 6, and 8. The

tonal organization of the example and its division into phrases are remarkably clear.

Ex. 16–5. Hindemith: *Sonata for Flute and Piano*, I. © 1937 by B. Schott's
Soehne, Mainz. Reprinted by permission.

**Other Factors
of Delineation
and Continuity**

Clearly defined cadences are absent from many contemporary works. When this is the case we usually can point to a variety of other factors that contribute to phrase and sectional delineation. For example, phrases may be marked off through a change of dynamics, harmony, tone color, or texture. All are involved at measure 7 of the following excerpt.

Ex. 16–6. Stravinsky: *Symphony in Three Movements*, I. © 1946 by Schott & Co., Ltd. London. Reprinted by permission.

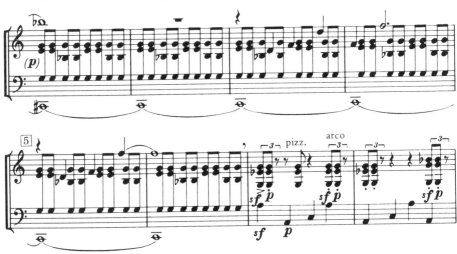

In the next excerpt four pairs of instruments (2 bassoons, 2 oboes, 2 clarinets, and 2 flutes) succeed each other in a series of short duets. These contrasts of colors help to delineate the form of the movement. The successive appearances of the instrumental pairs are further contrasted in the consistent use by each pair of a characteristic interval (6th, 3rd, 7th, 5th, respectively). In addition, each successive section is marked by a higher register, as the ranges of the different pairs suggest.

Ex. 16–7. Bartók: *Concerto for Orchestra*, II. Copyright 1946 by Hawkes & Son (London) Ltd. Reprinted by permission of Boosey & Hawkes, Inc.

In Ex. 16–8 the constant repetition of the accompaniment rules out a caesura until a change in rhythm occurs. The repetitious bass clouds the significance of the two melodic cadences of measures 7 and 14. The rests in measure 7 do help to punctuate the upper part; since this is not confirmed by the accompaniment, however, it is apparent that a decisive cadence is not intended here.

Ex. 16–8. Stravinsky: *Soldier's Tale*, Part II. By permission of the International Music Company, New York.

Ex. 16–9 contains a two-part canon at the octave. The contrapuntal texture of the excerpt provides no cadences in which both parts participate together, yet we perceive cadences in the separate voices at several points.

Ex. 16–9. Milhaud: *Quartet No. 9*, III. Reproduit avec l'autorisation des Editions "Le Chant du Monde," Paris.

It would be difficult to name any repetitive schemes found in twentieth-century music that are unprecedented. Literal, unmodified repetitions of motives, phrases, harmonic patterns, and other organizational units are found less often today than, for instance, in late eighteenth-century music. Repeated motives in recent music are more likely to be altered, as are harmonic patterns or sequences.

In Ex. 16–10 a simple motive has been spun out for several measures by adding and deleting pitches, so that in successive restatements different tones of the basic motive are stressed. The changing meters emphasize the regroupings of accented pitches that make this an interesting type of variation.

Ex. 16–10. Stravinsky: *The Rite of Spring,* Part I.

Motive repetition such as this has largely replaced the literal restatements that prevailed in earlier music. These kinds of repetitive schemes also conform with the asymmetrical phrase lengths that are characteristic of most current music.

Motive repetition dominates the extended development illustrated in Ex. 16–11. The rhythm of just one voice of the original four-part texture has been reproduced here.

Ex. 16–11. Bartók: *Quartet No. 4,* I. Copyright 1929 by Universal Edition; Renewed 1956. Copyright & Renewal assigned to Boosey & Hawkes, Inc. for the U.S.A. and to Universal Edition for all other countries of the world. Reprinted by permission.

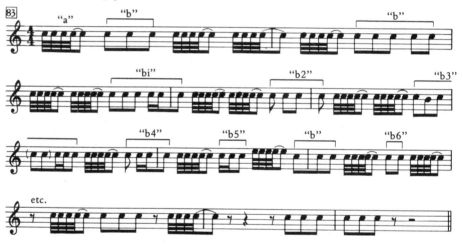

This line consists of two alternating motives. Motive "a" (♫♫♩) appearing first, followed immediately by "b," with which it will be grouped throughout the section. The six derivative patterns consist of fragments, extensions, repetitions, and minor variants of the initial form of "b."

The continuity of the passage results from the reshuffling of both patterns and the successive variants of "b" that occur in different metric positions.

Sequential repetition in twentieth-century music most frequently appears in modified forms, although instances of exact sequence occur. In Ex. 16–12, outlined seventh chords form a melodic sequence. Yet the harmonic accompaniment of this line is not sequential, although it is unified by an ascending eighth-note figure (heard twice in the celli and once in the violins) that outlines clear changes of harmony.

Ex. 16–12. Berg: *Violin Concerto*, I. Copyright by Universal Editions. Used by permission.

The Variation Process

As discussed in earlier sections, variation can be applied to both large and small formal units, to motives, phrases, or whole sections, to successive treatments of an initial theme, to a chord progression, or even to the return of a multithematic exposition. In a period of history when literal repetition of both large and small formal units has been largely abandoned, variation has been exploited in a vast number of ways.

Successive repetitions of an important motive are treated imitatively in Ex. 16–13. The motive, first heard in the highest part (Vln. I), is an octave lower in the second violin when it appears two measures later, then a rhythmic variant of the same motive begins in the viola in measure 4 (on the accented *e*). The viola version involves both an extension of the first note and a duple grouping of the remaining pitches. Our interpretation of the latter version as a variant of the first pattern is based on their similar contours; the variation is mainly rhythmic.

Ex. 16–13. Bartók: *Quartet No. 6*, I. Copyright 1941 by Hawkes & Son (London) Ltd. Renewed 1968. Reprinted by permission of Boosey & Hawkes, Inc.

Imitative dialogue based on a two-measure motive can be seen in measures 24–40 of Ex. 16–14. The different variants occur as interval expansions in which both duration and direction are altered, and restatements which contract the pitch span of the motive. Every subsequent entry of the motive is a variant of the first statement, which fills the octave a^1 to a^2.

Ex. 16–14. Ibid.

If we compare the preceding examples of motive variation with the next excerpt, we find a different, less obvious instance. Two phrases, each of which begins a different section of a movement in *A B A* form, are shown in the example. A careful study will show that (b) is derived from the rising melodic 3rd of motive (a). Both passages contrast tex-

turally, tonally, and rhythmically, but the melodic relationship of the
two is quite clear.

Ex. 16–15. Hindemith: *Chamber Music for Five Winds.* © 1922 by Schott &
Co., Ltd., London. Renewed 1949. Reprinted by permission.

A process typical of both tonal and atonal music can be found in
the next two excerpts. Both passages involve a textural variation of
essentially simple materials—a motive or a chord. In Ex. 16–16 a four-
note fragment, distributed between two pairs of instruments, is asserted in measure 1. The same pitches are immediately transformed into
a chord that is articulated three times.

Ex. 16–16. Webern: *String Quartet,* Op. 5, I. Copyright by Universal Editions.
Reprinted by permission.

Later, in the development of the same movement, this basic process
is reversed.

Ex. 16–17. Ibid.

Note how the end of the first measure of Ex. 16–17 contains two artic-ulations of a chord composed of superposed 6ths (augmented 5ths). Then the same intervals and the same pitch classes sound contrapuntally in a stretto. This stretto is a projection of 6ths in a completely different texture. Because it repeats one characteristic interval, the second measure of the example is a variation of the first.

Many large works of the twentieth century are unified through the reintroduction, in later sections or movements, of material that, while retaining some characteristic of the earlier appearance, is transformed into new patterns.

Stravinsky's *Symphony of Psalms* does not contain a movement called "variations." Yet the process of variation, along with other tech-niques of development, is partially responsible for the cohesiveness of this three-movement composition. The entire work seems to be or-ganized mainly through variation and contrast, rather than through repetition, although some repetitions do occur. Let us look at some of the most important materials of the first movement. (You may wish to consult the work's score for a more direct study.)

An *E* minor chord (a) begins the work and returns to mark off large sections of the movement. Stravinsky has voiced this chord in a way that highlights the interval of a third (both major and minor third).

(a)

Pattern (b) is an arpeggiated figure that further emphasizes the 3rd, joining 3rds with 2nds.

(b)

Item (c) slightly shuffles the 3rds of (a) and the 2nds of (b), while emphasizing its rhythm.

(c)

The horn theme (d), based on the 2nds of (c), is a variant of that previous theme's slower-moving pattern.

(d)

Motive (e) is an accompanimental ostinato that uses the 3rds of (a) and the 2nds of (b). This ostinato recurs, consistently varied, in all three movements, and it might be described as the nuclear theme of the entire symphony. The first fugue subject of the second movement, for example, derives its interval structure from this pattern. (See Ex. 16–18.)

(e)

Ex. 16–18. Stravinsky: *Symphony of Psalms*, II. Copyright 1931 by Russischer Musikverlag; Renewed 1958. Copyright and Renewal assigned to Boosey & Hawkes, Inc. Revised Version Copyright 1948 by Boosey & Hawkes, Inc. Reprinted by permission.

And notice how in items (f) and (f′) the 3rds of ostinato (e) flourish as they do in theme (g). Motive (h) is a soprano line, obviously built of the *E*-minor triad formed by (a).

It is difficult, because of the chain development established by these successive materials, to point to any one idea as basic, except for (a) because it occurs first. Stravinsky's music expands and develops through the introduction of a continuous chain of passages, each of which harks back to previous materials that are related through common melodic properties. The process is essentially variation, but it is a variation process that is more developmental than it is repetitive; the thread of continuity is more subtly woven into each variational segment than in most variation movements of earlier historical periods.

Serial composers have exploited different variation techniques, often treating a tone row as a kind of *cantus firmus*. Anton Webern's *Variations for Orchestra* does this and contains some unique treatments of the work's row. The main melodic theme of the *Variations* is presented in three groups of four notes, distributed among the contrabass, oboe, and muted trombone, as shown in Ex. 16–19. The note form of this work's row is shown following the excerpt. Another form of the row, transposed up a half-step, overlaps the first statement. It begins in the viola in the third measure.

Ex. 16–19. Webern: *Variations for Orchestra,* Op. 30. Copyright by Universal Editions. Reprinted by permission.

To understand better the relationships of the succeeding variations to the principal theme (the original form of the row), it is important that you recognize certain properties of the note series itself. A study of its three segments shows that certain intervals are emphasized, as marked in Ex. 16–20.

Ex. 16–20. The four-note segments of the row.

Segments 1 and 3 contain the pattern M7, m3, M7; segment 3 is a retrograde inversion of the intervals of segment 1. Segment 2 is different since it contains the M6th (b^2—d^2), but it also contains the M7 and m3. Both contrast and repetition are created by this arrangement of intervals into two same and one different units. Lines in Ex. 16–20 connect intervals that are common to all three segments. A great deal of the subsequent development to Webern's *Variations* exploits these intervallic properties.

Ex. 16–21. Ibid.

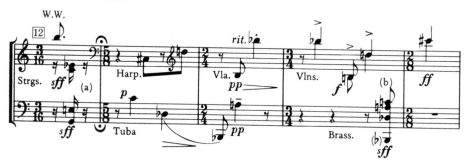

Two *sforzando* chords occur before the close of the exposition. Both are derived from simultaneous occurrences of members of the row. The chords shown in Ex. 16–21 obviously are derived from a verticalization of the pitches previously heard melodically. Chord (a) has the same interval content as the second four-note segment (the notes are transported up a semitone). Chord (b) has the interval *and* pitch class content of the first segment.

Webern's first variation (Ex. 16–22) begins at measure 21, posing a vivid contrast with the exposition because of its chordal texture. A single strand of melody "floats" over repeated chords. Note that the melody here uses the original segment 1 and its transposition, while the chords successively state segment 3 and then segment 2.

Ex. 16–22. Ibid. Variation I.

Variation II begins at measure 56. It is almost entirely chordal. The same basic intervals, reordered and contrasted by changes of orchestration and dynamics, are found here. Only measures 56–59 are shown in the reduction of Ex. 16–23. The original and transposed versions of the row are stacked one above the other to create this texture with the original retrograde.

Ex. 16–23. Ibid. Variation II.

Variation III is monophonic and involves tiny snatches of melody derived from reorderings of the row, tossed back and forth between isolated orchestral colors. Repeated rhythmic fragments, delineated by sudden changes of loudness, provide the contrasting effect of this section.

The tempo is twice as fast as Variation IV. Melodic fragments are couched in a contrapuntal texture, and the climax of the movement occurs toward the close of the variation. The reduction shown in Ex. 16–24 reveals how the composer treats the different voices (all derived from segments of the row) in a way that emphasizes interval types (M6 or m3; M7 or m2 or m9) that were stated at the outset of the movement.

Ex. 16–24. Ibid. Variation IV.

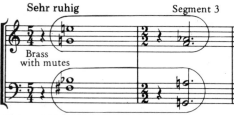

The fifth variation is short and very quiet, both chordal and contrapuntal in texture. It develops further the same properties of the row that we have seen. It is transitional in effect and leads quickly to the sixth variation, which is set off by a change of tempo and the muted statement of a chord progression that contains an interval that has been of no consequence heretofore, the tritone (*B-flat—E*).

Ex. 16–25. Ibid. Variation VI.

Segment 3 transposed up a semitone

The coda (sixth variation) recapitulates the different kinds of textures that have occurred earlier, and the row is unfolded melodically and chordally. The last melodic intervals heard echo the important first interval. Note the final three melodic intervals.

Ex. 16–26. Ibid. Measure 180.

The subtleties of this short work are startling. Still, in common with variations composed by earlier composers, it illustrates the development of material. But in this case the developed properties are the intervals of a tone row. The materials (and their treatment) have been economically chosen. They represent a distillation of musical ideas to a bare minimum.

Organization and Structure of Three Contemporary Works

Now that some of the materials and organizational procedures of recent music have been discussed separately, a study of whole compositions not only can reveal their elemental structure and organization but also will portray how analysis can disclose similar processes in other works.

The work quoted in Ex. 16–27 is a diminutive ternary design in which most sections are of different lengths, and in which the return is an abbreviated restatement of the opening section. Some of the most significant form-producing factors present are: (1) the strong cadences that close the first section and end the composition (measures 10 and 24); (2) the change of melodic contour and rhythm in measure 11; and (3) the abrupt change of texture (measure 19) that coincides with the beginning of the abbreviated return of the first section.

In addition to these features, tonality also is important. The work is framed by a *G* tonality (*G* because it appears both at the beginning and at the end). Within this framework other tonal regions are established, each associated with the beginning or end of a formal unit. For example, *C-sharp* clearly is tonic in measures 5–8, while *D* is tonic at the cadence of this section.

Ex. 16–27. Hindemith: *Ludus Tonalis*, Interludium in G. © 1943 by Schott & Co., Ltd., London. Reprinted by permission.

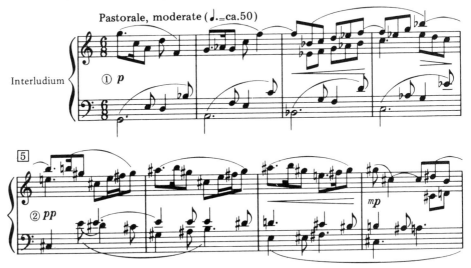

Tonality changes, together with sequences, are characteristic of the contrasting middle section (measures 11–18). Here contrasts are a result of the juxtaposed tonal regions—D (measures 11–12), F-sharp (measures 13–14)—and the bitonal separation of B and D-flat (measures 16–18), whereas in the first section, four measures elapse before a change of tonality occurs: G (measures 1–4), C-sharp (measures 5–8), and D (measure 10). In this sense, the middle section is less stable than the sections that precede and follow. As a matter of fact, instability is still present in the return gesture (measure 19). The restatement begins in *F-sharp* instead of *G*, then moves abruptly to *G* at the close.

The tonal form of this work shows a characteristic feature of many contemporary compositions: frequent tonality changes framed by a principal tonal center.

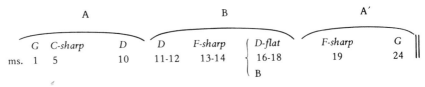

As the scheme shows, numerous tonalities occur within the span of twenty-four measures. Each of these coincides with the beginning or end of a formal unit, however, clearly delineating large formal sections as well as divisions within.

While the foregoing discussion reveals some gross features, other factors of organization come to light when the movement is reduced to a two-voice framework. (Before proceeding, the piece should be performed again, keeping in mind the broad aspects discussed earlier.) As you may recall, such a reduction contains only basic pitches, a skeletal pitch version of the actual work.

Ex. 16–28. Two-voice reduction and prominent step progressions of Ex. 16–27.

Octaves appear only four times between the outer parts of this piece, at the beginning, in measures 6 and 10, and at the end. In the two latter cases they help to establish the most stable parts of the work's form. In other words, the octaves at the beginning and at the end define the principal tonality, as well as the motion from the back to a point of repose. The octave in measure 10 creates the strongest secondary point of repose, a terminal cadence on *D*. A comparison with other cadential points, such as in measures 12 and 14, clearly shows another factor that contributes to the contrast of the middle section—the cadential intervals here are 4ths, which explains the effect of progressive cadences.

Another comparison can be made between the structural pitches that appear at the beginnings of formal units. For example, the phrases that begin in measures 5 and 19 have as structural intervals perfect 5ths. In contrast, the phrases that begin in measures 11 and 13 have as structural pitches minor 7ths. The contrast created by the middle section thus becomes even clearer: its beginning and ending structural pitches are less stable than those in the first and last sections.

A musical synthesis, made by restoring portions of the melodic overlay, discloses other organizational factors that are hidden in any reduction. Ex. 16–29 shows three instances of the elaboration of structural pitches.

Ex. 16–29. Melodic elaboration, measures 3–5 and 9–10.

In Ex. 16–29a both a 4–3 and a 6–5 suspension appear. The resolution of the latter is ornamented. In Ex. 16–29b the *E* is an appoggiatura, the *F-sharp* a basic associate.

If we continue our synthesis to include the harmonies associated with the structural framework, it is evident that tertian chords predominate. Here only a few instances will be cited. First, the opening four measures of the left-hand part consist entirely of parallel minor and major triads (note that the 5th of each chord is embellished by an appoggiatura). The result is essentially the same if both parts are considered in combination.

Ex. 16–30. Triadic parallelism, first four measures.

Second, the harmonic motion that immediately precedes the cadence in measure 10 involves a three-note quintal chord and a three-note seventh chord, both of which move to the cadential dyad of *d—a.*

Ex. 16–31. Cadential reduction, measure 10.

Ex. 16–32 shows the sonorities that appear in measures 14–16. The first chord is a perfect eleventh chord and the second a mM₇th. The third chord can be described as a mmM₉ chord, or as the stacked product of two different 3rds. Similarly, the next sonority can be described as a thirteenth chord (with an augmented eleventh) or as a bichord. The last chord of the example is the most complex in the work, appropriately located at the climactic point of the whole piece. It contains two tritones (*B—F, D-sharp—A*) but no perfect 5ths.

Ex. 16–32. Chords of measures 14–16.

Although the preceding discussion ignores more than it explains, it does suggest ways in which the principal organizational factors of a composition can be perceived through analysis.

Penderecki's *Threnody: To the Victims of Hiroshima* is representative of compositions in which musical properties other than melodic themes are the formative elements. Basic to this composition are events that have a "sustained" or a "nonsustained" quality.[2] Since the sustained sounds return, an arch-like design results; this design is made up of the *statement*, measures 1–25; the *contrast*, measures 16–61; and the *return*, measures 62–70.[3]

Loudness (dynamics) and silence are structural factors as well, particularly toward the end of the first section (measures 1–25). This section closes with a 50-second decrescendo from *fff* down to a silence of five seconds. This cadencing action is reinforced, in measures 20–24, by a change from *molto vibrato* to a very slow vibrato with a ¼-tone pitch difference, then even further to a tone of no vibrato. In addition to this, a change in the manner of performance, a reduction from 52 players to solo cello occurs (at measure 23).

Such clear separation of sections does not recur when the sustained-sound event returns. Rather, there is an overlapping of the contrasting section and the return, with different aspects of the initial material restated gradually beginning in measure 62. The composition closes with the full ensemble in a 30-second decrescendo, *fff* ═══ *ppp*.

Each of the large sections is characterized by processes of gradual change. Ex. 16–33 shows measures 1–2 of the movement.[4] As the notation indicates, groups of players enter at different moments in a pseudo-random fashion, playing the highest pitch of their instruments at an *ff* level without vibrato. Measure 2 introduces the sudden *f* and the two types of vibrato in the violins and violas;[5] measures 3–5 continue sudden dynamic changes and the two types of vibrato. (By measure 4, all of the instruments play either ⁓⁓⁓⁓ or ⁓⁓⁓⁓ In measure 5 the violins are without vibrato.)

Ex. 16–33. Penderecki: *Threnody: To the Victims of Hiroshima.* Copyright © 1961 by Deshon Music, Inc. & PWM Editions. Used by permission.

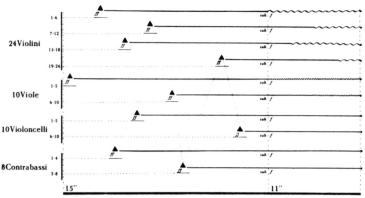

Different articulations of the sustained tone, a rapid alternation of pizzicato and arco played behind the instrument's bridge, are introduced in measure 6. These articulation changes are variants of the vibrato-like playing in the preceding measures. The result is *change*, the delineation of a new musical event.

Ex. 16–34. Ibid., measures 6–7.

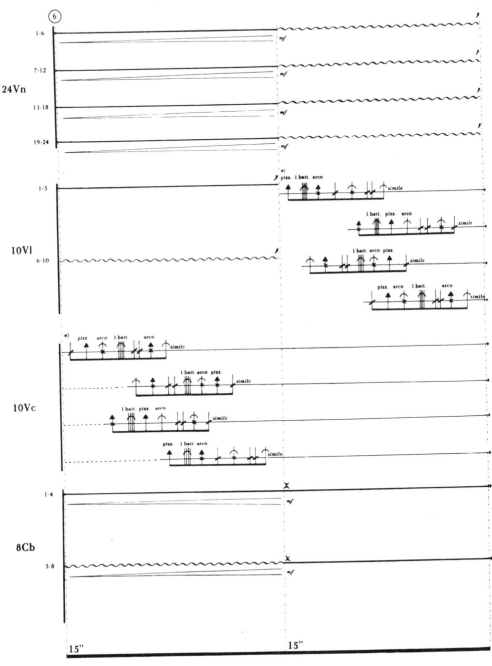

A distinctively new event is presented in measure 10. At this point the cellos are assigned notes in a lower pitch register. The phrase begins with a sustained unison that gradually is expanded, in the manner of a wedge, to encompass the pitch span of a perfect 4th. The phrase closes by gradually returning to unison. A similar idea is present from measures 10–20, even though the width of wedge is of different sizes. (See measures 11 and 14.)

Ex. 16–35. Ibid., measure 10.

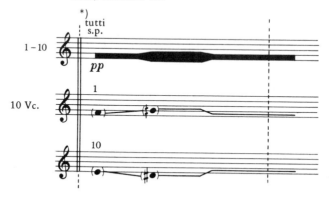

In measure 18 of our next excerpt, overlapping wedges are created by the individual entries of each of the players. Each sustains an assigned pitch, with a crescendo from *pp* to *f* (in the cellos) and to *ff* in all other instruments. By measure 19 this grows to *fff* in the cellos and string basses. Measures 18–19 contain the dynamic climax of this portion of the work. From measures 20 to 25 a decrease in loudness and in the number of participating players closes the section.

The formal section contained within measures 1–25 of this work is shaped, then, by changes in dynamics, articulation, texture, and pitch. Textural changes include the process of gradual change from several instruments playing a similar pitch to each instrument playing a different pitch, with a subsequent return to a single pitch (as at measure 23).

The section beginning in measure 26 does not introduce new materials, except that a drastic change in the density of attacks occurs. For example, in measures 26–34 very few attacks occur together, but by measures 35–37 simultaneous attacks and a sustained tone dominate the texture. Even so, the section is characterized by the attack-density change that begins in measure 26.[6]

---

[6] Although carefully notated, measures 26–34 and 38–46 create the effect of randomness, as if unfolding by chance. The element of chance is present for the performer, as in measures 10–12, and as a musical effect, as in measures 26–34 and 38–46.

Ex. 16–36. Ibid., measure 18.

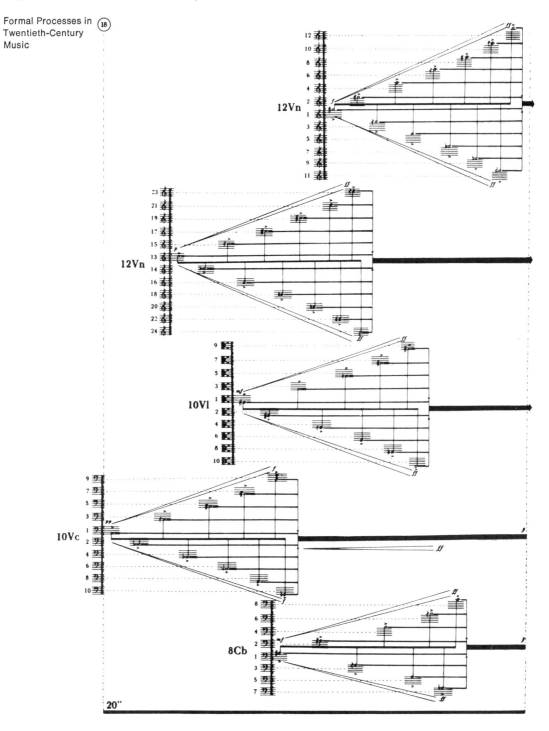

Ex. 16–37. Ibid., measures 26–31.

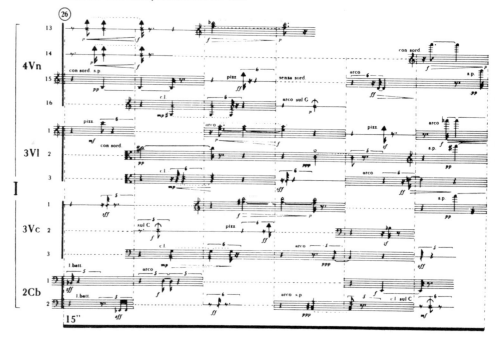

As in the first section, there is a gradual increase in the rate of articulation in this second section. This increase of textural density results in part from the change from twelve players (measures 26–37) to twenty-four (measures 38–43) to thirty-six (measures 44–61). By measure 65 all fifty-two strings are sounding, but each is performing a sustained tone rather than individual attacks.

The form of Penderecki's *Threnody* is the result of the interaction of properties—loudness, timbre, rate of articulation—that in earlier music play secondary roles. The formal process is characterized by changes that range from the subtle to the obvious.[7]

Aleatoric Scores

Although Penderecki's *Threnody* makes use, to some extent, of performers' decisions, the work's overall form is completely controlled by the composer.

In a few compositions of the past decade form is determined as much by the performer as by the composer. Thus, the concept of *open form* arises, in which the form of a composition depends largely upon decisions made by the particular performers to suit a particular set of conditions. The score for one such work is shown next.

This circular graph—the "score"—is divided into quadrants, each

[7] Note that many of the sounds employed by Penderecki are similar to those heard in electronic music.

Ex. 16–38. Ashley: *in memoriam . . . ESTEBAN GOMEZ.* Reprinted by permission of Source: Music of the Avant Garde.

quadrant further divided into sixteen equal units. Each of these sixteen units represents a constant unit of time (decided by the performers). Before a performance, each player assigns one sound dimension to each quadrant (i.e., pitch, loudness, timbre, and density[8]). Once assigned, the dimension must remain constant throughout the performance. Each performance begins with a reference sonority, prepared in advance, that serves as a constant reference for the other sounds that make up the composition.

Whenever any performer becomes aware of a deviant element (other than his own) in the reference sonority, his pattern of assigned sound elements (quadrants) shifts circularly so that the mode of devia-

[8] *Density* designates the mixing rate of performance ingredients, such as flutter-tongue, double-stops, etc.

tion he recognizes is assigned to the quadrant opposite that in which he is playing or will play next. (As the pattern of quadrants remains constant, thus all quadrants will be redesignated.) The pattern of quadrant designations remains in its changed position until the performer has played through the succeeding (newly designated) quadrant, after which it is subject again to transposition through the appearance of deviant elements in the sonority.[9]

[9] *Source: Music of the Avant Garde,* I:41.

Such a work evolves as it is performed, so any discussion of it as music must by necessity refer to a specific performance. Form and structure are realized anew with each performance; it is unlikely that any realization would duplicate another unless by conscious effort.

Exercises

For more detailed assignments see *Materials and Structure of Music II, Workbook,* Chapter 15.

Make aural and visual analyses of the large formal aspects of works such as the following, paying particular attention to how formal divisions are delineated, i.e., use of cadences, change of texture, change of tonality, change of chord types, changes of timbre, etc.

Bartók: *String Quartet No. 4,* III
Berio: *Circles*
Brown: *Available Forms*
Carter: *Piano Sonata II; String Quartets I, II, and III*
Davidovsky: *Synchronisms No. 1*
Erb: *Sonata for Harpsichord and String Quartet*
Hindemith: *Organ Sonata in E♭*
Kagel: *Sonant*
Lutoslawski: *Paroles Tissées*
Prokofiev: *Violin Concerto No. 2,* I
Schoenberg, *Piano Pieces,* Opus 11; *Pierrot Lunaire*
Stockhausen: *Studie II*
Webern: *String Quartet,* Op. 28
Xenakis: *Akrata*

Index of
Musical Excerpts

* Roman numerals indicate movement quoted.

Index

*Note: *Italic* type indicates pages on which the definition of a subject appears.